Food and Language

D1561502

Food and Language: Discourses and Foodways across Cultures explores in innovative ways how food and language are intertwined across cultures and social settings. How do we talk about food? How do we interact in its presence? How do we use food to communicate? And how does social interaction feed us? The book assumes no previous linguistic or anthropological knowledge but provides readers with the understanding to pursue further research on the subject. With a full glossary at the end of the book and additional tools hosted on an eResources page (such as recommended web and video links and some suggested research exercises), this book serves as an ideal introduction for courses on food, language, and food-and-language in anthropology departments, linguistics departments, and across the humanities and social sciences. It will also appeal to any reader interested in the semiotic interplay between food and language.

Kathleen C. Riley teaches linguistic anthropology at Rutgers University, USA. She has conducted fieldwork on foodways and language socialization in French Polynesia, France, Québec, and New York City. She has co-edited (with Christine Jourdan) a special issue of *Anthropologie et Sociétés* on food glocalization and (with Jillian Cavanaugh) a special issue of the *Semiotic Review* on food and language.

Amy L. Paugh is a Professor of Anthropology at James Madison University, USA. Her research investigates language and food, language socialization, and children's cultures in Dominica, Caribbean, and the United States. She is the author of *Playing with Languages: Children and Change in a Caribbean Village*.

Routledge Foundations in Linguistic Anthropology

Books in the **Routledge Foundations in Linguistic Anthropology** series serve as frameworks for courses on the sub-areas of Linguistic Anthropology. Each book concisely lays out the groundwork for instructors to introduce students to these topics and is structured in a way that enables the use of additional readings and resources to tailor each course. Serving as great jumping-off points for discussion, these books are ideal for undergraduate- and graduate-level Linguistic Anthropology courses.

Food and Language
Discourses and Foodways across Cultures
Kathleen C. Riley and Amy L. Paugh

For more information about this series, please visit: www.routledge.com/ Routledge-Foundations-in-Linguistic-Anthropology/book-series/RFLA

Food and Language

Discourses and Foodways
across Cultures

Kathleen C. Riley
and Amy L. Paugh

Routledge
Taylor & Francis Group

NEW YORK AND LONDON

First published 2019
by Routledge
711 Third Avenue, New York, NY 10017

and by Routledge
2 Park Square, Milton Park, Abingdon, Oxon, OX14 4RN

Routledge is an imprint of the Taylor & Francis Group, an informa business

© 2019 Taylor & Francis

Library of Congress Cataloging-in-Publication Data
A catalog record for this book has been requested

ISBN: 978-1-138-90700-3 (hbk)
ISBN: 978-1-138-90701-0 (pbk)
ISBN: 978-1-315-69523-5 (ebk)

Typeset in Sabon and Helvetica
by Apex CoVantage, LLC

Visit the eResources page: www.routledge.com/9781138907010

Printed and bound in Great Britain by
TJ International Ltd, Padstow, Cornwall

Contents

Illustrations

Tables

Figures

Preface

Many anthropologists and other scholars have looked at food, many have looked at language, and some have considered both. Yet few have made the kinds of connections between them that we are exploring here. They have recorded and analyzed social interaction around food but have not asked how the food came into play, or they have studied talk about food without considering how the discourse is structured. Much exploration of food as a kind of language does not examine how this meaningful food is made part of real life interactions, and much of the research about how language feeds or poisons us does not consider the full import of this metaphor. This book aims to gather the relevant research and generate a fruitful conversation about the interplay between these two things the mouth loves—food and language—across many social and cultural contexts.

Though this book is not meant to be exhaustive, our hope is that it provides a solid base for exploring how food and language come together in both universally human as well as culturally specific ways. We sprinkle vignettes, found in textboxes, throughout this book to tell the stories of how we and our colleagues discovered this expanding field of interest. The vignettes were written by the scholars themselves, who range from seasoned food and language scholars to students completing their graduate and undergraduate studies. We provide many additional resources on the eResources page that accompanies this book as well. In each chapter, there are callouts in the margins to specify online resources that are referenced in the text: 🕿. On the eResources page, links pertaining to these callouts can be found in the document called Online Resource Callouts. Additional information on the eResources page includes a list of resources for future exploration, a variety of exercises for delving into the field further, and some results from previous classroom projects.

The production of this book has benefited from support in a number of ways and from a number of sources whom we wish to acknowledge here. First, we must thank the institutional supporters of our fieldwork that led us to this fascination with food and language. The National Science Foundation and Wenner-Gren Foundation funded Riley's doctoral and follow-up research in French Polynesia; Johnson State College and Paris X Nanterre helped support her postdoctoral work in France; and the City College of New York and Queens College provided institutional backing for her research assistants at a school in New York City. Paugh's research in Dominica has been supported by the National Science Foundation, the Wenner-Gren Foundation, Fulbright-Hays, New York University, and James Madison University; her work in Los Angeles, California, was made possible by a postdoctoral fellowship at the UCLA Sloan Center on Everyday Lives of Families. Any views, findings, conclusions, or recommendations expressed in this book do not necessarily represent those of the any of the granting institutions.

We would also like to acknowledge the Vermont Studio Center in Johnson, Vermont, for facilitating our collaboration through a writing residency for Paugh in July 2017. It provided a deeply creative context full of excellent conversation and food, both for thought and taste. That sojourn was made possible by a Provost's Research Grant, and additional subvention funds were provided by the College of Arts and Letters and the Department of Sociology and Anthropology at James Madison University. Beth Eck and Sharon Loyd provided invaluable administrative and moral support throughout the project.

Several scholars who have worked with us over the years on this synthesis must be acknowledged. Two anthropologists who have mentored us throughout our careers and helped lead us down the path of food-and-language socialization are Bambi Schieffelin and Elinor Ochs. Three other scholars who have been key to this work are Christine Jourdan, Jillian Cavanaugh, and Martha Karrebæk. Riley and Jourdan started eating and talking together about these matters over a decade ago while teaching together at Concordia University in Montreal, a hub of multilingual and multiculinary exploration. Together they organized a panel on food and language matters at the American Anthropological Association annual meeting in Philadelphia in 2009, a topic which has continued to crop up ever since in various panels and conferences at different venues. Conversations in these settings (over food and drinks of course!) with Cavanaugh, Karrebæk, and Jourdan have been key to generating more panels and publications, allowing us to explore in collaborative ways the intersections of food and language across sociocultural contexts. Others who have influenced our thinking on this topic and benefited various chapters in this book through discussions, conference presentations, collaborations, publications, and feedback include Janet Chrzan, Leo Coleman, Anthony Graesch, Carolina Izquierdo, Alexandra Jaffe, Rich Lawler, Paul Manning, and Tamar Kremer-Sadlik.

We are also very grateful to a number of students and scholars who have specifically helped make this book possible. First, Riley has been developing the course on which this book is based for over 15 years. The first version, "Cultures through Cuisine," was co-taught with Cynthia West at Johnson State College in Vermont (Cynthia's vignette can be found in the final chapter of the book). Since then Riley has taught "Culture, Food and Talk" at Queens College and "Language, Food and Society" at Rutgers University. She has appreciated the curiosity, enthusiasm, and insights of these students, but wishes to thank several in particular for their critical reading of many chapters of this book at various stages of completion: Tracey Bobadilla, Natalie Brennan, Alysa Catalano, Brandon Fong, Asmeret Ghebremeskel, Carlie Hanlon, Sabrina Huwang, Sankeerth Kondapalli, Michelle Montenegro, Jeidys Noboa, Lilah Orengo, Sophia Pendleton, Eric Pereira, and Alyssa Vakulchik. Some of these students also generously contributed their results from classroom projects for publication on the eResources page. We thank our colleagues Martha Karrebæk and Jillian Cavanaugh for their astute comments on various chapters. Particularly, we would like to thank Karrebæk for using a draft and compiling comments from the students in her Fall 2017 class on communication and food. We also received useful responses from three anonymous reviewers of early drafts of the book as well as some very insightful line editing of the final draft by Riley's daughter, Anna Riley-Shepard.

The book has benefitted greatly from the original work of a number of scholars and artists: maps by geographer Eric Ross, cartoon by anthropologist Bernard Perley, artwork by Emily Leary (Paugh's daughter), and vignettes by Susan Blum, Garrett Broad, Jillian Cavanaugh, Parin Dossa, Anthony Graesch, Robert Jarvenpa, Christine Jourdan, Martha Karrebæk, Gwynne Mapes, Daniel Naumenko, Megan Tracy, and Cynthia West. We thank Leah Babb-Rosenfeld, Rebecca Novack, Judith Newlin, Kathrene Binag, and Elysse Preposi at Routledge for all of their help, patience, and editorial guidance.

Finally, we want to express the deepest appreciation to our families for their incredible patience and support throughout this process. Riley's partner, Neil Shepard, has followed the book since its inception, forwarding along relevant cartoons, news articles, and poems, chewing over titles and ideas, and sharing the meat of the matter whenever she was not at her desk. And Riley's daughter Anna has inspired this book with her inquisitive palate (sometimes vegan) and ever-supportive presence. Paugh's husband, Thomas Leary, provided sustenance through both food—in the form of much needed meals—and discourse—through discussions of insights and hurdles in the writing process—while nurturing children, chickens, gardens, and bees as Paugh focused on the research and writing. Paugh's daughters, Kathryn and Emily, inspired and kept the process fun by trying new foods and foodways, baking delectable treats, and creating endless food puns during dinnertime conversation. Of course, despite all the valiant help and support of all of those mentioned here, the remaining errors of fact and judgment are entirely our responsibility.

Copyright Acknowledgements

We are grateful to the following for their permission to reproduce copyright material in this volume:

Figures

Text

Chapter 1

Introduction
Talking Food Across Cultures

The many connections between food and language seem obvious once we think about it: infants cry to communicate their need for milk, foods are labeled in ways that shape our consumption habits, and many of us talk on the phone while preparing dinner or Instagram the amazing dish we are about to eat. Talk about food comes in so many forms from grocery lists and TV cooking shows to nourishing coffee chats and famine relief websites. But despite the everyday co-occurrence of food and language in our lives, the two have only recently begun to be diced, mixed, and kneaded together by scholars.[1]

In this book, we bring together research from many disciplines to map out this emergent field of study. Our own approach comes from the discipline of **anthropology**, which is the holistic study of human beings and their many different ways of giving meaning to experience, past and present. We emphasize linguistic anthropology, the branch of anthropology that looks at language use as a social activity across cultures.[2] This focus has drawn a number of linguistic anthropologists toward examining social interactions in which people are also engaged in making, eating, sharing, or simply talking about food.

1.1

In this introductory chapter, we sample many ways in which food and language are similar. We define several terms from the field of **semiotics**, the study of signs, needed to make sense of these food-language connections. Finally, we outline the four facets of the framework we use to organize the book: language *through* food, language *about* food, language *around* food, and language *as* food.

Food and Language: Exploring the Parallels

Perhaps the most obvious similarity between food and language is that both are oral obsessions; the mouth is the primary medium through which we savor them. But whereas language is apparently produced within us and exits the mouth to be consumed by others elsewhere, food is apparently produced elsewhere and enters the mouth to be consumed by us. The principal goal of this book is to probe how the production and consumption of both food and language are intertwined and circulated in complex ways both within and beyond ourselves.

First of all, neither food nor language is experienced *only* by way of the mouth. Every sense in our bodies is involved in producing and consuming them, making our engagement with both a **multisensual** experience. We feel the texture of both with our lips and tongues and teeth. For example, the crunch of a chip and the expletive "Damn!" are both palpable experiences of the mouth. But we also use our hands to prepare and eat food, feeling the flora and fauna that we harvest and butcher, dice and stir-fry, ladle out and bring to our lips. Similarly, we use our hands to nuance or sign our language and to feel the pages of a book, the texture of the keyboard, or the raised dots of Braille for the visually impaired. We comprehend language with our ears, from whispers to oratory, as well as with our eyes when we read a book, understand sign language, or interpret body language. But we also use our eyes and ears to appreciate food: the shapes and colors in the garden and on the plate as well as the sounds of peas snapping, meat sizzling, soup slurping . . . And, of course, taste and smell have everything to do with enjoying or rejecting food, but do these two senses have any role to play in language?

1.2

Well, if we expand the term **language**, as we will be doing in this book, to include the many ways in which humans communicate, it becomes clear that taste and smell have roles to play in "language" as well. For instance,

Figure 1.1 Copenhagen street food market, Denmark

Credit: Photo by Shane Rounce on Unsplash

think about the use of perfume or cologne to signal physical appeal and the use of food gifts such as a jar of homemade jam or a donation of a Heifer International water buffalo to an impoverished family to express emotions and social concerns.

Our multisensual experience of both food and language points to a second fundamental parallel: our language and food habits both live within us as embodied forms of knowledge and practice that we acquire through everyday social interactions. This is what the sociologist Pierre Bourdieu (1977, 1985) called **habitus**, referring to the deeply embedded ways of being and understanding the world. Because of our constant exposure to our own community's tastes and speech patterns, we rarely question the essential rightness of these ways of doing, thinking, and feeling. Anthropologists refer to this phenomenon as <u>ethnocentrism</u>.

1.3

For instance, many Americans believe that they speak English without an accent and sometimes enjoy acting out the accents of people from other parts of the United States or from Australia or India because we feel in our gut that they are the ones with the real accents (an attitude known as **linguacentrism**). Similarly, in the case of food, we may feel a visceral disgust at the thought of eating certain foods that we have not grown up eating. American students in our anthropology classes sometimes react with horror-stricken faces when offered taste-tests of seaweed, snails, or crickets, all items that are considered consummately edible elsewhere in the world. In other words, what we think and feel about food and language is unconsciously socialized and stored in our bodies at a time that predates memory, making it sometimes difficult for us to learn or even consider other ways of speaking or eating. Have you ever struggled to acquire a second language or to enjoy a new ethnic cuisine? What is clear to researchers is that our **linguistic** (language-related) and **alimentary** (food-related) habits and attitudes are not only acquired early but also in interwoven ways.

Finally, both food and language serve to bind communities, to define differences between communities, and to resolve or escalate conflicts across boundaries. And they both do this in **multimodal** ways. That is, the many sensual aspects—tastes, smells, sounds, sights, and touch—of both food and language circulate between individuals and communities using a number of modes, channels, or media. These modes include vocal and facial expressions, hand and body gestures, spoken or manual language, paper and electronic writing, music and dance, visual images (from petroglyphs to film) and, of course, food. Multimodal flow can occur face-to-face around a campfire with an exchange of smiles, an interjection of 'yum,' and a toasted marshmallow on a stick. Or it can happen virtually via electronic media. For example, think of how those who live transnationally use both language and food to stay in touch with their friends and family at home: texting transmits verbiage only, phones add the aural qualities of the voice, and Skype offers up the situated visuals.

"I discovered coffee!"

Figure 1.2 Caffeinated cave art

Credit: Danny Shanahan/The New Yorker Collection/The Cartoon Bank. Reproduced with permission.

Yet these same sights, sounds, smells, and tastes may also set these new-comers apart from their neighbors, who may not only mock the incom-prehensible "gibberish" of the immigrants next door, but also complain about what is cooking in their kitchen or what their children are bringing to school in their lunch boxes. This is a perfect example of how the produc-tion and consumption of both food and language are not only multisensual and multimodal processes, but also governed by habitus in ways that lead sometimes to revelry and sometimes to bigotry. Thus, this book explores the intertwined roles played by food and language as communicative media across cultures past and present around the globe.

Foodways and Discourses, Material and Symbolic

In order to understand how food and language operate as multisensual and multimodal systems, we need to introduce and define a few terms here that will be essential to our discussion throughout the book, beginning with the words material and symbolic. Material is used to refer to the concrete stuff of the world, those tangible factors that have a real impact on our actual lives. Foods are material objects that we take into our material bodies. Symbolic is used to mean the abstracted notions and ways in which we think and communicate about our lives. Language, for instance, is a system consisting of conventionally agreed upon symbols used for communication. However, it will quickly become obvious that although the material and symbolic are traditionally presented as a dichotomy, along the lines of the so-called mind-body divide, they are not opposites and are in fact intermingled as commonly as are food and language.

Another two technical, but indispensable, terms for our discussion of food and language are **foodways** and **discourses**. The word **foodways** covers *all* the material and symbolic ways in which humans "do food" in both everyday and formal settings. In other words, it includes how we grow, cook, exchange, store, eat, compost, and communicate through, about, and around food, constructing both actual food as well as the notion of nourishment. The term foodways is more all-encompassing than food alone. Additionally, it indicates the cultural specificity with which we give meaning to the fulfillment of this critical human need.

Similarly, the term **discourses** can be used to refer to *all* the material and symbolic ways in which we "do language" in both everyday and formal settings. By "doing language" we mean engaging in communicative practices of all kinds, linguistic and **paralinguistic** (meaning alongside language). Linguistic communication includes written, signed, and spoken **acts**, such as jokes, compliments, or complaints, as well as **genres**, such as prayers, gossip, or lectures. Paralinguistic communication includes voice qualities, vocalizations such as sighs and gasps, facial expressions such as smiles and winks, and body language such as a thumbs-up or timid crouch, as well as dress, hairstyle, perfume, and so on.

We use the term **discourse** to refer to the activity of communicating. We use the plural of this term, **discourses**, to refer to the specific **discursive** acts circulated as well as the **ideologies** carried by the utterances. Ideologies include cultural beliefs, values, and assumptions that we pick up unconsciously from others, whether or not they are in the best interests of ourselves or others; ideologies are made powerful by both big media pronouncements and our own daily interactions. Some scholars use two terms, big D Discourse(s) and little d **discourse(s)**, to distinguish between these public and private spheres of interaction and the resulting ideologies.[3] However, in this book we will adopt the big D usage primarily to index the Foucauldian notion (even though Foucault did not capitalize the term) that certain ideological formations take on power not only because of how pronouncements are performed in particularly powerful ways by particularly powerful persons, but also because of how these Discourses accrue power when circulated and negotiated through everyday discourse as well (see for instance Foucault 2002 [1969]). In other words, we will use the small d discourses to encompass both the activity of discourse and the ideological

Table 1.1 Foodways and discourses

Foodways	Material and symbolic practices related to the production and consumption of food and food ideologies in both everyday and formal settings	
Discourses	Material and symbolic practices related to the production and consumption of language and language ideologies in both everyday and formal settings	
	discourse = communicative activity → linguistic (written, signed, spoken, etc.) → paralinguistic (vocal, facial, body, dress, food, etc.)	Discourse(s) = dominant ideology or ideologies circulated via discourse (both everyday and formal)

Discourses established via this activity, whether in the form of everyday chats or formal pronouncements. See Table 1.1 above for a graphic representation of these terms and what they cover.

For the most part, we will be using the two terms discourses and foodways in parallel ways to highlight how people engage in discursive and alimentary activities that are both material and symbolic in nature. That is, while food may seem more immediately concrete than language and language may seem a lot less tangible than food, both have material and symbolic sides. For instance, words off the lips or print on the page are equally as sensuous as food at the market or on the plate. Additionally, both foodways and discourses involve embodied actions or practices, which are made meaningful through abstract systems of thought and emotion. Both involve the production of something of substance, for instance, pronouncements in an interaction and ingredients for a dish. But these are only possible because individuals have acquired various forms of symbolic knowledge or competence, for instance, how to turn a phrase and how to prepare a meal. Finally, both discursive and alimentary products are received or consumed by **interlocutors** (conversational partners) and fellow diners in a variety of ways based on individuals' shared or differing foodways and discourses. A shared habitus can lead to mutual appreciation of a rhetorical flourish or a chef's signature dish, and different linguistic and culinary standards may lead to shock at "salty language" (the use of crude words or cursing) or disgust in response to some particularly "slimy" or "smelly" ingredient.

The Influence of Material and Symbolic Factors on Foodways and Discourses

Let's look now at how both material and symbolic factors contribute to the construction of culturally distinctive foodways and discourses. Table 1.2 graphically represents various relevant factors, moving from most material

Table 1.2 Material and symbolic factors

	Material factors		
F O O D W A Y S	Biology → what the species is able to eat	Biology → how the species can communicate	
	Geography → what foods can be procured in a given environment	Physical health → how individuals can communicate	
	Technology → how food is produced and processed	Technology → how discourses are formulated and broadcast	**D I S C O U R S E S**
	Economy and capital → who produces which foods for whom to consume	Economy and capital → who produces which discourses for whom to consume	
	Commodity marketplace → how foodways are valued and marketed	Linguistic marketplace → how discourses are valued and circulated	
	Political regulations → who has the right to eat what	Political citizenship → who has the right to say what	
	Religious/aesthetic rules → how we should eat	Religious/aesthetic rules → how we should speak	
	Socialization, education → how we learn to eat	Socialization, education → how we learn to speak	
	Symbolic factors		

at the top to most symbolic at the bottom, as these influence humans' various foodways and discourses.

Starting from the top with the material level, we can see how biology and genetics, our own as well as the flora and fauna we feed on, determine to some degree what is edible in that it will not kill us but make us healthy. Similarly, our human biology and morphology, such as the brain, vocal apparatus, and hands, have provided us with the capacity for human language. Relatedly, on the next line down, it is the health and diversity of various geographic environments that constrain what foods are available for humans to hunt, gather, grow, and husband. And our physical health as individuals is fed by resources and nutrients that provide us with the strength and cognitive power to communicate with others.

Technology, one more line down, is another concrete way in which humans engage with the world. Once invented, various technologies such as tools, energy sources, and laboratory techniques have been put to work to produce, process, and preserve more and better foods—or worse foods, depending on how you feel about chemicals and genetically modified organisms. Similarly, various forms of linguistic technology, including the printing press, radio, phone, and the internet, have all facilitated our ability to formulate and broadcast our discourses around the globe, ushering in new forms of cultural and linguistic contact and change in the process.

In reference to the fourth line, the ability to produce and store food has led to a world of unequal access to material wealth. That is, those with financial capital have the ability to organize the tangible acts of labor by which food is produced, and these elite also generally capitalize on their positions to eat more or better forms of the food that is produced. For example, as explained in the film *Cowspiracy* (Andersen and Kuhn 2014), the explosion of factory-farmed meat produced in the 20th century has led not only to the degradation of our global environment but also to an increased disparity in health, wealth, and social mobility as an elite controls the corporate proceeds from the ever-increasing global desire for meat. They also have access to the health benefits of eating more of it as well as the education and medical resources needed to guard against the health risks of eating too much of it. Similarly, and not surprisingly, those people with wealth and health are in turn provided with greater opportunities to produce and shape both the everyday and powerful discourses that affect everyone and help them retain global power themselves.

All the discursive and alimentary factors discussed so far begin with an apparently material basis yet proceed to have social and even spiritual impacts. Continuing to move down the chart to the more obviously symbolic factors, we see how the economic market impacts our foodways in a variety of ways—from the relative sizes of our paychecks and the price tags on the products we consume to the ways in which advertising and packaging influence the commodities and brands we develop a taste for. Similarly, our opportunities to acquire and use various **sociolects**—the ways of speaking that signal where we come from regionally, ethnically, socioeconomically, and so on—are structured by the **linguistic marketplace**, a term used to describe the social structures that organize how linguistic varieties are valued or not according to the prestige of those who speak them and constrain who has access to the more valuable ones (Bourdieu 1991).

On the next line down, political regulations control or at least constrain who can produce, exchange, and consume what foods. For instance, both the United States Food and Farm Bill and global trade agreements now have a significant impact on how farmers are allowed to grow crops, and who then gets to buy and eat them. Similarly, our political right to speak out (aka "have a voice") is governed in part by laws that define our citizenship status and the nature of the nation to which we belong. We will consider many of these political and economic issues having to do with food and language in Chapter 8.

On the next to bottom line, we see that a variety of religious and aesthetic rules shape our sense of what can be eaten and with what etiquette. For example, kosher and halal are the names of the dietary regulations prescribed in the Jewish Bible and the Muslim Qur'an. In many societies, various diets and food fads move in and out of popularity over time, impacting eating habits and perceptions of "healthy" or enjoyable foodways. Individual practices and beliefs with respect to these food restrictions and fads depend not only on how one was raised, but also on the community context (for instance, whether one's group is marginalized or not), as well as the immediate social setting (for instance, peer pressure to drink or become a vegetarian). Similarly, various religious and aesthetic regimes also determine to some degree what speech genres we learn to use to express the beliefs and values attached to those regimes. For example, the African-American style of preaching made famous by Martin Luther King Jr. may be associated by many with his civil rights message, and the musical genre of rap has been associated with a range of social messages from black pride to misogyny.

Finally, at the bottom of the table comes the general issue of **socialization**.   1.4 Socialization is the process by which we learn from parents, teachers, and peers at home, school, and the workplace as well as via mass media. **Language socialization** is the means by which we are socialized into our understanding of language and how to use it; similarly, **food socialization** is the process by which we are socialized to learn our food knowledge and food practices. We use the term **food-and-language socialization** to refer to the interlinked processes by which food and foodways are learned through language and language is learned through food and foodways. This term highlights the interconnections between how we are socialized to do both food and language, separately and together. The symbolic meanings of food and their socialization are major topics of Chapters 4 and 7.

Just as all of the discursive and alimentary processes at the top of the chart clearly begin with material factors but end up influencing our symbolic universe—our feelings, thoughts, and perspectives—so do the processes at the bottom of the chart start with symbolic factors but obviously have a material impact on individuals, their communities, and their environments. To understand this consequential relationship, we explain foodways and discourses in terms of semiotics.

Foodways and Discourses as Semiotic Systems

The term **semiosis** has been used over the last century and a half by a range of philosophers, linguists, and anthropologists and refers to a wide variety of processes involving **signs**.[4] A sign is, basically, something that stands for

something else. Both words and food items are signs. For example, think of the English term 'chocolate.' The word itself is a sign that refers to that   1.5 yummy comestible made from cacao. In addition, the food itself has also become a sign with different meanings at different times. First cultivated in Central America, chocolate was valued as a form of currency by Mayans

and Aztecs. Now, in its physical form mixed with milk and sugar, it is a sign used to signify "I love you" on Valentine's Day.[5]   1.6

Some signs are very closely linked to what they represent, such as the classic example of smoke indicating fire—smoke is attached in space and time to the fire, which causes it. It is thus a **non-arbitrary** connection. By contrast, many signs are **arbitrary**; they have no self-evident connection to what they signify but come to be linked through conventional usage. Language is considered a classic example of a system of arbitrary signs, in fact, a system of sub-systems made up of **phonemes, morphemes,** and **syntax.** Phonemes are the contrastive bits of sound that we use to form words. Humans combine phonemes in verbal language, as they combine manual forms in sign language, into morphemes, the smallest meaningful units of a language. These include both words and elements of words (such as the free morpheme *food* and the bound morpheme -*s* marking plurality in *foods*). These morphemes can be further combined into sentences according to syntax, the rules that govern the structure of sentences in a language.[6] The grammatical rules for combining phonemes into morphemes and morphemes into syntactic units are not set in stone but change over time in ways that are somewhat arbitrary, being just the conventions of a given language.

1.7

Thus, words are perfect instances of how the relationship between the form and meaning of many signs is arbitrary. That is, the material form (sounds, letters, or hand gestures) used to transmit the meaning or concept that speakers associate with that word have no necessary connection to that meaning. For example, the sound /b/, the letter <b>, and the hand gesture for 'b' do not in any way naturally lead one to think of the ideas behind *beef, bonjour,* or *Beijing.* In semiotic terms, we refer to these arbitrary signs as **symbols,** and most languages are primarily constructed out of wholly conventional symbolic signs, whether sounds or words. There is no intrinsic reason why we should call a tree *tree* instead of *arbre* (as the French do) or *tumu* (as Marquesans do). It is just a long-standing contract among the worldwide community of English-speakers to do so.

However, even language employs some signs with more or less non-arbitrary meanings, and this provides a good illustration of how semiotic systems combine both material and symbolic components. Think, for instance, of onomatopoeic words such as *buzz, bam,* and *burp* that do sound a little like the physical sounds they signify. Similarly, some hand forms in sign language do look a bit like what they mean. For example, the American Sign Language (ASL) sign for the concept of drinking looks like someone bringing a cup to their lips, as seen in Figure 1.3. And in some forms of writing, the signs used may resemble what they mean, as when the Egyptian hieroglyphic for 'day' looks like a simplified sun or when the emoticon ;) looks like a wink and means something like 'just kidding.' In

1.8

semiotics, signs whose meanings are based in part on some form of natural resemblance, as in these examples, are called **icons.**

Figure 1.3 The ASL sign for "drink" (© Shutterstock)

Next, consider how sentences (aka a string of linguistic signs) are produced by people within specific here-and-now settings that allow people to be "in touch" whether in the living room or on the internet. These utterances are formulated and interpreted through linguistic codes, those things we refer to as English, Urdu, Tahitian, etc. Within those codes, many of the signs point to meanings inferred from the immediate setting. For example, when I use the word *you*, I probably mean the one or more people to whom I am presently speaking, but if you respond to me using *you*, you probably mean me, not you. We call these signs **shifters** because they shift their meaning depending on the situation—in this case, who is speaking to whom. Even more complicated, in French one of the words for 'you,' *vous*, may refer to the multiple people I'm speaking to, but sometimes it refers to only one person, in which case, this signals that the situation and/or the relationship between me and my interlocutor is somewhat formal. And if I suddenly use *vous* with someone I normally address as *tu*, the informal form of 'you,' everyone knows that the situation has become official (or I've completely changed my feelings about the 'you' I'm speaking to). In other words, the material situation is indicated or even transformed by this semiotic usage. Semioticians call these signs **indexes** because they work a little like an index finger pointing at some meaning in the spatial and temporal vicinity of the finger.

Foodways can be seen to operate as semiotic systems in some very similar ways. We will go into this at greater length in Chapter 4 but provide

ﾟere a couple of brief examples. First, consider how the meaning of the food we eat is in many ways arbitrary and conventional, just like language. That is, humans do not all agree about the best ways to grow, cook, or eat food, much less what is considered "healthy" or "tasty" or "classy" food. Some of what is happily ingested as "food" by some people does not look, smell, or taste like "food" at all to others. Think, for example, of termites in Mozambique, horse meat in France, fermented shark in Iceland, or the mechanical objects eaten by Muzzy, the fuzzy green alien on the BBC's animated language-learning program. That is, what we eat does not necessarily *iconically* resemble the essence of food, nor are its food-like qualities always *indexed* within a particular setting. Instead, many edibles only come to take on the properties of 'food' by contrast with non-food because we grow up with the conventions of procuring, preparing, and thinking of them as food—that is, they carry the *symbolic* meaning of being 'food.'

Nonetheless, there are some food characteristics that are inherently tasty to humans. For instance, the widespread attraction to sweet and more limited interest in bitter is apparently an evolutionary adaptation of the tongue that allowed humans to find the calories we needed while avoiding foods that were poisonous. Similarly, many conventionally meaningful ways of producing and consuming foods that are very effective—such as using digging sticks to grow corn, boiling stew over a fire, or transporting food to our mouths with our fingers—take on alternative indexical meanings in different times and places. Farmers in Ohio use tractors to grow corn and might consider the digging stick "primitive," while Americans could hardly imagine life without microwaves but still grill hamburgers and steaks on the Fourth of July. And Europeans who teach their children to use forks and knives "properly" will consume a sandwich with their hands or a whole meal at an Ethiopian restaurant. These situations are associated with particular foodways, which in turn *index* different feelings, ideologies, or levels of formality.

The Semiotic Value of Wine

Let's clarify the connections between foodways and discourses by briefly tracing how the semiotic value of one food commodity, wine, is impacted by both material and symbolic factors. Grapes, from which wine is produced, were first grown only in very particular environmental conditions: the right kind of semi-sandy soil and the right kind of temperate climate. While wild grapes sprouted both in Asia and North America and were no doubt foraged by early humans, the earliest archaeological proof that humans pressed and fermented them into something intoxicating is based on ceramics with resin dating back to 6000–8000 years ago in Georgia and Armenia. From there, technology has been needed not only to produce

Figure 1.4 Lavaux terraced vineyards in Saint-Saphorin, Switzerland
Credit: Photo by Samuel Zeller on Unsplash

wine, but also to store, package, and transport it, from amphora to corked bottle to waxed cardboard carton.

Over time, some individuals acquired more of the capital to produce and consume the finest vintages while others ended up selling their labor (as farmworkers or factory workers) in order to buy rotgut. But the knowledge of how to cultivate, press, and ferment specific varieties of grapes into various kinds of wines has been semiotically developed, refined, and transmitted over many centuries from European monasteries in the Middle Ages to the vineyards of Napa Valley, and has most recently extended to parts of the world from South Africa to Siberia where grapes and wine production would once have been materially impossible. Nonetheless, certain material conditions can still wipe out whole cultivars and send the industry into a slump; for example, an aphid called phylloxera was imported from the United States and caused the Great French Wine Blight of the 19th century.

Similarly, a range of material but semiotically translated objects continues to influence the physical qualities of wine as well as our "taste" for them. First, there are the specific soils and climates where certain cultivars are grown (frequently referred to by the French term **terroir**), the chemicals and techniques used to grow or ferment them, and the labor practices found on various vineyards. These material factors are in turn semiotically translated into linguistic labels that certify and advertise various properties

Table 1.3 Commodity value of wine

Material	Symbolic
Grape cultivars (botanical properties based on biochemical composition)	Taste (a culturally socialized, multisensuous form of desire)
Land (soil, climate, etc.)	Locale/*terroir* (AOC)
Technology and practices for growing, pressing, fermenting, and storing	Health and environment (certified organic)
Capital and labor (means and relations of production)	Just (fair trade)
Experience of inebriation (taste-testing only to extreme intoxication, recreational to ritual, etc.)	Social values (age restrictions, notions of alcoholism, ideologies of distinction, etc.)

(e.g., "organic," "fair trade," and "AOC" from the French *appellation d'origine contrôlée*, meaning that the geographic origin of the product is certified; see more about labels in Chapter 5). And these along with other cultural values mediate a consumer's evaluation of a given bottle of wine, a particular label, wine in general, or the entire experience of inebriation itself, whether as a Bacchanalian rite or an afternoon of wine tasting. Thus, the material preconditions and practices involved in accessing a glass of wine as well as the social relations that organize the value of the commodity from taste to pricing are clearly infused with human symbolism.[7] This material/symbolic relationship is illustrated in Table 1.3.

Connecting Discourses Through, About, Around, and As Foodways

It is not uncommon for researchers to recognize the co-occurrence of food and language. Many studies of language incidentally include data about growing, sharing, cooking, eating, and advertising food; similarly, many studies of food include linguistic data such as words and media that represent food, speech acts and discourse genres that organize its production and consumption, and written texts that detail its preparation and distribution. By contrast, this book explores the many ways in which foodways and discourses are semiotically intertwined across a range of social and cultural settings. We use four phrases to organize our approach: language *through* food, language *about* food, language *around* food, and language *as* food.

Language through food encompasses the many ways in which people express personal and sociocultural meanings through their foodways. We consider structural approaches that employ language as a metaphor for how food communicates meaning and value, as well as studies of the social and semiotic ways in which food reflects and instantiates sociocultural ideologies and practices, identities and relationships. These studies are the focus of Chapter 4.

We use the phrase *language about food* to focus attention on how food becomes a topic of both everyday discourse and ideological Discourses. In Chapter 5 we explore various approaches to this topic ranging from semantic and etymological analyses of food words to aesthetic and rhetorical analyses of food genres such as ads, poetry, cartoons, recipes, policies, art, and films. All of these discourses about foodways give voice to a wide range of topics from health and environment to gender and ethnicity.

Language around food refers to the notion that language is used in specific ways in the presence of food while producing, marketing, preparing, and consuming it. In Chapter 6, we look at how communication is interwoven with food in various settings: kitchen, coffee shop, trailside meal, factory, grocery, and family dinner table.

Finally, the phrase *language as food* points out how discourses are often viewed and consumed like sustenance. That is, different ways of interacting are frequently understood metaphorically as nurturing (or not). For instance, language appears to function in language socialization studies as a medium of cultural transmission from one generation to the next. Chapter 7 explores this type of food-and-language connection, focusing in particular on how food-and-language socialization occurs in homes, schools, community, and fieldwork settings.

Cooking Our Model

To bring our model to a tasty simmer, we turn now to Michael Pollan's (2013) *Cooked*. Like all of his books about food, this one is written with an informed lay readership in mind and does a wonderful job of exploring four of the fundamental ways in which humans prepare food using fire, water, air, and earth. For our purposes, we find in his book examples of how food and language are entangled in the human imagination in ways that can be understood through our four-part model of language through, about, around, and as food.[8]

First of all, Pollan spices his writing with lots of what we recognize as language-through-food analogies. That is, he explores how food operates like language in having rules and dialects. He also writes that food itself tastes best when it works through metaphor. For example, the cooking pot, he says, stands in for family (2013:157), and the smell of fresh baked bread symbolizes our sense of 'home' (2013:209). Further, he discusses the semiotic processes by which all living creatures use food to speak to each other. In the case of barbecue, the same nutty, fruity, and vegetal signals that originally attracted animals to eat and thus transport a plant's seeds are transmitted again when meat cooks over fire, indexically drawing us in in ways that seem innate but have a long, conventional history. In the case of fermentation, the microbiota, whether of bread starter, cheese, or sauerkraut, incite us to feed them by sensually alluding to matters that are presumed to be naturally disgusting—the smells of death, sex, feces, and dirty socks. Paradoxically, these become semiotically transformed instead into the iconic foods of our communities: smelly cheese, kimchee, stinky tofu, etc. We use these acquired tastes to index—both signaling and constructing—our cultural identities by contrast with those of others (Pollan 2013:368–370).

Secondly, he considers how language *about* food can be used to manipulate us. For example, he examines how in the United States bread is no longer the singular product of certain ingredients and techniques but has proliferated into what he refers to as "notional breads" because of all of the research, development, and advertising that have gone into them. They are semiotically shaped by "nutritional conceits, clever ways to work the words 'whole grain' or 'whole wheat' onto a package, now that those magic words constitute an implied health claim" (Pollan 2013:271). We also recognize that Pollan's book is itself an instance of language *about* food, adding to a growing list of very popular literature on this subject.

Third, language *around* food is illustrated by his discussion of how human language may have first developed in prehistoric times around the hearth in the form of gossip. He mentions that talk takes place not only when eating and drinking but also while cooking, and that this food-based interaction supports communal sociality rather than individualism (Pollan 2013:182, 195–201).

Fourth, Pollan claims that the poetic imagination is not only fed by but also symbolized by alcoholic fermentation (2013:400–402), which fits into our concept of language *as* food. For example, Pollan writes: "Just as we take pleasure in enriching our language with layers of metaphor and allusion, we apparently like to trope what we eat and drink, too, extracting from it not only more nourishment but more meaning as well—more psychic nourishment, if you will" (2013:361).

As is clear from this analysis of these examples from Pollan's book, our framework of relationships between food and language inevitably overlap. For example, a study of language *around* food may well include some investigation of how talk *about* the food at hand emerges while also paying attention to how communication *through* the food is occurring in that setting. In this book, we pay close attention to when and where more than one angle on the food-and-language relationship is coming into play because we believe this is the most productive way to fully digest how food and language are semiotically intertwined.

Summary

Having explored how both foodways and discourses function similarly as embodied and signifying media through which humans negotiate their material and social existence, we turn now to look more closely at the many ways in which the two are semiotically intertwined. In Chapter 2, we explore how foodways and discourses have operated semiotically in human societies from the distant to more recent past. In Chapter 3, we explore some of the methods and settings for finding and analyzing data about the relationship between food and language. As mentioned above, Chapters 4, 5, 6, and 7 focus on the four types of food-language relationships: through, about, around, and as. Finally, in Chapter 8, we explore some of the ways in which the food-and-language model can be put to use in the world of food activism.

In each of the chapters, we provide two brief vignettes written by researchers about how they got into the business of studying food and language. Many of our contributors are linguistic anthropologists, but we have also elicited stories from scholars in other related fields such as cultural anthropology, archaeology, biological anthropology, and communication studies. The vignettes demonstrate the variety of paths that we and our colleagues have taken on our way to studying the fascinating relationship between food and language. In addition to the vignettes found in the book, readers will find a wide assortment of other resources and exercises on the companion website. In particular, we have included examples of data collected and analyzed by our students when responding to some of the food and language exercises.

Notes

1. See Karrebæk, Riley, and Canvanaugh (2018) for a recent overview of this burgeoning field.
2. Useful introductions to the field of linguistic anthropology can be found in Duranti (1997); Ahearn (2017); and Wilce (2017).
3. This big D little d distinction is explained well in Gee (1999).
4. The concepts we are using here are derived from Saussure, Peirce, and a host of other interpreters of their work. For a selection of relevant writings, see Innis (1985).
5. For a good account of the origins and spread of chocolate, see Coe and Coe (1996).
6. For a comprehensive overview of the field of linguistics, see Crystal (2010).
7. For the origins of wine, see McGovern (2013), and for a more general history, see Unwin (1991). Silverstein (2006) has analyzed the semiotic processes by which we assess wine.
8. To be clear, Pollan himself does not use this model, but we are using his work to illustrate the model.

References

Ahearn, Laura. 2017. *Living Language: An Introduction to Linguistic Anthropology*, 2nd edition. Malden, MA: John Wiley & Sons.

Andersen, Kip, and Keegan Kuhn. 2014. *Cowspiracy: The Sustainability Secret*. A.U.M. Films & Media and First Spark Media.

Bourdieu, Pierre. 1977. *Outline of a Theory of Practice*. Translated by Richard Nice. Cambridge: Cambridge University Press.

Bourdieu, Pierre. 1985. "The Genesis of the Concepts of Habitus and Field." *Sociocentrum* 2(2): 11–24.

Bourdieu, Pierre. 1991. *Language and Symbolic Power*. Edited by John B. Thompson. Translated by Gino Raymond and Matthew Adamson. Cambridge, MA: Harvard University Press.

Coe, Sophie D., and Michael D. Coe. 1996. *The True History of Chocolate*. London: Thames & Hudson.

Crystal, David. 2010. *Encyclopedia of Language*. Cambridge: Cambridge University Press.

Duranti, Alessandro. 1997. *Linguistic Anthropology*. New York: Cambridge University Press.

Foucault, Michel. 2002 (1969). *The Archaeology of Knowledge*. Translated by A. M. Sheridan Smith. London and New York: Routledge.

Gee, James Paul. 1999. *An Introduction to Discourse Analysis: Theory and Method*. New York: Routledge.

Innis, Robert E., ed. 1985. *Semiotics: An Introductory Anthology*. Bloomington: Indiana University Press.

Karrebæk, Martha Sif, Kathleen C. Riley, and Jillian R. Cavanaugh. 2018. "Food and Language: Production, Consumption and Circulation of Meaning and Value." *Annual Review of Anthropology* 47: 17–32.

McGovern, Patrick E. 2013. *Ancient Wine: The Search for the Origins of Viniculture*. Princeton: Princeton University Press.

Pollan, Michael. 2013. *Cooked: A Natural History of Transformation*. New York: Penguin Books.

Silverstein, Michael. 2006. "Old Wine, New Ethnographic Lexicography." *Annual Review of Anthropology* 35: 481–496.

Unwin, Tim. 1991. *Wine and the Vine: An Historical Geography of Viticulture and the Wine Trade*. London: Routledge.

Wilce, James M. 2017. *Culture and Communication: An Introduction*. New York: Cambridge University Press.

Chapter 2

The Communicating Eater

Food and language are meaningfully intertwined in numerous ways. But how and why has this come to be? In this chapter, we explore the idea that wherever human foodways and discourses co-occur they are entangled via **semiotic mediation**, that is, through their mutual engagement in mediating human forms of social interaction, social organization, and cross-cultural communication.[1] We consider how this entanglement differs from how other animals do food and communication. We present some suggestive hypotheses and examples researched by biological anthropologists, paleo-anthropologists, archaeologists, and ethnohistorians concerning the ways in which food and language became entangled in specific times and places around the world and over the course of human history. We focus in particular on how various foodways and communicative modes emerged in relationship to one another in the recent past: the advent of agriculture and writing, the spice trade along with trade languages, colonialism and the printing press, and finally commercial agriculture and the internet. The two vignettes in this chapter detail some of the relevant projects explored by biological anthropologists and archaeologists.

Foodways and Discourses as Semiotic Mediation

Semiotic systems like food and language are particularly good for mediation, that is, for translating and negotiating meanings across contexts. Consider how language allows us to abstract ideas out of their material settings, examine them, and attach new meanings that materially change the situation. Here is a simple example of this: you put a pot of stew on the stove to simmer and return to your room. Sometime later, your partner yells to ask if something is burning. You come running back to turn off the stove before your dinner is completely ruined. In this case, language *mediates* the situation by using symbols to transmit information that is not materially, multisensually apparent to you because you left the room. You don't hear the soup bubbling over or smell it burning, but as a result

HAVING RESERVATIONS

By Bernard C Perley ©2017

Figure 2.1 "Having Reservations"

of the language used by another person you return and affect the situation, salvaging your meal.

Furthermore, language is particularly good for mediating situations in which people who hold contradictory understandings or have opposing interests come into contact, as when negotiating financial contracts or brokering political treaties. We easily recognize this meaning of mediation in the sphere of law and politics, but it may also be applied to the everyday ways in which we confront and attempt to resolve oppositional forces, whether on the playground, at work, or at a store. Because our daily lives are filled with small differences in understanding, we are constantly using language to manage miscommunications and ambiguous social interactions.[3]

However, language is not the only semiotic system used for everyday semiotic mediation as we are exploring it here. Our foodways too offer us a range of semiotic resources for bridging perspectives, soothing ruffled feelings, and forging new understandings. Think, for example, of cases when European explorers were greeted in the Americas with offerings of food by the inhabitants. While these food encounters rarely ended well for the indigenous peoples, the initial intention was to mediate an unpredictable situation in which no shared language was available to bridge the human divide.

Given that foodways and discourses both function as semiotic mediators, it is perhaps not surprising to find that their connection is also mediated by the use of signs. Like all biological creatures, humans need to eat in order to grow, heal, work, and rear their offspring. The calories, nutrients,

Figure 2.2 Unmediated grazing (© Shutterstock)

and medicinal properties absorbed through food are very material properties. But there are some meaningful differences between how we and other creatures obtain these nutrients.

For example, animals are capable of communicating *about* and *around* food to some degree.[4] That is, bees dance to indicate distance and direction of nectar, wolves use body language to organize the hunt, and dolphins organize fishing expeditions using clicks and whistles and body gestures. Monkeys use specific screeches to indicate what kind of predator is approaching the group, while elephants provide their calves with milk in response to the calves rubbing their trunks and emitting rumble calls. Your dog or cat uses both vocal signals and body language to let you know it is time for dinner. When grazing together, zebras express satisfaction by a blow through the lips (Estes 2012). While these communicative acts do represent a form of semiotic mediation separating the creature from the nutrients they will feed on, they do not involve the sorts of technological mediation humans engage in when they use a hoe to grow corn, buy groceries from the store, or cook food over a fire. For instance, consider how grazing zebras as seen in Figure 2.2 have almost unmediated access to the food they need by putting their mouths to the ground and ripping grass up with their teeth (see also Vignette 2.1 for an example of the intimate relationship between orangutans and their food).

2.3

Vignette 2.1   Daniel Naumenko: Orangutans in the Rainforest

Daniel Naumenko completed his senior thesis at Rutgers University under the direction of Dr. Erin Vogel and is now working on a Ph.D. in Biological Anthropology at the University of Colorado—Boulder.

I started in a lab, as nervous and timid as any new undergrad, analyzing urine samples from wild orangutans in Indonesia. For years, field workers had been collecting these samples along with numerous other data detailing their diets, destined to be sent thousands of miles away to a giant freezer. Little did I know I would soon catch a glimpse of a grand discourse over food, not between two people, but between an individual and their environment.

The lab analyses I conducted that first year sought to determine how biological functions changed with diet. The orangutans we study, along with most other members of their species, live in a particularly difficult environment. For short spurts of weeks or a few months, fruit, orangutans' preferred food and primary source of energy, bursts into abundance, leading to a veritable feeding frenzy. But soon, this high-fruit period gives way to a long period where little, if any, fruit is available. The orangutans are then forced to rely on leaves, bark, and anything else they can find for many months or years.

The unpredictable availability of fruit, and the poor quality of what orangutans are left to rely on, begs the question of how they respond to this boom-and-bust environment. Using urine samples, we can take a look at the balance of energy within each individual over time, including when they are sick or stressed. All organisms need to eat to provide themselves with enough energy to function; fighting infections and coping with stress add to that bill. But with fruit so scarce for such long periods, maintaining this balance is no easy task for orangutans.

To further my understanding of how orangutans respond to these changes in diet dictated by their fluctuating environment, I set out to study them in person. Deep within the rainforests of Borneo sits the Tuanan Orangutan Research Station, our camp for year-round field studies. Each morning, we hike out to a nest in the pitch blackness, with a small headlamp to light our way and a machete to clear a small path. By 4:30 am, we reach the nest, high up in a tree, and wait. Through the cacophony of birds, the chorus of insects, the singing of gibbons, we hear the rustle of leaves, and then a splattering stream. Time to catch a urine sample!

Once out of the nest, the orangutan we are waiting for starts her day. For the next 12 or so hours, we follow her and her three-year-old son at a distance and watch, recording their behaviors and everything about their diet: what plant parts they eat, how much, how long, how fast. Orangutans spend nearly the entire day on their own and eating, with the occasional nap mixed in. The quality of food is so low and fruit so scarce during these low-fruit periods that they can't do much else except eat and look for their next meal. In fact, during the rare periods when fruit is abundant, orangutans prioritize it in their diet, building up fat stores to help carry them through the lean low-fruit season. And although mothers spend several years with their offspring, teaching them the skills necessary to forage and feed, this is one of the few social relationships orangutans ever engage in. Food is so scarce and of such poor quality that orangutans cannot live and forage in close proximity without competing. It was clear from my observations that there was little for them to eat and that they struggled to make ends meet.

Striving to understand their diet, both in the lab and the field, has only increased my interest in how food connects individuals to their environment. For all species (except to some degree humans), diet is dictated by the environment. Organisms must learn to respond to the inherent and sometimes unpredictable fluctuations in food, and they must strategize in order to survive. Additionally, it is likely that signal molecules respond to the orangutan's environment and diet along with their behavior. Even humans are still engaged in a dialogue with the environment over food; and a growing number are aware that they live at the mercy of a changing climate. For me, I can't wait to get back into the forest and continue to delve into the biological conversation between rainforest and orangutan, and to learn just how orangutans manage to survive.

By contrast, humans have devised a range of tools and techniques, social relationships, and communicative media for transforming our environment into the sustenance that we require. In other words, although zebras may show some awareness of other animals while eating, and may even pass messages among themselves about approaching predators or the availability of better grasses elsewhere, this communication is not essential to the direct consumption of ingredients from their environment. As with other animals, there is not much in the way of semiotically mediated tool use or foodways transmission. These other organisms do not engage in the sort of discursively mediated interactions displayed in the images in Figures 2.3 and 2.4: humans celebrating as they eat their fill and humans caregiving even as they themselves are starving.[5]

Among our closest primate relatives, we see some use of semiotically designed food technologies as well as the socialization and maintenance of foodways practices. For example, gorillas hum and sing when foraging and feeding as expressions of contentment, while baby gorillas scream when being weaned to indicate displeasure (Salmi, Hammerschmidt, and Doran-Sheehy 2013). Studies of chimpanzees also suggest that they may exhibit some symbolic mediation. Consider for example a chimpanzee coming upon and eating some ants climbing out of an anthill onto a stick; this would not be a semiotic act. However, once our close relative looks around for an appropriately shaped stick, pokes it into the termite mound, waits for the termites to march out, licks the stick clean, and then reinserts the stick to obtain another mouthful, semiotic mediation has occurred. The stick functioned as a piece of technology used to deliver this delicacy because the chimp was capable of interpreting a material object as a form filled with symbolic meaning: a termite-extraction instrument.

2.4   With respect to the semiotic acquisition of food production strategies, Whiten, Horner, and de Waal (2005) discovered in a series of field observations and experiments that several foodways were successfully transmitted by one individual to others in a chimpanzee group. These practices

Figure 2.3 *The Feast of the Bean King* by Jacob Jordaens (1593–1678)
Photo courtesy of KHM-Museumsverband, Austria. Reproduced with permission.

Figure 2.4 Starving people huddle together during the peak of India's Bengal famine in 1943 (© Shutterstock)

included nut-cracking, termite-fishing, and accessing food from a machine. Sometimes more than one variation on the technique was discovered, such as using a long or short stick for the termites, using stone or wood for cracking nuts, and using the poke or lift method for accessing the food in a machine. In these cases, individuals would tend to conform to the leader's choice of technique, and groups would diverge over time in their choice of one food practice or another. In other words, foodways were used to semiotically mediate group bonding, possibly indexing an incipient cultural identity. Another recent study reports that a group of chimpanzees used leaves fashioned into spoons and gathered around to drink from a naturally occurring pool of palm wine being tapped by humans in West Africa. Unfortunately, the report does not discuss if and how the chimps communicated during their drinking sessions (Hockings et al. 2015).

2.5   For now, we will take a closer look at the foodways and discourses that mediate humans' access to their food. First, it is clear that we depend on soil, water, sunlight, flora, and fauna, like other organisms, yet the fact that

Figure 2.5 Chimpanzees using sticks as tools to fish for termites in Uganda

we tend to refer to these as environmental "resources" signals a semiotic interpretation of these natural objects as items awaiting extraction and manipulation by us, their interpreters. Similarly, technologies, while existing as a host of material objects, are also the result of semiotic engagements. That is, ploughs, factories, and chemical pesticides do not exist until we use our semiotic skills to transform objects into "useful" objects. So, while chimpanzees may demonstrate their capacity for semiotic mediation by modeling for their offspring how to use a stick to fish for termites to eat, the human production of arrowheads and microwaves requires quantitatively more and qualitatively different forms of semiotic mediation at the level of both production and transmission.

Consider some of the human forms of physical, mental, and discursive labor involved in procuring, processing, storing, and distributing food. We procure food, sometimes by shopping at the market and sometimes by gathering, scavenging, fishing, or hunting for berries, nuts, rabbits, fish, and other flora and fauna. We may also produce food via agriculture, animal husbandry, genetically modifying organisms, or manufacturing chemical flavors. We process foods for storage and transport by fermenting or pickling, drying or salting, canning or freezing; for instance, beets are transformed into sugar, milk into cheese, and grain into pasta. We use these and other techniques (roasting, baking, boiling, etc.) to prepare foods for more immediate consumption. We package foods for storage, transport, and sale (in calabashes, reusable canvas bags decorated with ads, plastic containers with labeling, etc.), the better to distribute food via feasts, markets, and internet shopping. For example, food circulates through heirloom tomato tastings at farmers markets, sushi-grade tuna flown into mountain ski towns, and sugary cereals sold via "advergaming" (advertising via video games; see Thomson 2011). We then serve and consume our food from a common pot around the hearth, with fine cutlery on a yacht, with chopsticks on the couch, from a travel mug while texting, etc. And we do all this before we eliminate the remains in doggy bags, composts, dumps, and sewers.

These foodways are organized by human thought and social interaction, and the diversity of these practices helps define the contours of our sociocultural differences. The ways we produce food are governed in part by political institutions and ideologies. How we process, store, and distribute food reflects and reinforces our political and economic systems, including related inequities. Our cultural categories and beliefs influence what we eat and how we prepare and consume our foods. And the ways in which we socialize our children at home and in various institutions affect how all of these other forms of social organization are transmitted from one generation to the next. In short, unlike most creatures, humans around the world engage in socioculturally diverse and symbolically mediated foodways. In the next section, we explore some of the theories and some of the history of how humans arrived at this state of affairs.

The Emergence of Foodways and Discourses in the Human Past

This brief survey of the role of semiotic mediation in human foodways is suggestive of a long and complex relationship between language, food-ways, and cultures in the human species. Yet the story of the origins of these relationships is much harder to tell. The Linguistic Society of Paris threw up their hands in dismay in 1866 at the impossibility of ever knowing the truth about the origins of human language and banned all subsequent scientific exploration of the question. Nonetheless, research continues and though inconclusive, one hypothesis is that spoken language began 100,000–50,000 years ago.[6] Similarly, the record of early human food-ways, although continually clarified by new paleoanthropological findings based on early tools, food remains, and fire pits, is not yet fully written and may never be. After all written records do not appear until approximately 5,000 years ago. Nonetheless, hypotheses abound as new evidence about our ancestors and near primate relatives continues to be collected and ana-lyzed. From this evidence, it is likely that the material and symbolic sides of food and language have been entangled throughout evolutionary time and across human cultures.

2.6

What we do know is that at some point in the past, humans began to use a finite number of phonemes or manual signs to communicate an infi-nite number of propositions about the world, thus setting human language apart from the closed systems of other communicating creatures, who use at best a limited number of signs to transmit a limited number of ideas to each other (although several non-human primates have learned to commu-nicate with humans, and sometimes each other, to varying degrees through sign language and other means). As a result, our human ancestors were able to communicate not only about the here and now, but also about the past and future, a feature of language known as **displacement**.

2.7

Prayers and myths, laws and spells, lies and jokes all became possible as humans began to engage in **conviviality**, that is, taking lively pleasure in the company of others (from Latin *com* = 'with' and *vivere* = 'to live' and *com-vivere* = 'carouse together'). A form of conviviality known as **commensal-ity,** the act of eating together (from Latin *com* = 'with' and *mensa* = 'table'), has been much studied in recent years by both archaeologists and cultural anthropologists (see for example, Kerner, Chou, and Warmind 2015). We surmise that sharing foods and words, tastes and tales (language *through* food and language *around* food) could have provided the pretext, context, and medium for social and emotional bonding. One recent hypothesis hav-ing to do with food consumption and the emergence of language proposed by Van Esterik (2015) is that in utero feeding and breastfeeding are the **ontogenic** (related to individual development) and **phylogenic** (related to species evolution) precursors of commensality.[7]

But while the interactions between human foodways and discourses in the distant past may never be wholly known, more can be said with some certainty about our more recent prehistoric ancestors. Evidence for this comes from archaeological investigations of **ecofacts**, or the remains of what people ate; **artifacts**, or the utensils they used to produce, cook, and eat food; and the spatial organization of the sites where they flaked tools and hunted, processed tubers and feasted. Additionally, scholars have used the data collected by early explorers and contemporary ethnographers who made contact with non-literate peoples to hypothesize about the lives of our ancestors. It must not be presumed that these groups were living unchanged for thousands of years until their lives were impacted by modernity; however, the food-and-language patterns of small-scale hunter-gather and horticultural groups can be explored for clues and models of how our early ancestors adapted to similar environments as they migrated and occupied more and more diverse ecosystems. See Vignette 2.2 for a peek at how archaeologists use material evidence from the past and present to understand how human social life has varied over space and time.[8]

2.8

Vignette 2.2   Anthony P. Graesch: An Archaeological Window on Foodways and Food Talk

2.9

Anthony Graesch is an Associate Professor and Chair of the Anthropology Department at Connecticut College, whose research focuses on the archaeology of North America, past and present.

My interest in archaeological anthropology didn't begin with an explicit desire to study foodways. Nevertheless, much of my scholarship has been related to the role of foodways and food-related discourses in the organization of everyday life in past and present societies. My first research projects, beginning with a summer field school in California as an undergraduate, explored the archaeological past through colonial entanglements between indigenous North American and European societies, manifestations of political economy, and organization of household labor. Inevitably, almost all of these projects came to include smaller-scale studies of both ancient and recent foodways. This is because much of our material world, especially the objects we regularly discard, is related to the foods we routinely acquire, process, and consume.

For example, in one study, I collaborated with two other archaeologists to examine the impacts of 18th- and 19th-century European colonialism on everyday life in western North America. This project included the comparative analysis of vertebrate faunal remains (i.e., animal bone) recovered during excavations in three indigenous North American cultural settings: Emigdiano Chumash and Island Chumash in California and Stó:lō-Coast Salish in British Columbia. Our research suggests that while altered foodways are often privileged as evidence of cultural change in studies of cultural entanglement, continuity in foodways can also be regarded as an active process and a response to new power dynamics. That is, in the face of mounting colonial pressures, the persistence of longstanding food procurement, processing, and consumption practices can be viewed as a marker of ethnic and group identity and even a covert symbol of resistance. Indigenous food choices in present-day North America still echo the political and ideological impacts of colonialism; like language, foodways simultaneously reflect and define indigenous reactions and responses to changing power structures.

In practice, archaeological approaches have proven to be particularly useful for investigating economic, ecological, and certain social dimensions of past foodways. Preserved plant foods, hearths, fishing knives, and cooking stones have all constituted primary datasets in some of the various research projects I've pursued. However, in the absence of a textual record, food discourses are difficult if not outright impossible to examine in the pre-present, even if we recognize that such discourses were probably just as important in daily social life then as they are now. But archaeological concepts, methods, and theory can add considerable analytic and interpretive value to anthropological studies of the present, especially those that examine the shaping roles of objects, language, and embodied action in the organization of everyday social behavior.

Some examples of the latter are evident in research I conducted while participating in a nine-year study (2001–2010) at the UCLA Sloan Center on Everyday Lives of Families (CELF). On this project, we applied data collection methods traditionally reserved for archaeological research—systematic mapping of physical spaces, digital photography, and assemblage cataloging—to the study of work-family balance in present-day dual-earner families with children. Our analytic emphasis on issues of materiality, or the dialectic of social life and objects, soon made clear that kitchen spaces are something special in the lives of working families. Not unexpectedly, food preparation is an activity that anchors much of parents' time in the home to kitchen spaces. However, we were somewhat surprised to learn that all family members gravitate to kitchens to accomplish a wide range of activities—homework, bill paying, scheduling, conversations, child socialization, etc.—during their waking hours at home. Indeed, our data demonstrate that while family members enjoy only an average of four to five waking hours per day under the same roof, most of this time is spent in the kitchen. This centripetal force of kitchens in families' hyper-busy daily lives is evident in the complex assemblages of objects docked or staged in these spaces: mobile phones, schoolwork, backpacks, schedules, multiple calendars, bills, and books, among numerous other objects unrelated to meal preparation and anticipating daily life outside of the home. Simultaneously shaped by and reflecting something of the hyper-paced lives of working families in the 21st century, these intersectional spaces are also where children are recurrently exposed to parents' notions of appropriate food choices, taste, edibility, preparation, and purchasing habits as a result of frequent congregation in kitchens and not just at mealtimes.

Based on the available evidence, what we know is that until approximately 10,000 years ago, all human groups lived in small-scale societies that were nomadic and relatively egalitarian, in that status distinctions were based primarily on age and gender. These groups relied on hunting, gathering, and fishing for their subsistence. We can also assume that by this point humans had organized themselves into culturally and linguistically distinctive social groups.

Beginning some 13,000–10,000 years ago, possibly due to the need for new subsistence strategies due to increasing population density and other factors, they began to domesticate the plants they had been previously gathering, including tubers such as yams and grains such as millet, as well as the animal products they had been foraging, from snails[9] and honey[10] to sheep and goats. They began to preserve foods, such as dried fruit, salted fish, and smoked meats, and engage in increasingly longer-distance exchange, using established trade routes to access different forms of valued foods, such as shellfish from the sea, birds from the mountains, and salt wherever it could be found.

2.10

We also know that our prehistoric ancestors were using visual symbols to record their lives and signal their cultural differences. These included rock art and portable sculptures, especially of animals they hunted or feared, and female figures they may have worshiped for their fertility (as in Figure 2.6), as well as decorated tools and ornaments, trade items such as obsidian and beads, lunar calendars, and other forms of tabulation.

As humans began to live in sedentary agricultural societies in many parts of the world, food would have been increasingly used to index forms of social differentiation and ranking. The archaeological record suggests

Figure 2.6 Venus of Willendorf, Austria (© Shutterstock)

that with growing population density and social stratification, the quality, quantity, and diversity of foods were unequally distributed and consumed at sites decorated to represent the grandeur of some over the poverty of others. From comparative and historical linguistics, we know that distinctive languages had already proliferated as a consequence of social groups migrating over vast geographical distances and thus diversifying through natural linguistic processes over time. But as culturally distinct social groups came into contact, distinctive linguistic varieties may have become part of the toolkit for distinguishing one group from the next.[11] In other words, foodways and discourses were probably being intensified not only as markers of cultural identity between "us" and "them," but also as an index of social status, both reflecting and helping to construct newly emerging forms of social inequality.

D'Anna and Jauss (2015), for instance, analyze the functional specialization of cooking pots and their association with different sites where they were made and/or used by Uruk communities in western Asia 6,000 years ago as evidence for growing complexities in the social relationships and levels of authority being used to organize these communities. Similarly, Fletcher and Campbell (2015) read the social and symbolic significance of the remains of food consumption and disposal (ceramics, animal, and human bones) collected from 6,000-year-old domestic and mortuary sites in Turkey. They conclude that **anthropophagy** (in other words, cannibalism) occurred in ritual form—that is, humans consumed specific parts of other humans for symbolic reasons, but in ways that were strongly controlled by social sanctions. Additionally, the finding of pots depicting similar seasonal scenes dispersed throughout a large region speaks to the existence of a widespread network of communities joined by ritual feasting. Kerner (2015), also working at 6,000-year-old domestic and ritual sites in the Near East, examines drinking and churning vessels and their possible contents (water, milk, wine) for evidence of social distinction in small-scale societies and the possible foci of celebration, such as fertility.

In ranked societies, elite men would have been expected to eat more, eat better, and control whether others ate at all via **redistributive feasts**—that is, lavish occasions at which leaders were able to collect food produced by others and then redistribute it in ways that manifested others' affiliation to them. Their power to do this was still achieved rather than ascribed in that they did not inherit their positions, depending instead on their ability to inspire support from their followers. Graeber (2001) has explored how potlatches, a form of competitive feasting, were being used to negotiate power among the Indians of the Pacific Northwest contacted by explorers and early ethnographers and involved not only the gifting of food but also other valuables, such as blankets and copper ornaments, that were sometimes even destroyed to display the leader's power and wealth.

We read all of these cases as instances of language *through* food, or that is, of humans using food to communicate who they are with each other. What of language use *about* and *around* food? Despite the lack of any written record of what people were discussing during much of this time, we can assume that language about food was on the rise, including specialized vocabularies to facilitate food procurement as well as ritual genres to lubricate interactions with the food-providing gods. Similarly, opportunities to engage in language around food while producing and consuming it would also have been increasing. Especially as humans began to inhabit more permanent settlements and establish new food-centric spaces (gardens and pastures, kitchens and **middens** (refuse heaps), longhouses and feasting areas), the exchange of both food and talk would have been common.

Semiotic Mediation of Foodways and Discourses in Cities and Empires

Some 5,000 or so years ago, larger populations gathered in expanding urban centers in early state societies, fueled by increasingly intensive agriculture of crops such as wheat, corn, rice, and legumes, as well as animal husbandry of goats, sheep, pigs, chickens, and guinea pigs. New ways of processing and storing staples were developed; for example, fermented beer and wine could be kept in ceramic pots, and grains could be stockpiled in stone buildings, protecting against times of drought and pestilence. But these developments also led to sanitation problems and plagues, the specialization of labor (farmers, builders, metalworkers, soldiers), and gross forms of social inequality. Stratification was violently enforced by those who inherited power and wealth (kings) over those who were born without (slaves) or were forcibly stripped of privilege when their community was overpowered by a marauding group next door. Fernandez-Armesto (2002) provides a good overview of the pluses and minuses of agriculture and settlement as compared to hunting-gathering and nomadism.

Neighboring groups continued to exchange foods based on what they could not get in their own vicinity, for example, exchanging shellfish for grain. However, this is also the time when longer-distance trading routes were established across land by camels and sea by boats for the exchange of rare or "exotic" commodities, such as gold and silk, but especially aromatic spices and scents such as salt, pepper, frankincense, and turmeric. These latter, lightweight comestibles were valued not only because they came from afar but also because they were ephemeral in their effects—lit as incense, applied as perfumes, and ingested for their taste and not because they filled the belly. By 3,000 years ago these spice routes and silk roads were fueling the wealth of emperors and filling their heads with strategies for controlling access to these exotic tastes. As Nabhan (2014) explains, these spice routes developed over thousands of years into the present forms of what we now know as **globalization,** to be explored at more length below. The map in Figure 2.7 shows the major Old World trade routes prior to European expansion.

2.11

So, although the first empires (such as Sumer, Yangtze, Indus, Olmec, and Roman) arose in various corners of the world where food could be predictably produced and amassed, the expansive and appropriative mechanisms of empire were driven by an ever-growing urge to extract both staples and delicacies from tributary neighbors. The elite used enslaved labor and tribute from dominated regions to amass and display their wealth through visible signs of power, such as personal ornamentation (gold, silk, and incense) and monuments (ornate palaces and megalithic tombs), as seen in Figure 2.8. Urban centers emerged at the crossroads of trade, and empires expanded over the perceived need to control the spice routes and silk roads.

Writing and math arose in conjunction with cities and empires, partly to keep track of the accumulating wealth and partly to record the conquests of emperors for posterity. For these tasks, **orthographies** (writing systems) proliferated: Sumerian cuneiform on clay tablets around 3000 BCE, Chinese ideographs on bone around 2000 BCE, the Phoenician alphabet on papyrus around 1500 BCE, and Mayan hieroglyphs on stone around 1000

Old World Trade Routes circa 1340

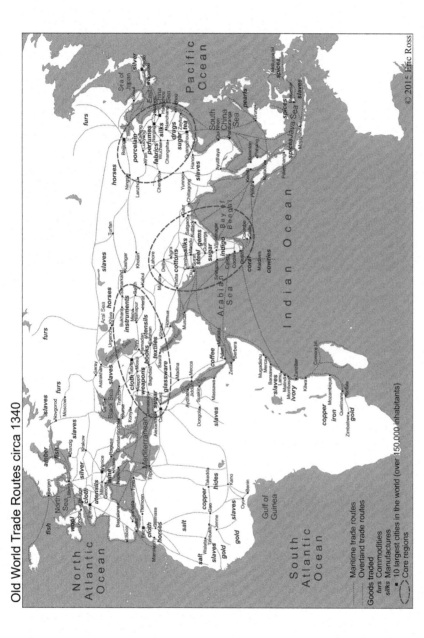

Figure 2.7 Map of Old World trade routes circa 1340

2.12

Figure 2.8 Terracotta Warriors in Xi'an, China (© Shutterstock)

2.13

2.14

BCE (see Gnanadesikan 2009 for a good history of writing). Additionally, the occupation of writing specialist, including scribes and historians, as well as institutions for the storage and transmission of these texts, such as libraries and schools, emerged. Simplified trade languages or **lingua francas** were established by traders to facilitate communication along the trade routes. Some of these were simplified versions of languages already spoken by some powerful group along the trade route, such as Aramaic or Swahili, and others were developed out of bits and pieces of many languages, such as Sabir, a language created around the Mediterranean. However, it was also during this period that grammars were honed to index respect and submission (these linguistic features are called **honorifics**) while formal registers were codified in order to distinguish them from informal ways of speaking, and thus used to index status and formality in political, religious, and educational spheres. Xiong et al. (2014), for example, attempt to trace the development of honorifics over a period from feudal to contemporary China.

Food too was used to index status. That is, language *through* food is apparent in how food was produced, prepared, served, and consumed. Class stratification was reflected and reinforced by the fact that laborers ate simply and worked hard, frequently producing and preparing food for others, while the elite signaled their wealth by enjoying sumptuous feasts made of diverse and exotic prestige foods brought from afar and prepared in elaborate ways by underlings. The most extreme example of the imperial power to consume whatever they wanted was that of anthropophagy, an infamous example of this practice being the Aztec rulers' predilection for sacrificing war prisoners and eating select parts to manifest their power (Coe and Koontz 2008). Additionally, Freedman (2015) discusses how the excess in amount and diversity of foods and social hierarchy on display in medieval European banquets has continued in varying forms into the present day even as, in principle, we laud the democratizing forces of commensality. But political commensality is complicated. For instance, even a cursory reading of the 20,000 cuneiform tablets used to tabulate the administrative commands and receipts of Zimri-Lim, the Amorrite king of the Mari of Old Babylon (reigning 1775–1761 BCE), would indicate that the king had an avid taste for locusts and truffles, foods associated at that time with the nomadic Hana herdsmen who were deemed uncivilized by the urban, beer-and-bread eating Mari. However, upon careful analysis, it is equally possible that the king was actually stockpiling these uncouth foods to serve at feasts he held to keep the fealty of the Hana who served as his military (Nymann 2015).

As this last example bears witness, written language *about* food had also begun to appear: storehouse and mercantile records were etched onto clay tablets, Judaic food prescriptions were recorded in the Bible, recipes were written down early in China, and travelers (for example, Herodotus and Marco Polo) reported on the "strange" foodways of others. In an analysis of documents from the early Christian era, Gilhus (2015) explores how religious sects used written representations of how they ate to distinguish themselves from others throughout the ancient Mediterranean world. In particular, meat-eating became the means for identifying the Other: "savages" ate raw meat, Christians refused to eat sacrificed meat, and for some others, the smoke from this meat was what fed the gods.

Language *around* food began to be formulated: rules of etiquette were required by the elite, monastic silence was imposed at meals, and domestic kitchens became associated with domestic gossip. This is also the period when the language-*as*-food ideology that people must be purposefully educated via language outside the home first emerged. Schools, temples, guilds, and other institutions for explicitly instructing youth (of a certain age, class, and gender) first appeared in socially stratified societies. Embedded in these institutions was an understanding that specialists could not be expected to learn through peripheral participation and observation all of the knowledge and practices they would need to know to fulfill their social roles. Instead, it began to be believed that youth must be nurtured via language into full-fledged membership in their society.

Mercantilist World Economy, ca. 1530–1776

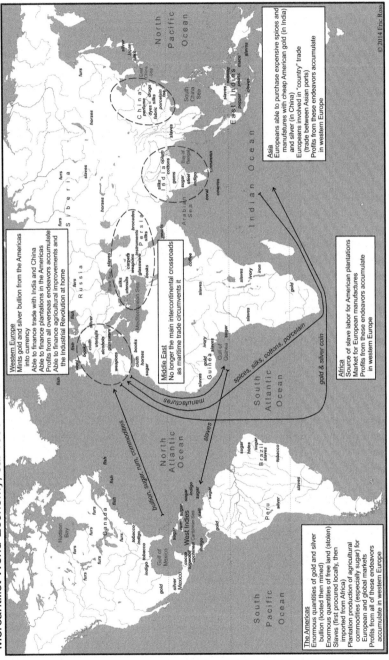

Western Europe
Mints gold and silver bullion from the Americas into currency
Able to finance trade with India and China
Able to finance plantations in the Americas
Profits from all overseas endeavors accumulate and the Industrial Revolution at home
Able to finance agricultural improvements and the Industrial Revolution at home

Middle East
No longer the main intercontinental crossroads as maritime trade circumvents it

Asia
Europeans able to purchase expensive spices and manufactures with cheap American gold (in India) and silver (in China)
Europeans involved in "country" trade (trade between Asian ports)
Profits from these endeavors accumulate in western Europe

Africa
Source of slave labor for American plantations
Market for European manufactures
Profits from these endeavors accumulate in western Europe

The Americas
Enormous quantities of gold and silver bullion (looted then mined)
Enormous quantities of free land (stolen)
Slaves (first procured locally, then imported from Africa)
Plantation production of agricultural commodities (especially sugar) for European and global markets
Profits from all of these endeavors accumulate in western Europe

© 2014 Eric Ross

Figure 2.9 Map of the mercantilist world economy circa 1530–1776

Copyright © Eric Ross, Al Akhawayn University, Morocco. Reproduced with permission.

2.15

Semiotic Mediation of Foodways and Discourses During Colonialism

Approximately 500 years ago, the fledgling empires of Europe, eager to corner the market on the spice trade, launched their globe-changing investment in exploration and colonization of other areas of the world. As explained in the last section, the original spice routes formed the precursors of the first global network of exchange. Medieval Europeans' desire for the smell and taste of these lightweight exotics (Freedman 2008) drove exploration and acquisition across three continents and finally the whole world, as mapped out in Figure 2.9. Fueled by resources extracted from the colonies and the labor exploited by capital, a new political economic formation was forged: the capitalist nation-state. Here, the ideals of freedom and equality were spawned during the Enlightenment while new forms of competition over resources and new forms of international warfare were simultaneously created.

This desire for spices launched what has come to be known as the **Columbian Exchange**, a term that refers in particular to the circulation of foods, but also diseases, between Europe and the Americas as a result of Columbus sailing in 1492 from Spain to the Caribbean in search of India (Crosby 1972). Many others followed or were forcibly transplanted, and as a result of the increased flow in people, goods, and ideas, foods from around the globe were naturalized—not just imported, but also implanted 2.16 in the soil—in new places. Tomatoes and chili peppers from Central America were slowly incorporated into the cuisines of southern Italy and southeast Asia, potatoes from South America became the overwhelming staple of Ireland, beef and dairy from Europe and rice from Africa came to be

Figure 2.10 An assortment of spices and herbs at market (© Shutterstock)

deemed essential throughout the Americas, and breadfruit was borrowed (on a second try after the mutiny on the *H. M. S. Bounty*) from the Pacific and taken to the Caribbean to keep the enslaved populations fed.[12]

Colonialism operated through the control of colonized territories and their peoples via political, economic, cultural, and ideological domination. The **plantation system** of using enslaved labor from Africa and indentured labor from Asia and Oceania to produce a few valued food commodities was instituted in the colonies at this time. This system made it increasingly difficult for indigenous peoples to hold onto their land and labor, a fact that has continued to make it difficult for peoples throughout the Caribbean and Central and South America to grow the crops they need to subsist on, despite that most former colonies were granted independence by the mid to late 20th century. The merchant capital acquired through colonialism laid the foundation for the Industrial Revolution and the rise of capitalism in Europe (Wallerstein 1974, 1980; Wolf 1982).

New industrial means for producing and processing various resources through manufacturing were created, turning iron into guns, cotton into cloth, and sugar cane into sugar and rum. In *Sweetness and Power* (1985), Mintz traces how over the course of a couple of centuries, sugar was transformed from a scarce, highly valued resource available only to the European elite via the spice trade into a mass-produced commodity for consumption by the European laborers who fueled the Industrial Revolution. The power-inflected taste for sugar in Europe drove what has come to be known as the transatlantic trade triangles. Europeans began to enslave and transport West Africans to the Caribbean and southern United States, where they were forced to grow sugar cane, coffee, and cotton. The sugar cane was then processed into rum or refined into white sugar and sent back to England where the industrial working class became hooked on these now low-cost commodities (that still carried an upper-class connotation). Revved up (if not nourished) by these "hunger killers," along with tea from the other British colonies, the workers produced the steel tools, guns, and cotton textiles so valued in Africa and needed and used as currency in exchange for enslaved Africans.

2.17

With respect to language, the invention of the printing press by Johannes Gutenberg in the 15th century unleashed a flood of new ideas and information to wide sectors of society via mass-produced newspapers and novels, which promoted the ideals of national citizenship and hopes for social mobility. Anderson (1983), in fact, argued that print capitalism changed the way we think about and organize society. Although schools and universities were originally developed to keep track of specialized knowledge by knowledge specialists such as priests, during this period the republican ideal emerged that schools should be used to close the literacy gap between rich and poor. Similarly, standard forms of speaking and writing were developed out of the liberal ideal to increase rational expression and democratic inter-comprehensibility, but were also then used to rationalize centralized governmental control. In other words, these formal registers, as well as a range of specialized **jargons** (such as the technical language used in legal documents), were linked to and used to articulate wealth and power. By contrast, people began to be conscious at this time of the signifi-cance of their **vernaculars**, the informal languages used at home and in the local community rather than at work or in the capital; they began to main-tain and use these like comfort foods to express local warmth. Cavanaugh's (2016) work on food and language provides a good example of how this worked in tandem in 19th- and 20th-century Italy as she explores how the Bergamo dialect is used to market "authentic" salami at a farmers market in northern Italy. We will return to this issue of "authentic" heritage foods in Chapter 4.

Language *through* food is found in this period, especially in the West, in the proliferation of foodways conventions communicating binary distinctions: "civilized" versus "savage," national versus regional cuisines, food for the masses versus foods of the rich, and most recently home-cooked comfort foods versus institutional cooking. Texts *about* food began to proliferate in the form of cookbooks, nutrition tracts, and ethnographic descriptions of exotic foodways. Further, the terminology for discussing food was refined, such as for discussing wine tasting, cheese, and sushi. Middle-class notions concerning polite conversation *around* food—that is, etiquette for table talk—and notions of conviviality and commensality began to be standard-ized via etiquette books and newspaper columns. Finally, language *as* food can be seen in the growth during this period of the middle-class belief that children should be socialized at school and at the table while eating. Addi-tionally, health education to teach people to "eat right" began in the 19th century, and by the 20th century advertising helped to inspire the consump-tion of processed foods with questionable nutritional value.

Semiotic Mediation of Foodways and Discourses in the Age of Globalization

Over the last century, the globalizing forces that were gathering for mil-lennia and particularly during the past 500 years have crystallized into a number of structural processes we now label globalization. Both wars and neocolonial economics have been fueled by the increased ease of transpor-tation and communication across national boundaries, which have in turn allowed for the circulation of ideas, commodities, and people from multi-national CEOs to refugees.

With respect to food, beginning as early as the 19th century, war and industry triggered new technologies for producing, storing, and trans-porting food, including canning and freezing, steamships, and trains. For example, the American Civil War was made possible by canned goods, and chemical warfare during WWII morphed into the pesticides that have made large-scale commercial agriculture possible. Some iconic foods have spread around the globe (e.g., Coca-Cola), and yet these same foods are also **glocalized,** or transformed for local taste buds. For example, McDonald's burgers are made with soy sauce in Beijing (for more on McDonald's in East Asia, see Watson 2006). Meanwhile, the consumer's taste for authentically exotic food grows, even when these are actually the **creolized** (blended or mixed) foods of ex-colonies or immigrant communities, such as *gumbo* in New Orleans and *adobo* in the Philippines. It is fascinating to explore the **food chains,** that is the global chain of events leading to individual food commodities reaching our plates.[13] This concept, also sometimes referred to as **food paths,** may include both the historical and present-day paths traveled by a particular ingredient such as corn. Additionally, particular dishes such as rice-and-beans (Wilk and Barbosa 2012) may vary in fascinating ways as they make their way around the globe.

2.18

And all of these food changes have been paralleled by globalizing changes in the arena of language as audio-visual and electronic media are increasingly produced and consumed around the world. The overlap with food can be found everywhere. Language *about* food includes a range of multimodal "foodie" discourses: food and wine magazines, lush food films, seductive food ads, and Instagram posts of our latest meals. Discussions of dietary restrictions, allergies, and anti-bacterial soaps pervade the blogosphere, as do discourses—in the form of petitions, newsletters, and conference notices—about food insecurity, food justice, and food sovereignty, among other things. One can order food online, from exotic ingredients (for example, acorn flour and snails) to full meals (ready to eat or ready to prepare as family meals). One craze we recently heard of: Uber drivers will take you to *their* favorite ethnic restaurant. Of course, not everyone has access to all of these discourses and media, nor may they desire to take part in them.

2.19

The received wisdom for many brought up within a certain class of Western culture is that language *around* food—that is, talking while cooking and eating—is a hallmark of our humanity and more particularly of our "civilization." Now, however, these practices may seem old-fashioned or even classist to many, while others are in a sort of moral panic over the fear that the family meal, and therefore civilization, is disappearing. And yet new media have also allowed for talk in the presence of food to proliferate in new ways—for example, Skype calls between family members on different continents as they open and sample food sent from home (De Leon 2015).

Language *through* food is also doing well in this brave new world as we self-consciously contrast authentic/traditional and inauthentic/modern cuisines. We worry about the semiotic effects of foods on bodies in the form of obesity, emaciated children, and dieting. In the United States, sustainable foodies vie with freedom-eaters in school cafeterias and PTAs as explored in Riley's school food study (forthcoming). These discourses feed into contemporary notions of language *as* food, as we worry about what our children are consuming and digesting from the airwaves.

Tracing the Origins of Fusion Food

As discussed in the last two sections, food has long been a medium of semiotic (mis)communication for peoples arriving at the doorstep of others. Whether in the form of spice trades, colonialism, or globalization, innumerable cross-cultural encounters have been instigated by and organized around food. For instance, spices became invested with power-laden values of status, hierarchy, and ethnic difference, and as a result transformed into a meaningful currency of cross-cultural dialogue. And the sorts of food-focused exchanges that took place in caravansaries and bazaars so long ago continue to unfold in consequential ways around the world today. These take place due to a range of migratory experiences, from the first acquisitive journeys of discovery by Europeans to the inquisitive jaunts of jet-setting tourists and the difficult treks of immigrants and refugees today. We now explore a few specific examples of how language through-around-about-as food have contributed in specific times and places to the production of what many of us would refer to as **fusion foodways**, that is, food practices that are the melded consequence of cross-cultural contact and semiotic mediation.

First, consider the reactions of New England Protestant missionaries to the foodways they encountered in the kingdom of Hawai'i during the early 19th century (Kashay 2009). Due to the expense and difficulties of preserving and transporting corn and wheat by boat from New England and the ecological impossibility of producing these familiar ingredients in the Pacific islands, they were forced to eat what Hawaiians ate. Some missionaries even enjoyed local foods such as pineapples, breadfruit, and taro, according to the letters and reports they sent home; the only food they rejected as "uncivilized" was dog meat. The difficulty of procuring familiar foods became evidence—a sign—of their piousness as compared with the Hawaiians, whom they considered dirty, lazy, and gluttonous. They judged the Hawaiians for their manner of preparing and consuming food—peeling potatoes with their fingernails instead of knives and eating with their hands from a communal plate—believing these were signs of the indigenous population's "savagery." By contrast, the missionaries maintained their home foodways, using individual plates, forks, tablecloths, etiquette, and restraint as signs of their higher, "civilized" status. In other words, out of necessity, these missionaries filled the foods they adopted with acceptable meaning, while investing local foodways with negative symbolism, thus rationalizing the destructive impacts of their missionizing on the Hawaiians' culture and sociopolitical autonomy. Over the last two centuries, Hawaiians have created a **creole** language out of a mix of their indigenous language and the

English introduced by missionaries, as well as a wide variety of creolized Hawaiian dishes, such as chicken-and-pineapple kabobs and taro chips.

Immigrants from post-colonial settings have also engaged in complexly layered symbolic food encounters. For instance, Tuomainen (2009) sought to understand why immigrants from Ghana to London were eating as they did at the turn of the 21st century. In Ghana, foodways had been affected by British colonialism in a number of ways, from the early introduction of agricultural crops such as maize, rice, and sweet potato to the importation of canned and frozen foods, and finally by major changes in land tenure, urbanization, and transportation. As a result, colonial food items, such as canned fish, bread, and sauces, and ways of eating, such as consuming family meals in courses using silverware, and with turkey at Christmas, became status symbols both for the educated elite and for others who aspired to this status. When Ghanaians first emigrated to London, they used traditional Ghanaian recipes and available ingredients to prepare **hybridized** dishes for dinner in the home; however, they also began to eat British foods for breakfast and lunch. This was partly because they wished to fit in and partly because these breakfast and lunch foods, which had operated as status markers back home, were cheap and plentiful in London. Thus, just as many Ghanaian immigrants became linguistically bilingual, **code-switching** back and forth between English and their home language(s) on a daily basis, so did many also become **food bilinguals**. However, since the rise of multiculturalism in the 1980s, traditional ethnic foods (or rather their hybrid cousins) have been symbolically re-invested with pride in pan-Ghanaian identity and celebrated at public functions and restaurants.

Frequently, **syncretic** foods result from colonial imposition—that is, a new food is created out of a mix of the meaningful foodways of the colonial settlers and those they settle among and learn from. Foods such as these may then be re-filled with symbolic meaning as a local, **heritage** food—that is, a food handed down through the generations and celebrated as symbolic of this particular tradition. Let's look for instance at the Virginia ham. Based on journals, letters, how-to manuals, and recipes from 17th–18th-century coastal Virginia, Edwards (2011) examines how Algonquian Indians, Africans (by way of the Caribbean), and the British all contributed materially and symbolically over the course of 200 years to the construction of this "local" ham. In the beginning, starving British men were completely dependent upon Indians for food, and the absence of European women cut the lines of culinary transmission to the colonies. Then, over time, this growing European middle class replaced their European indentured servants with enslaved Africans. In the Chesapeake Bay, the environment was perfect for raising pigs brought from Europe and preserving the meat: the woods provided plenty of forage for the pigs to eat and wood for smoking the meat, which proved to be a better preserving method than pickling in a hot and humid climate. However, all three peoples contributed their techniques for processing and preserving meat: smoking and drying meat or fish in smoke houses using fire was borrowed from the Indians, other smoking methods from the Afro-Caribbeans, and salt rubbing and bathing from the British. In other words, intercultural exchanges between these peoples all contributed to the syncretic creation of Virginia ham, a heritage food that now enjoys high global market value, both symbolic and economic.

Interestingly, foods found by European explorers and colonists in the "Orient" or "New World" were also brought back to the "Old World" and glocalized, given both a new form and significance in this new context. A relevant instance is the process by which "Indian curry" was produced. As Maroney (2011) explains, the "real" story begins when Portuguese explorers brought chili peppers to India in the 16th century, providing an alternative to the Tamil spice *kari* used in the spicy sauces of the subcontinent at that time. When British colonials (mostly male) took power, they adopted and appreciated hot Indian dishes that were saucy and made from fresh vegetables and spices, calling them all curries and rices while living there. Returning to Britain, these *nabobs*, Europeans enriched by their colonial exploits, trained their servants to prepare "curry" for nostalgia's sake and sought out the taste at the coffeehouses where they gathered to reminisce. Over time, women domesticated the dish to satisfy their husbands' longings, at first following recipes that called for simple spicings of black pepper, onion, and coriander, later adding turmeric and cayenne, thereby marking it through heat and color as exotic. Eventually, they came to rely on curry powder, commercially produced and exported from India specifically for this market and sometimes laced with lead to make it red. Thus, the mobility and encounters of foodstuffs and persons contributed to the production of this spice, turned dish, turned commodity, influencing both its form and meaning. The dish that never existed as such in India came eventually to symbolize the exoticism of the colonial experience there for the British.

An instance of how a specific food may be materially transplanted and symbolically transubstantiated can be seen in the success of rice throughout the Pacific. The food was first introduced by Europeans in the 19th century, effectively marketed by Chinese traders because it was easy to store, transport, and cook, and has now become a valued staple. Jourdan (2010) explains the glocalization of rice in the Solomon Islands in three stages. Early on, the elite sought it out as a form of symbolic capital, trying rice as a new prestige food and index of modernity. Next, rice was made to fill a niche in the local foodways in several steps: it was distributed as a ration to those working on plantations in Australia, then the British government doled it out following the destruction of the islanders' taro-growing gardens during World War II, and finally world marketing strategies brought the price of rice lower than that of local produce. Most recently, rice has accrued new symbolic meanings. Given the ease of procuring and preparing it in urban settings and the quick and inexpensive comfort and satiety it brings in an insecure wage-labor market, rice has become the best means of upholding kinship ties of reciprocity and expressing concern for hungry, unemployed family members. However, as Jourdan explains, this symbolic reanalysis may be shifting once again as new factors to do with market prices and global ideologies about health and the value of indigenous foodways, as explored in the next section, may be influencing the local meaning of rice once again.

Finally, the ongoing global flow of persons and goods and foods and languages creates **assemblages** of different meanings in different places, thus mediating human interactions in different ways. In small stores in Sydney and Tokyo, dried and frozen freshwater fish from South Asia are assembled alongside cell phones, SIM cards, and distinctive languages. According to Pennycook and Otsuji (2017), river fish are an example of **boundary objects**—that is, objects that work to both define a cultural community that values them while also mediating the boundary between communities. In the Japanese and Australian stores, the river fish clearly carry significance for the Bengali immigrants who discuss (in Bengali) details about the fish, but they also *become* significant for other immigrants (e.g., Fijian or Ghanaian) who ask (in English) to know more about these fish that are unfamiliar to them—what species or how they are processed. The authors also call these fish "assembling artifacts" because of how they can show up in new places, associate with new objects (in this case, phone cards), and transmit new meanings (for instance, how sweet or clean the fish is) for the people who are called to read them in these settings. As with the ancient spice routes, intercultural trade creates sometimes-chaotic social spaces in which symbolic meanings are carried by sensuous tastes and smells, negotiated via human interaction and desire, and fused in new and unfamiliar ways.

Summary

In this chapter, we have explored the semiotic mediation of foodways and discourses. We began by comparing human and animal activity and communication, speculated on some prehistoric connections, and traced some major social, political, economic, and technological changes related to both food and language in more recent history. We suggest that human foodways and discourses have played mutually reinforcing roles in human social organization and exchange because food and language are fundamental to the processes and development of social systems—economic, political, religious, and communicative. On the one hand, patterns of food production, preservation, preparation, and consumption are the material foundations of human societies while, on the other hand, linguistic communication is the filament without which much of this would have been impossible. In other words, food has been the stuff through which societies have interacted during contact—through trade, colonialism, capitalism, globalization—frequently in the absence of a common language, becoming instead the bases on which new languages were created.

The latest period covering the globalizing interpenetration of food and language is the context for most of the rest of this book. But before we plunge into that story, let us first turn in the next chapter to the various methods used to study how these phenomena unfold in a variety of contemporary settings.

Notes

1. See Mertz (1985) for a good introduction to the concept of semiotic mediation.
2. Suggested readings for more on this topic are Gumperz (1982) and Agar (1996).
3. For more about differences between how humans and other animals communicate, see Scheibel and Schopf (1997).
4. Bernard Perley is Maliseet from Tobique First Nation, New Brunswick, Canada. He is also an Associate Professor of Anthropology at the University of Wisconsin-Milwaukee where he teaches courses in linguistic anthropology and American Indian studies. He uses humor and creative media as critical components of his ethnographic work.
5. And this does not even consider the mediation work exemplified by the artist and photographer who rendered these images, or those discourse-managers who recycled them onto the internet, where we in turn found them to use in this book.
6. Some suggest that language first took the form of sign language, rather than spoken language, because it seems that our vocal apparatus developed more slowly than our brains (Corballis 2009).
7. Several other scholars have hypothesized relationships between the evolution of language and foodways: for instance, that hunting and gathering encouraged humans to engage in instrumental speech (Falk 2009), that fire and cooking allowed for a smaller jaw that permitted speech (Wrangham 2009), and that cooking and eating around the fire allowed for the evolution of speech in the form of gossip (Dunbar 1998).
8. For more about archaeological methods for studying foodways, see Moore 2013 and Twiss 2015.
9. For more about early snail husbandry, see Lubell (2004).
10. For research on how the body parts of bees in raw honey offer a great protein source for foragers, see Crittenden (2011).
11. For instance, in the highly multilingual region of the Amazonian basin (Jackson 1983), social groups use their **linguonym,** or the name of their language, as their **ethnonym,** or name of their group (Sorensen 1967), much as we find in European nations. By contrast, in Papua New Guinea, another highly multilingual area of the world (Salisbury 1962), this is not the case and in fact social groups who might otherwise share many linguistic features point to specific words to indicate their extreme cultural differences from their neighbors (Romaine 2000:9–10), much as happens in inhabitants of the different boroughs of New York City.
12. See, for instance, the role played by codfish in the rise and fall of the European system of colonialism (Kurlansky 1997).
13. See Balasco (2008: 60-65) for a discussion of the pros and cons of using this seemingly unilinear term for such a complex notion and how "web" might be preferable.

References

Agar, Michael. 1996. *Language Shock: Understanding the Culture of Conversation*. New York: William Morrow.
Anderson, Benedict. 1983. *Imagined Communities: Reflections on the Origins and Spread of Nationalism*. London: Verso.
Balasco, Warren. 2008. *Food: The Key Concepts*. Oxford: Berg.
Cavanaugh, Jillian R. 2016. "Talk as Work: Economic Sociability in Northern Italian Heritage Food Production." *Language and Communication* 48: 41–52.
Coe, Michael D., and Rex Koontz. 2008. *Mexico: From the Olmecs to the Aztecs*. London: Thames & Hudson.
Corballis, Michael C. 2009. "The Evolution of Language." *Annals of the New York Academy of Sciences* 1156: 19-43.
Crittenden, Alyssa N. 2011. "The Importance of Honey Consumption in Human Evolution." *Food and Foodways* 19(4): 257–273.
Crosby, Alfred W. 1972. *The Columbian Exchange: Biological and Cultural Consequences of 1492*. Westport, CT: Greenwood Press.
D'Anna, Maria Bianca, and Carolin Jauss. 2015. "Cooking in the Fourth Millennium BCE: Investigating the Social via the Material." In *Commensality: From Everyday Food to Feast*, edited by Susanne Kerner, Cynthia Chou, and Morten Warmind, 65–85. New York: Bloomsbury Academic.
De Leon, Conely. 2015. "Transnational Filipin@ Kin Networks and Intergenerational Circulations of Care and E-Motional Labour." Paper presented at the CASCA Conference, Laval, QC.
Dunbar, Robin. 1998. *Grooming, Gossip and the Evolution of Language*. Cambridge, MA: Harvard University Press.
Edwards, Megan. 2011. "Virginia Ham: The Local and Global of Colonial Foodways." *Food and Foodways* 19: 56–73.
Estes, Richard. 2012(1991). *The Behavior Guide to African Mammals: Including Hoofed Mammals, Carnivores, Primates*. Berkeley and Los Angeles: University of California Press.
Falk, Dean. 2009. *Finding Our Tongues: Mothers, Infants, and the Origins of Language*. New York: Basic Books.
Fernandez-Armesto, Felipe. 2002. *Near a Thousand Tables: A History of Food*. New York: The Free Press.
Fletcher, Alexandra, and Stuart Campbell. 2015. "It Is Ritual, Isn't It? Mortuary and Feasting Practices at Domuztepe." In *Commensality: From Everyday Food to Feast*, edited by Susanne Kerner, Cynthia Chou, and Morten Warmind, 109–125. New York: Bloomsbury Academic.
Freedman, Paul. 2008. *Out of the East: Spices and the Medieval Imagination*. New Haven, CT: Yale University Press.
Freedman, Paul. 2015. "Medieval and Modern Banquets: Commensality and Social Categorization." In *Commensality: From Everyday Food to Feast*, edited by Susanne Kerner, Cynthia Chou, and Morten Warmind, 99–108. New York: Bloomsbury Academic.
Gilhus, Ingvild Sælid. 2015. "Ritual Meals and Polemics in Antiquity." In *Commensality: From Everyday Food to Feast*, edited by Susanne Kerner, Cynthia Chou, and Morten Warmind, 203–216. New York: Bloomsbury Academic.

Gnanadesikan, Amalia E. 2009. *The Writing Revolution: From Cuneiform to the Internet*. Malden, MA: Wiley-Blackwell.

Graeber, David. 2001. *Toward an Anthropological Theory of Value: The False Coin of Our Own Dreams*. New York: Palgrave.

Gumperz, John J. 1982. *Discourse Strategies*. Cambridge: Cambridge University Press.

Hockings, Kimberly J., Nicola Bryson-Morrison, Susana Carvalho, Michiko Fugisawa, Tatyana Humle, William C. McGrew, Miho Nakamura, Gaku Ohashi, Yumi Yamanashi, Gen Yamakoshi, and Tetsuro Matsuzawa. 2015. "Tools to Tipple: Ethanol Ingestion by Wild Chimpanzees using Leaf-Sponges." *Royal Society Open Science* 2: 150150. DOI: 10.1098/rsos.150150, accessed April 29, 2018.

Jackson, Jean E. 1983. *The Fish People: Linguistic Exogamy Tukanoan Identity in Northwest Amazonia*. Cambridge: Cambridge University Press.

Jourdan, Christine. 2010. "The Cultural Localization of Rice in the Solomon Islands." *Ethnology* 49(4): 263–282.

Kashay, Jennifer Fish. 2009. "Missionaries and Foodways in Early 19th-Century Hawai'i." *Food and Foodways* 17(3): 159–180.

Kerner, Susanne. 2015. "Drink and Commensality or How to Hold on to Your Drink in the Chalcolithic." In *Commensality: From Everyday Food to Feast*, edited by Susanne Kerner, Cynthia Chou, and Morten Warmind, 125–135. New York: Bloomsbury Academic.

Kerner, Susanne, Cynthia Chou, and Morten Warmind, eds. 2015. *Commensality: From Everyday Food to Feast*. New York: Bloomsbury Academic.

Kurlansky, Mark. 1997. *Cod: A Biography of the Fish That Changed the World*. New York: Penguin Books.

Lubell, David. 2004. "Are Land Snails a Signature for the Mesolithic-Neolithic Transition?" *Documenta Praehistorica* 31: 1–24.

Maroney, Stephanie R. 2011. "'To Make a Curry the India Way': Tracking the Meaning of Curry Across Eighteenth-Century Communities." *Food and Foodways* 19: 122–134.

Mertz, Elizabeth. 1985. "Beyond Symbolic Anthropology: Introducing Semiotic Mediation." In *Semiotic Mediation: Sociocultural and Psychological Perspectives*, edited by Elizabeth Mertz and Richard J. Parmentier, 1–19. New York: Academic Press.

Mintz, Sidney W. 1985. *Sweetness and Power: The Place of Sugar in Modern History*. New York: Viking.

Moore, Katherine M. 2013. "The Archaeology of Food." In *Routledge International Handbook of Food Studies*, edited by Ken Albala, 75–86. New York: Routledge.

Nabhan, Gary Paul. 2014. *Cumin, Camels, and Caravans: A Spice Odyssey*. Berkeley: University of California Press.

Nymann, Hanne. 2015. "Feasting on Locusts and Truffles in the Second Millennium BCE." In *Commensality: From Everyday Food to Feast*, edited by Susanne Kerner, Cynthia Chou, and Morten Warmind, 151–163. New York: Bloomsbury Academic.

Pennycook, Alastair, and Emi Otsuji. 2017. "Fish, Phone Cards and Semiotic Assemblages in Two Bangladeshi Shops in Sydney and Tokyo." *Social Semiotics* 27(4): 434–450.

Riley, Kathleen C. Forthcoming. "'Don't Yuck My Yum': Semiotics and the Socialization of Food Ideologies at an Elite Elementary School." *Semiotic Review* 5: *The Semiotics of Food and Language.*

Romaine, Suzanne. 2000. *Language in Society: An Introduction to Sociolinguistics,* 2nd edition. Oxford: Oxford University Press.

Salisbury, Richard F. 1962. "Notes on Bilingualism and Linguistic Change in New Guinea." *Anthropological Linguistics* 4(7): 1–13.

Salmi, Roberta, Kurt Hammerschmidt, and Diane M. Doran-Sheehy. 2013. "Western Gorilla Vocal Repertoire and Contextual Use of Vocalizations." *Ethology* 119(10): 831–847.

Scheibel, Arnold B., and J. William Schopf, eds. 1997. *The Origin and Evolution of Intelligence.* Boston: Jones and Bartlett Publishers.

Sorensen, Arthur P. Jr. 1967. "Multilingualism in the Northwest Amazon." *American Anthropologist* 69: 670–684.

Thomson, Deborah Morrison. 2011. "Play with Your Food: The Performativity of Online Breakfast Cereal Marketing." In *Food as Communication/Communication as Food*, edited by Janet M. Cramer, Carlnita P. Greene, and Lynn M. Walters, 23–37. New York: Peter Lang.

Tuomainen, Helena Margaret. 2009. "Ethnic Identity, (Post)Colonialism and Foodways: Ghanaians in London." *Food, Culture, and Society* 12(4): 525–554.

Twiss, Katheryn C. 2015. "Methodological and Definitional Issues in the Archaeology of Food." In *Commensality: From Everyday Food to Feast*, edited by Susanne Kerner, Cynthia Chou, and Morten Warmind, 89–98. New York: Bloomsbury Academic.

Van Esterik, Penny. 2015. "Commensal Circles and the Common Pot." In *Commensality: From Everyday Food to Feast*, edited by Susanne Kerner, Cynthia Chou, and Morten Warmind, 31–42. New York: Bloomsbury Academic.

Wallerstein, Immanuel. 1974. *The Modern World-System, Vol. 1: Capitalist Agriculture and the Origins of the European World-Economy in the Sixteenth Century.* New York and London: Academic Press.

Wallerstein, Immanuel. 1980. *The Modern World-System, Vol. 2: Mercantilism and the Consolidation of the European World-Economy, 1600–1750.* New York: Academic Press.

Watson, James L., ed. 2006. *Golden Arches East: McDonald's in East Asia*, 2nd edition. Stanford, CA: Stanford University Press.

Whiten, Andrew, Victoria Horner, and Frans B. M. de Waal. 2005. "Conformity to Cultural Norms of Tool Use in Chimpanzees." *Nature* 437: 737–740.

Wilk, Richard R., and Livia Barbosa, eds. 2012. *Rice and Beans: A Unique Dish in a Hundred Places.* London and New York: Berg Publishers.

Wolf, Eric. 1982. *Europe and the People without History.* Berkeley: University of California Press.

Wrangham, Richard. 2009. *Catching Fire: How Cooking Made Us Human.* New York: Basic Books.

Xiong, Dan, Jian Xu, Qin Lu, and Fengju Lo. 2014. "Recognition and Extraction of Honorifics in Chinese Diachronic Corpora." In *Chinese Lexical Semantics*, CLSW 2014, edited by Xinchun Su and Tingting He, 305–316. New York: Springer.

Chapter 3

Procuring and Processing
Food-and-Language Data

Having surveyed many rich connections between food and language throughout the human past to more recent times, we now review some of the most fertile ways to study this topic in contemporary societies. First, we detail the many methods for collecting data, both discourse-based and sociocultural, that may be utilized to probe how food and language are interrelated.[1] Second, we explore some of the ethical dilemmas linguistic anthropologists confront while collecting sensitive food and language data, whether in homes or factories, at school cafeterias or farmers markets. The chapter offers a taste of the kinds of studies that we sample at more length throughout the book. We provide examples from our own field-work, including vignettes explaining how we both were drawn into the study of language and food. In addition, the Appendix and the companion eResources page give readers a chance to experiment with some of the research methods explained in this chapter through suggested exercises and projects.

Ethnographic Techniques for Studying Food and Language

In order to see beyond the surface of human activity, cultural and linguistic anthropologists spend an extended amount of time doing **ethnographic fieldwork** in the contemporary societies they study. Ethnographic fieldwork consists of consistent, intensive, on-the-ground research with a social group over an extended length of time. For example, anthropologists tend to live in a community for at least 12 months, which helps the researcher get a sense of how daily life unfolds throughout the year and across the seasons. **Ethnography** (*ethnos* = 'people' and *graphy* = 'writing') is both a method of investigation and a process of creating a written account based on this activity of working to understand and document another culture.

3.1

3.2

During fieldwork, food-and-language activities serve as key ways for anthropologists to establish positive working relationships, referred to as **rapport**, with community members. For instance, we may be welcomed with a village feast, offered a meal in someone's home, or simply given a share of the staple crop. If not, we may make our own inroads by purchasing, preparing, and consuming local foods to demonstrate our interest and commitment to the culture, while simultaneously trying our best to speak the local language. Sometimes we make mistakes that clarify the **norms**, or unspoken social rules or conventions, we are breaking, and sometimes we accidentally adhere to local norms in ways that subsequently facilitate our entry.

Cultural anthropologist Bruce Knauft (2016) describes how he negotiated conventions of conviviality with the Gebusi of Papua New Guinea when they offered him a heaping pile of starchy cooked bananas upon his arrival to a village. First, he ate from the mound, accepting their welcome gift and pleasing them by consuming their food. Then, he shared the rest of the massive platter, inadvertently following local social conventions. As his hosts began to eat and engage in friendly conversation with one another, he was able to relax a little and learn more. By contrast, John Barker (2016), when he first arrived to work with the Maisin in Papua New Guinea knowing nothing of the norms of reciprocity, inadvertently broke these rules by "paying" with rice and sugar for the fresh food that a friend brought him unasked on a regular basis. However, over time, the amount of food he received kept diminishing, and the relationship was becoming strained, until one day another friend who brought him food rejected the "payment" and explained in a pained way that his attempt to offer immediate reciprocity was hurtful and indicated that they were not real friends. In other words, there are always foodways we cannot guess from afar; thus, we learn "on the job" and in the process establish the rapport we will need to continue our fieldwork.

Along with finding a way to eat, anthropologists entering an unfamiliar culture also attempt to become competent in the language(s) of the community—not only to be able to communicate for practical reasons, but also as a way in to understanding the culture and its rules. And this can be true even when studying our own "home" culture using a linguistic code we thought we knew. Often we must acquire new ways of speaking and find ourselves questioning the meanings of linguistic forms and patterns of interaction we might otherwise have taken for granted. This applies to how language is used in the presence of food as well.

For example, Paugh was struck by a strong sense of familiarity when observing dinnertime food interactions among middle-class families in one project in Los Angeles, California. Regular "battles" between children and their parents over what children should eat seemed like a normal part of American childhood. It was only after carefully analyzing the mealtime discourse data did she and her colleague Carolina Izquierdo begin to see the complex interactional foundations behind those battles. In many ways, adults were undermining their own efforts to encourage "healthy" eating practices through the ways they framed food, eating, and child/adult status interactionally (Paugh and Izquierdo 2009).

Additionally, we may need to acquire some of these unfamiliar social conventions surrounding food and eating ourselves, including how to politely request, refuse, or express appreciation for the foods that are being prepared and offered. As anthropologists, we try new foods that we may not even categorize as food, and in turn come to understand why those foods are eaten and enjoyed by locals, thus confronting our own hidden pockets of ethnocentrism and demonstrating a capacity for **cultural relativism** (that is, opening our minds to other worldviews).[2] For instance, Riley had a hard time wanting to taste *fafaru*, the fermented fish that is a specialty in French Polynesia, because it smells like excrement. Once she managed to close her nostrils and chew, she was amazed at how succulent and sweet it was. Fermented breadfruit paste, or *mā*, originally made by throwing peeled raw breadfruit into a hole in the ground to rot (now made similarly in plastic garbage bags), was another taste she came to acquire while living there.

Participant Observation and Field Notes

Consuming local foods and communicating in the local code is part of the primary ethnographic fieldwork method known as **participant observation**, the act of observing while participating in everyday life. The objective of participant observation is to engage as fully as possible in the everyday lives of those being studied, while simultaneously observing what is going on in order to richly describe it in **field notes** for later analysis. Although anthropologists can and do sometimes use some other methods, such as the lab-based experimental techniques of psychologists or the language-elicitation interviews of linguists, we do this to augment, not replace the primary tool in our toolkit: ethnographic research. In the process of participating in daily life and observing what others do, researchers come to understand how language is used to talk about and around food as well as use talk to nurture membership in the community and access food there.

Because of the central role of food in human social life, even anthropologists who are not primarily focused on it have described and analyzed the food talk that they witnessed or took part in. For instance, Riley came to realize the salience of fish for Marquesans in the course of catching and cleaning, preparing and eating so many different kinds, raw or cooked over an open fire or in coconut milk—the variety mind-boggling and tasty. In the process, she also learned the Marquesan words for the dishes, the fish, and the many stages in the life of a coconut, as well as how to properly interact while catching fish and eating them.

We document such patterns and keep track of the data we collect in our systematic field notes. These notes become the groundwork upon which we base the ethnographic analyses that we write and publish about the people

Figure 3.1 Eating with hands in Mabalacat, Phillipines
Credit: Photo by Avel Chuklanov on Unsplash

we study. Notes may be taken on the spot during ongoing events, often in the form of short jottings or voice recordings that will be expanded later, or they may be written up at the end of the day from memory. They elaborate upon the relevant dimensions of everyday life and provide full descriptions of one-time events of obvious significance; but they may be accompanied by the researcher's personal reflections as well. For instance, researchers grapple with feelings of embarrassment when having inadvertently violated local norms of eating etiquette, or ethical concerns regarding the consumption of particular foods, such as dolphin or monkey—and field notes give us a time and place to reflect.[3] Field notes highlight some of our insights as we take note of the words people use to describe their foods and foodways, the routine interactions they engage in around food, and the significant narratives that people tell about food.

Contexts for the Study of Language and Food

Linguistic anthropologists seek to identify patterns in the co-occurrence of food and language through their repeated participant observation in and careful description of food-centered discourse events situated within their cultural and linguistic **contexts**. Context consists of the overall circumstances surrounding a communicative act or event: the immediate physical and social setting, the cultural organization of space and material objects, the historical background, the participants and their roles, and the talk that came before or after an event or utterance.

We also insist on studying language in its contexts of use because we view language as **multifunctional**, that is, serving many functions. At the semantic level, language encodes information and is used to describe the world; this is its **referential** function. At the pragmatic level, language enacts things and is used to do things in the world; this is its **performative** function (Austin 1962). The pioneering work of British social anthropologist Bronislaw Malinowki (1884–1942) highlighted the importance of language operating as a form of social action at the pragmatic level, and the related need to study it in context.

Malinowski (1935) examined food and language in everyday speech and gardening spells used to grow yams and other crops in the Trobriand Islands in the South Pacific. Among his many insights, he demonstrated the importance of language in the production of food in context, particularly how specific formulas pronounced by a village garden magician (*towosi*) were considered essential for crops to thrive. Malinowski (1935:7) described language as "an indispensable ingredient of all concerted human action," and demonstrated that it was essential in Trobriand ideology to urge food to grow:

> Let us once more listen to the Trobriand magician while he addresses spirits and animals, plants and soil. The spell in the belief of the natives is a verbal communion between the magician and the object addressed. The magician speaks and the objects respond. The words are launched into the things—sometimes even the surrounding world gives the sign that the words have been received by the essence of things: the *kari-yala*, 'magical portent', awakens, the thunder rumbles in the skies and lightning appears on the horizon.
>
> (Malinowski 1935:240–241)

For the Trobrianders, the use of magical words and the practical work of gardening are intertwined and inseparable in food production. Malinowski was one of the first scholars to make explicit such connections between food and language by studying both in context.

Following in his footsteps, linguistic anthropologists have demonstrated the importance of context in enabling the emergence or deterrence of certain kinds of language or the preference for one language over another in a given social situation, such as the use of sacred religious registers within temples and the use of non-standard dialects at home and not at school (Duranti and Goodwin 1992). The place, material objects, tasks at hand, and salient social identities of those involved all contribute to constructing the context for social interaction.

Figure 3.2 Photo of Bronislaw Malinowski with local consultants in the Trobriand
Islands

Courtesy of the Malinowski collection at the LSE Library. Reproduced with permission.

More recently, two other terms have been introduced that point to similarities in the way scholars approach food and language in specific contexts.
Linguistic landscapes refers to the many ways in which the world is now
inundated with written signage, whether as official warnings, billboard
advertising, or even a trashed newspaper on the ground. Some sociolin-
guists have used linguistic landscape studies to identify the usage of more
than one language in urban neighborhoods, while others have expanded
this methodology to investigate how the forms, functions, and contexts
of signs can tell us about the history, future goals, and social stratification of groups in a given area (Blommaert 2010). Similarly, **foodscapes** is
used to refer to the world of food we look out at every day, both actual, in
our refrigerators at home or the supermarkets in our neighborhood, and
virtual, the plethora of food images in the media. These foodscapes may
vary hugely across geographical space and time as well as across town
in the many social settings we find ourselves in throughout the day. For
instance, Riley found it truly shocking to survey the well-stocked shelves
of suburban supermarkets back in the United States after spending a year
in a village in the Pacific where the biggest store sports a few shelves with
canned fish and crackers. On the other hand, some rural areas and neighborhoods in major cities in the United States are considered **food deserts**
for lack of nearby stores offering healthy foods (or any foods at all). Food

3.3

information inundates our linguistic landscapes and foodscapes with great regularity, influencing us with discourses about what foodways are good for our health, our environment, and/or our taste buds.

Finally, foodways and discourses may change as foods and linguistic forms, whether written or not, are **decontextualized** (removed from their original contexts of use) and **recontextualized** (shifted into new contexts). For instance, when Riley introduces her students in New Jersey to eating breadfruit, it is a very different experience than when she eats it with her friends in the Marquesas; similarly, it takes some linguistic sleight of hand to make her students feel the weighty significance of the myth of the god Atua who created breadfruit. Thus, the contexts of data collection are also relevant for both conducting and evaluating ethnographic research and writing. In the next two sections, we expand upon different ways of collecting food discourses in both naturalistic and research-constructed contexts.

Analysis of "Naturally" Occurring Food Discourse

Participant observation and detailed ethnographic notes are central to the anthropological toolkit, but one method that distinguishes linguistic anthropological approaches (and related fields, such as sociolinguistics, conversational analysis, linguistic ethnography, and discursive psychology) from other forms of anthropology is the audio and visual recording and analysis of **discourse events**. Discourse events are occasions in which people engage in some form of contextualized social interaction. Audio and visual recording entails using a tape recorder or electronic recording device to capture what is said during an interaction, or the use of visual recording devices that capture both sounds and visuals. Such techniques provide researchers with a more life-like record of what was actually said and done, so that they do not need to rely solely on their notes or people's self-reports for the analysis of the event.

Linguistic anthropologists consider these recorded data to be **naturalistic** in that we attempt to record people going about their daily lives, whether at home or market, in the break room at work or the school cafeteria, or at ritual events, such as religious feasts or heritage festivals. While many researchers use audio/video recordings for interviews and oral histories, as will be discussed below, what is unique about this approach is its focus on social interactions that are not elicited by the researcher. In naturalistic research, participants are not asked to do anything in particular as they might be in experimental studies, such as those often used in psychology. However, even the mere presence of the researcher and/or the recording device has an impact on our subjects' interactions, producing what is called the **observer's paradox**, so called because observers alter the very reality they came to observe. And yet, recordings of naturalistic events allow us to access actual linguistic forms as they are produced in their associated

Figure 3.3 Soho restaurant in London, United Kingdom
Credit: Photo by Clem Onojeghuo on Unsplash

contexts, rather than relying on researcher prompting, perspectival constraints, or participant memory.

The Ethnography of SPEAKING-and-FEEDING

Following in the ethnographic tradition, linguistic anthropologist Dell Hymes developed in the 1960s a key framework for attending to naturally occurring speech events. Initially called the **ethnography of SPEAKING,** based on the mnemonic explained below, it is now frequently referred to as the **ethnography of communication** in order to include other communicative modes beyond the spoken word: written, signed, and embodied. Nonetheless, Hymes's initial goal was to create a roadmap for how to describe and analyze language use in context, both beyond the level of grammatical description and across cultures (Hymes 1964). Thus, he designed the acronym SPEAKING to call attention to seven key foci when studying a communicative event:

Setting: when and where the discourse event takes place
Participants: who is present and participating in the discourse event
Ends: goals, intentions, and effects of participants' specific discursive acts and of the discourse event as a whole
Acts: smaller discursive actions (such as requests or insults)
Keys: moods or emotions during specific interactions or the whole event
Instrumentalities: channels (such as writing and speaking) and codes (such as languages and dialects) used
Norms: discursive rules and expectations governing the event
Genres: the types of discourse genre used (such as narrative, sermon, or gossip)

Frake's (1964) classic analysis of how Subanun men in the Philippines engage in competitive drinking events is a good example of how the ethnography of SPEAKING methodology can be applied to analyzing food—or in this case drink—consumption in a specific setting. Among the Subanun four stages of competitive talking-and-drinking can be discerned. First, there is the tasting round when invitations are offered and permission asked in prescribed ways. Second, there is 'jar talk' devoted to predictable forms of talk about the drink being consumed in a Chinese jar. Third, the discussion expands to local gossip and informal adjudication of other events. And fourth, there is a display of verbal art, frequently sung, in which form wins out over content. Frake was able to use Hymes's tool to analyze the setting and participants, the norms and communicative genres, and the goals of various speech acts as they reflected and helped construct the stages of the drinking event.

Additionally, this model allows us to discern and tease out the patterns and expectations that underlie **communicative competence**—the ability to communicate across a variety of social situations in ways deemed appropriate by a given social group, including sociocultural norms about when, where, and how to produce an utterance. This can be distinguished from **linguistic competence**—the knowledge needed to put together a well-formed and grammatically meaningful sentence in a particular language. For instance, you may know enough English to form the sentence "Pass the peas," but you may not know enough about your dining companions to know that if you want to be asked back for another meal, you will need to make your request at the right time (such as after grace and without interrupting the host), without pointing and with a pleasant smile, hinting indirectly with a compliment instead of asking directly: "Wow, those peas look delicious!" In other words, a simple interaction such as this benefits from a specific form of communicative competence that we call **alimentary competence**—the knowledge of what specific foods and foodways mean and how to interact around and with them in a particular context, depending on the participants' relative social statuses and relationships. In the situation sketched here, it might also be helpful to know in advance that the kids at the table will think you are crazy to want more peas, but that your adult hosts will take you for a cultivated person because you appreciate these peas from their garden cooked this evening with onions and cumin.[4]

The development of communicative competence has been studied in depth within the approach we introduced in Chapter 1 known as language socialization, the study of the process by which children and other novices simultaneously learn linguistic and cultural practices and beliefs (Duranti, Ochs, and Schieffelin 2012; Ochs and Schieffelin 2012). Because the cultural knowledge acquired in this way frequently revolves around food—how to produce, prepare, share, and consume it—this research often includes explicit or implicit consideration of how alimentary competence is linguistically socialized via what we call food-and-language socialization, also introduced in Chapter 1 and explored at length in Chapter 7.

Language socialization research is both ethnographic and **longitudinal**, that is, researchers examine how children learn linguistic and cultural practices and ideologies as interrelated processes over a considerable length of time in order to understand how individuals develop into competent members of their community. A hallmark of the method is the audio- and video-recording of talk between novices and experts within everyday contexts so as to understand the interactive practices that lead to the transmission and transformation of local knowledge. Attention to micro-level exchanges, when contextualized by the ethnographic study of macro-level Discourses, allows researchers to analyze how cultural and linguistic reproduction and change occurs.

Building on Hymes's paradigm and the language socialization approach, Riley has developed an additional set of research foci, FEEDING, to be used alongside SPEAKING for the study of food-and-talk events specifically. These include:

Food: food items present during the event
Employment: activities to do with procuring, preparing, serving, and eating the food
Etiquette: cultural food rules shaping the food-focused event

*D*isplay: arrangement and presentation of food

*I*mplements: equipment used to produce, prepare, package, serve, consume the food

*N*otions: ideas and beliefs about food expressed or manifested during the event

*G*ender: participants' rights and obligations based on identities and roles

With the ethnography of SPEAKING-and-FEEDING model, the researcher's attention is drawn to how food and talk-in-interaction co-occur in meaningful, context specific ways. For example, *etiquette* points us to the varied expectations that shape food interactions, including rules for social politeness, the organization of religious rituals involving food (such as the blessing of the bread on Shabbat), and health or safety guidelines. *Implements* reminds us to take account of material objects such as gardening tools, a bread knife or ladle, the family china, chopsticks, TV tables, and so on. *Notions* helps us attend to the ways in which participants engage in interactional moves that construct food as good, tasty, or healthy, and might index political principles regarding, for example, animal rights, environmental sustainability, or food justice. *Gender* cues researchers to consider the ways participants' perceived sociocultural identities (age, gender, sexuality, ethnicity, class) and/or social roles (boss, mother, family clown) influence their rights and obligations within a particular communicative event. For more detailed instructions on how to apply the SPEAKING-and-FEEDING model, see the Appendix and student research examples on the website.

Vignette 3.1   Kathleen C. Riley: Food-and-Language Socialization in France, the United States, and the Pacific

3.4

Kathleen C. Riley is a linguistic anthropologist teaching at Rutgers University.

I conducted my first ethnographic fieldwork in 1993 on the island of Nuku Hiva in French Polynesia. I chose this setting because I was interested in understanding how children simultaneously acquire two languages and two cultures (French and Polynesian) and how the particular Polynesian language and culture on that island (Marquesan) was faring given the colonial power of French. I found that despite a strong cultural and linguistic revival movement, many Marquesan children were learning French at home, many adults were using a mix of codes for everyday interactions, and many students were acquiring cosmopolitan values even while living on an island in the middle of the Pacific Ocean. However, over time another interest emerged from this work.

I did not know how obsessed I was with food until I arrived in the field and encountered the indigenous diet—based on starches, fish, and meat (many now tinned or frozen)—and the difficulties of procuring and preparing the foods I most value—green vegetables. Though frustrated, I didn't yet know that I would translate this fixation into a new lens for focusing on the study of food and language. At the time, I started a vegetable garden on a friend's land to feed my need, and only later discovered that a lot of my informal data revolved around fishing, hunting, gardening, sharing, acquiring, cooking, eating, and talking about and around food.

Ten years later I conducted another ethnographic study of language socialization, this time in France. My purpose was to gain a firsthand understanding of what was French and what Polynesian about my friends in Nuku Hiva by conducting a very similar study with French people in a privileged suburb outside Paris. This time (perhaps because French people share my obsession with food) I recognized that I was specifically attuned to the differences in how French and Marquesan people interact around food in particular, not just culture in general. Again, my American sensibilities about food and childrearing were sometimes jarred by what I discovered in France. For instance, I found these bourgeois parents to be highly structured about how they fed their children and was put off by the formal behaviors they expected from them at dinner. Of course, I reminded myself to stay open-minded. Instead, I focused on what a culture clash this was with what I had come to understand as a far more Polynesian way of relating to food: the lack of talk while eating, the use of fingers as utensils, the pre-chewing of tough foods to feed babies, and the unstructured mealtimes. All of this was and continues to be anathema to the French priests, teachers, doctors, and administrators who have attempted to "civilize" the Marquesans for the last 150 years. I was fascinated with the ways in which the big-D Discourses flowed in and out of the little-d discourse of my friends in these two places on opposite sides of the globe; although connected by a language and an ongoing colonial relationship, many of their ideologies and practices around language, food, and life in general were diametrically opposed.

Finally, all of this experiential immersion in food and language in the field led me to formalize my methods for studying food-and-language socialization in order to conduct a new research project, but within a culture that I presumed I knew far better: the United States. Of course, the United States is a big place, so it is impossible to be a native anthropologist of the whole country, much less one subculture within it. But this is what I attempted by choosing to study an independent school in New York City where I myself had gone as an adolescent and where my own daughter was presently enrolled. Here, in 2010–2012, I purposefully put language and food on the table together for the first time, studying how children were digesting among themselves the food and food education being introduced at the school as a consequence of the school food change movement, despite the opposition of some of the parents and staff.

Transcription of Recorded Food and Language Interaction

In order to analyze audio/video recordings in detail, researchers engage in the method of **transcription**. This entails writing down what has been said according to particular conventions, with varying degrees of contextual details added. Ideally this is done collaboratively with the assistance of a participant from the recorded interaction, or at least a family or community member with greater cultural and linguistic knowledge than the investigator. This participant-assisted transcription can generate rich **metalinguistic** (communication about language) and **metapragmatic** (communication about how language is used) reflections that allow for exploration of **food ideologies** and **language ideologies** (that is, ideologies about the nature of and practices related to food and language) in greater detail than may be generated by formal interviewing or participant observation alone. For instance, working with participants on recorded data naturally elicits their commentary on the effects of language use during the recorded food activities. Collaborative transcribing helps researchers to get a more accurate understanding of what took place, what was said (especially in a foreign language), and why. It also can elicit explanations of the interaction and evaluation of participants' behavior, manners, tastes, etc.

For the food-and-language researcher, the same methods of recording and transcribing are used as in other linguistic anthropological research, however the settings may differ in that we specifically focus on moments of food-and-language interface: the dinner table, the market, the farm, or a food activist event. These contexts may include both the school lunchroom as well as the PTA meeting where new lunchroom policies are discussed. Video recordings offer both visual images that allow researchers to see what is going on while also hearing the conversations about and around food. Video recordings capture more, but never all, of the context and

Figure 3.4 Busy street in Koenjiminami, Suginami, Japan
Credit: Photo by Alex Knight on Unsplash

facilitate analysis of non-verbal communication that accompanies food talk, such as nodding or shaking the head, facial expressions of pleasure or disgust, hand gestures and body posture, and so on.

There are particular challenges with using audio/video-recording as a method. Transcription can be quite time-consuming and requires choices as to what will be included in the final transcript. Details include non-verbal actions and sounds that accompany speech and eating (lip smacking, sounds of appreciation) as well as vocal tone, pitch, and volume. Capturing the talk around food often comes with the drawback of picking up sounds that may make it difficult to interpret what is said, such as noises from stove-top frying, utensils clattering, or mouths chewing. Further, any form of photographic image and sound recording raises ethical issues concerning the use and storage of sensitive data, as will be discussed later in this chapter. Although such ethical and logistical concerns must be addressed, the benefits of these methods for accessing actual interaction are manifold.

Analyzing Written and Mediated Texts

One other key source of food discourses, which is neither elicited nor even influenced by the observer's paradox, is that of written documents and, more recently, **mediated texts** that include both written and audio-visual materials found on the radio, TV, or internet. The gathering and analysis of food-related documents offers another research method for examining ideas about food, the linguistic forms they take, and the **intertextual** links that are created when discourses are circulated (de- and re-contextualized) via written documents, everyday gossip, or mediated proclamations.

Researchers can investigate both historical and contemporary food-based textual materials through an anthropological lens. Examples include but are not limited to primary historical sources such as missionary and colonial accounts of food practices; food-related diaries, letters, blogs, and other forms of social media; cookbooks, recipes, and menus; and official documents related to modern food production such as brochures, labels, certifications, and advertising. These materials may be gathered in many ways from archival research to internet searches, and reveal documents from many types of organizations ranging from governments to corporations. Through the analysis of textual food-and-language data, researchers can investigate the construction of authenticity and the cultural and economic value of foods, as is discussed at more length in Chapters 4 and 5.

Eliciting Food Discourses

Linguistic anthropologists are interested in collecting a range of food discourses: the local names of foods, dishes, and food-related events, the linguistic routines and clichés people use about or around food, and the various communicative genres that focus on food from myths to Instagram posts and jokes to oral history memories. While ethnographers may have a chance to participate in some of these food discourses, they can explore them more fully by eliciting this material from willing participants. Important interviewing techniques in the anthropological toolbox include the elicitation of word lists, photo elicitation, oral history interviews, focus groups, and foodways journals.

Gathering Words, Stories, and Images

First of all, much research on language and food has sought to explore the words used to talk about food and the ways in which people categorize foods into food groups and preparations into cuisines. This has been done through the methodical elicitation, recording, and transcription of lists of **lexemes**, or vocabulary, for food-related items and actions, and the sorting of these into culturally relevant categories or **domains**. Levi-Strauss, whose work will be considered in Chapter 4, is considered the forefather of this attempt to categorize the foodways practiced in different cultures, and this has given rise to the subdiscipline of **ethnosemantics**, which collects, classifies, and taxonomizes local terms related to a number of domains, food being a particularly productive one.

Secondly, food-focused **interviews**, whether highly structured, semi-structured, or informal, can be used to collect participants' ideas about their food practices and beliefs. Interviewees' reflections about what they eat, how, and why, can provide not only some reliable information about what they do and do not do, but also some of their thoughts and feelings—including how they wish they ate or think they ought to behave around food—even if that is not what the researcher actually observes happening during participant observation. Carefully collected food-focused **narratives** (stories) may offer insights into individuals' foodways, as well as into the food patterns and ideologies in the society at large.

Carole Counihan, for example, conducted **food-centered life histories** in Italy and the United States as a method to get at her consultants' personal and social histories through describing their most significant food memories. These semi-structured interviews used discussion of food, eating practices, and food-related contexts as a window into broader sociocultural change experienced over an individual's lifetime. In *Around the Tuscan Table*, Counihan (2004) provided lengthy transcribed narratives of 23 Florentines to get at changes in Italian culture through the changes in diet, cuisine, meal routines, and food labor that her consultants engaged in. Her interviewees highlighted the importance of food in constructing relationships, primarily through regular meals with immediate family,

Figure 3.5 Producing talk around food

Credit: Photo by rawpixel.com on Unsplash

but also through less frequent meal-sharing with friends and daily shopping in their neighborhoods. In *A Tortilla is Like Life*, Counihan (2009) explored similar themes and again provided transcribed narrative excerpts from interviews with 19 Hispanic-American women in Antonito in rural southern Colorado, detailing their foodways and botanical knowledge as well as their gendered roles in food production, preparation, and consumption. Counihan was able to use these food-focused interviews as a means of accessing and giving voice to marginalized subjects, especially women.

Written reporting about foodways may be collected via **surveys** and **questionnaires**, both systematic methods for gathering information from participants through pre-determined questions. For initial research this may prove to be very productive, giving us a preliminary overview of the concerns and orientations of a population. However, anthropologists do not rely wholly on these results because of how the format limits the subjects' responses: the researcher may know too little about the cultural context to word the questions in ways that make sense to the subjects, or the response frame (yes-no questions, tiny spaces for responding) constrains the answers. By contrast, in literate societies, researchers have fruitfully employed **foodways journals** to elicit data. In this method, participants keep track in written form of how they procured, prepared, consumed, and talked about food on a regular basis for a period of time. Foodways journals, which may also include drawings or photographs of food, can give a more accurate impression of a person's everyday food behaviors than self-report during an interview. Jourdan was able to use this method in both the Pacific and Canada to track food transformations across three generations. In the Solomon Islands, she learned from weekly journals kept in 20 urban households that people were eating rice at almost every meal, including breakfast, replacing the root and tree crop staples of earlier times (Jourdan 2010). In Montreal, she used foodways journals and found that the principal meal of the day (*souper*) had not disappeared for the younger generations but had been simplified from several courses to a single-course meal (Jourdan and Poirier 2012).

In another productive technique, referred to as **photo elicitation**, pictures are used as a point of departure for probing people's opinions and beliefs concerning food. Sometimes researchers take photos of their subjects processing, preparing, distributing, and consuming food; other times they ask their subjects to actively participate in the data collection by taking photos themselves with cameras provided by the researcher. This method has proven very useful in getting at children's understandings of food. For instance, Salazar, Feenstra, and Ohmart (2008) examined children's food preferences by taking photos of the salads that they created at school lunch and eliciting commentary afterwards.

Similarly, Johansson and colleagues (2009) examined the foodscapes of Nordic children in Denmark, Sweden, Norway, and Finland by providing the children with disposable cameras to document food on their own. These images were then used to prompt small group discussions about "healthy eating" and other food-related topics among the children in relation to what they deemed important in their lives. In these recorded discussions, the researchers found that the children recognized a variety of foodscapes, including home meals, school meals, and store displays, and their photos expressed a range of food meanings, such as healthiness, attractiveness, tastiness, and accessibility. Photos of their favorite foods included healthy and unhealthy foods, but food at home was always considered better than school food because of a sense of intimacy linked to the home. They contrasted everyday and festive foods as well, creating moral contradictions between the healthy foods they were taught to eat and the unhealthy foods they were exposed to through child-targeted ads, kid menus, and messages about fun weekend foods. Nevertheless, Nordic children seem to have imbibed a notion of balance regarding bad and good, healthy and unhealthy, and mundane and festive foods.

Focus groups with or without photos involved is another means to engage both children and adults in talk about their foodways. Researchers seek a group of participants to discuss various questions, whether open-ended or directed, about food. When focus groups consist of members of an existing social group or strangers from similar backgrounds, the sharing of common experiences and perceptions (or disagreements about these) often sparks rich conversation. For example, Cosgriff-Hernández and colleagues (2010) used this technique to explore the diet and food concerns of Mexican Americans at a community health center in Texas. Many of the participants expressed an awareness of what makes food "healthy" (low-grease, little processing, necessary nutrients) and where to acquire this knowledge (doctors, WIC, schools, media, friends/family), but also reflected on why putting this knowledge into practice was not always easy (fill a piñata with veggies?!). While they preferred their traditional Mexican cuisine of tortillas, beans, and chili, it included more fresh vegetables than they could afford in America (in Mexico they could grow them) and relied on cooking with unhealthy lard. Similarly, healthy eating on a budget took strategic planning, but their busy American-style work schedules contributed to a reliance on fast foods. The focus group discussions provided insights into the challenges faced and strategies devised by this population.

Finding Naturalistic Data in Food Elicitation Research

Typically, researchers focus on the *content* rather than the *form* of the data collected via elicitation methods. That is, the primary goal of these methods is to garner information about the participants' foodways or their

beliefs about food. However, even though the data resulting from elicitation procedures are decontextualized from their "natural" settings, linguistic anthropologists are always eager to analyze discursive data in multiple
ways—we want to know not only *what* people say but also *how* they say
it. We understand that as subjects become increasingly comfortable with
the situation, they manifest more complicated feelings and ideas about
food, rather than only the normative thoughts and feelings they assume
the researcher is looking for. As this happens, they also express themselves
in ways that "normally" co-occur with those feelings and ideas. Further,
focus groups or interviews conducted with family, friends, or other community members as co-participants can elicit conversations that may manifest more ordinary forms of communicating, as was likely the case in the
two focus studies discussed above involving Nordic children and Mexican
Americans.

It is also possible to purposefully situate interviews in ways that allow
the researcher to capture something closer to naturalistic discursive data. In
the case of food-discourse interviews, it is productive to conduct interviews
in food-related settings. For instance, Riley found in her study (forthcoming) of a privileged school in New York City that interviewing parents
about their families' foodways while sitting in their kitchens or at their
dining tables facilitated their ability to talk about food-related matters,
such as what and how they cooked and took their meals. In many of these
families, nannies or housekeepers procured and cooked food, while many
of the children actually ate separately from the adults.

Additionally, it may be helpful to interview participants in the presence
of and engagement with actual food, such as by interviewing over snacks,
coffee, or tea—or at least with photographs of food as in the food elicitation method. Food-focused interviews, contextualized in this way, may
elicit richer data since the interviewees' senses and memories are awakened
by gustatory, olfactory, textural, visual, and auditory stimuli. The conversational styles, including degrees of formality and informality character-
izing the interactional event, will also vary more in natural settings. And
the actual food may bring out explicit reflections from participants, as
Szatrowski (2014) found when she brought "taster meals" to elicit conversations about how participants experience and identify with food from the
United States, Japan, and Senegal.

By setting up situated food-discourse events of this kind, anthropologists
have the opportunity to examine not only how people talk about food during the event but also how the setting and the co-participants, including the
researcher, influence the way the communication happens. In other words,
putting some forethought into how we construct our elicitation events
can overcome some of the limitations of employing such methods. And
when used in conjunction with participant observation and audio/video

recordings of everyday life, researchers can compare what people say they do with what they are observed doing with respect to food and language.

Mixed-Methods and Team-Based Food-and-Language Research

Finally, it is worth noting that many researchers combine more than one of these methods. For instance, striving to link micro-level discourse with macro-level Discourses about nutrition and food knowledge, Riley (forthcoming) examined language socialization and the school food change movement in a New York City elementary school through a mixed-methods study. She employed participant observation, the SPEAKING-and-FEEDING method described above, interviews, family foodways journals, recorded food chats with children, and adult focus groups using food and photographs as prompts with the children. Multiple methods targeted both situated food talk and larger cultural discourses in ways that allowed for an analysis of connections between small-d discourse and large-D Discourses about health, sustainability, and freedom of food choice. Specifically, it was possible to identify intertextual links between discourses in the media, playgroups, classrooms, cafeteria kitchens, and parent meetings. Her research benefitted immeasurably from the collaboration of 13 undergraduate research assistants,[5] who brought their own culturally diverse perspectives to bear on analyzing this field site.

3.5

Team-based projects that bring together researchers from a variety of disciplines often combine multiple methods, thus allowing for exploration of many dimensions of food and talk in daily life and official contexts. For instance, the UCLA Sloan Center on Everyday Lives of Families, directed by linguistic anthropologist Elinor Ochs, investigated many aspects of the everyday lives of 32 middle-class families with children in Los Angeles, California (see Ochs and Kremer-Sadlik 2013 for an overview of this study). Paugh participated in this team-based project that employed diverse methods to get at the organization of family life through daily interaction and practice. Videographers filmed family members over a period of one week. During filming, families prepared and ate meals and snacks, dined at restaurants, got takeout, and shopped for food. Researchers also interviewed parents about their families' health and eating practices, and couples provided narrated tours of their refrigerators and kitchens. Paugh and Izquierdo (2009) have analyzed this data to examine how food-related conflicts build sequentially in dinnertime interaction and how they relate to families' perceptions of their food socialization practices (also see Ochs and Shohet 2006). Similar centers were established in Italy and Sweden, allowing cross-cultural comparison. Such multi-method, team-based study is very fruitful in researching the relations between language and foodways.

Vignette 3.2   Amy L. Paugh: Negotiating Food and Language in the Caribbean and United States

3.6

Amy L. Paugh is a Professor of Anthropology at James Madison University.

My interests in studying language and food emerged from other projects that did not begin with but led to a focus on food interactions. My first project, which began in 1995, explored language shift and children's multilingual play on the eastern Caribbean island nation of Dominica (not to be confused with the Dominican Republic). In Dominica, there has been a societal shift away from Patwa, an Afro-French creole language, to English, the official language, despite a national creole revitalization movement. In order to investigate this complex situation, I video-recorded six families with young children at home and in their community over the course of a year. I also interviewed parents, teachers, and government officials, and spent a lot of time participating in daily life in the village. My focus was on how people alternated between Patwa and English, which adults often did for gossiping, cursing, and joking. Caregivers frequently used Patwa for disciplining children even though the children were not permitted to speak it. In turn children used Patwa in their peer groups to boss one another around and to pretend to be farmers, fisherman, and other primarily adult male roles. Only later did I begin to pay attention to how jam-packed the activities that I recorded were with talk about and around food, including the role play mentioned previously. Further, a daily socializing activity concerned teaching children to overcome greediness (*vowasité* in Patwa) and to learn to share food with others.

In addition to recording village interactions, I investigated public discourses about the loss of the creole language and other traditional practices. As I followed these public exchanges about language both during my early fieldwork and in recent years, what also came to the fore was how creole foodways were losing out to more processed, imported foods that were considered to be "modern." Public discourses lamented this shift and promoted the consumption of local foods, but what I found in the home was the daily socialization of children to prefer imported processed foods versus locally sourced foods such as root crops and fish. For example, adults used packaged snacks and foreign foods as rewards for good behavior, or threatened to withhold them as punishment for bad deeds. Adults also denigrated local foods by claiming that they had "no food" when they could not afford to buy bakery bread, tinned meat, frozen imported chicken, or macaroni and cheese. It became clear that shifting foodways are key ingredients in larger processes of linguistic and cultural change.

A second project deepened my growing interests in food, but in a different cultural context among middle-class dual-earner families in Los Angeles, California. In 2001, I became a postdoctoral fellow in a multi-year interdisciplinary project at the Sloan Center on Everyday Lives of Families (CELF), housed at UCLA and directed by Elinor Ochs. There I developed several smaller projects examining family interaction at the dinner table. In one project, I analyzed narratives about work told by parents in the presence of or to children while eating during dinnertime. These stories were fostered by the shared mealtime experience, and they exposed children to the world of work, and how to talk about it, long before beginning work themselves.

In a related project, I collaborated with Carolina Izquierdo, a medical anthropologist, to compare self-reports about eating practices with what was actually happening at the dinner table. We found that in interviews, parents prized eating as being central to good health. They took responsibility for their children's food choices and eating habits, while often feeling that they fell short in practice, largely due to children "not wanting" the healthy foods they claimed to prepare. When we examined food interactions, however, we were struck by the extensive negotiations about food and eating that took place. Parents debated with children about what they should eat and when, sometimes arguing over the exact number of pieces of food to consume. While these interactions immediately concerned food, they also constituted a terrain for the negotiation of relationships, status, and authority. For example, when seven-year-old Michael Reis asked for "a night without vegetables" because he had eaten so much fruit, his mother firmly replied, "There's never going to be a night without vegetables." He continued to protest and evoked sibling fairness, complaining that his sister, Ally, ate only vegetables and was not forced to eat fruit. In the end his mother conceded, "Well he, he, he does have a point there Ally . . . . Okay so you get two bananas tomorrow." In other interactions, parents asked children what they "wanted" to eat but then told them what they "needed" to eat instead. Caregivers used threats, rewards, conditional promises, nutrition lessons, and various forms of bargaining to try to get children to eat or not eat particular foods. Thus, through analyzing the turn-by-turn construction of food interactions from the video data, we demonstrated how conflicts over food build sequentially as family members co-construct and evaluate one another's eating choices and preferences.

Novices in both of my studies were learning how to engage in eating practices and how to talk and bargain about those practices. Food talk thus emerged as a key site for socializing children, constructing and contesting identities, and negotiating a frequently fraught moral and social terrain.

Studying Food Talk Ethically

Anthropologists have been struggling for over a century with our ethical obligations to our subjects and scientific colleagues, as well as to the greater human community. Linguistic anthropologists may be very sensitive to this issue because we are so attuned not only to the micro-politics of everyday interactions, but also to the ramifications of framing and representing issues on the larger discursive stage. Issues related to equality and justice come up in a range of food-and-language settings from international debates over food access to dinnertime discussions of what kids ought to eat. In this section, we consider how researching food talk requires ethical considerations both while collecting the data in the field and when publishing it afterwards.

3.7

How to Treat Subjects Ethically in the Field While Collecting and Analyzing Data

As we have seen, linguistic anthropologists do their work by engaging first-hand with people's communicative selves as they go about their everyday lives in their homes and schools, places of work and worship. That is, we observe and participate in interactions, ask questions and listen to replies, record conversations and later query participants about what they meant by that or that or that. We keep our eyes and ears ever alert. Similarly, food anthropologists do their work by engaging with people as they produce and consume the basic ingredients of life in a multisensual landscape. We observe and participate in hunting and gardening, shopping and marketing, cooking and processing, eating and composting. Our own bodies and tongues are ever-engaged. Put these two together and you meet some very nosy researchers interested in using all of their senses to figure out how individuals and communities make meaning out of food and talk.

To do all this, we enter spaces that our subjects may never have imagined anyone would want to enter, observe events that no outsider to that situation had attempted to watch before, and ask questions they may have never asked themselves before much less considered discussing with anyone else. For the anthropologist, these acts of observing and engaging are the only way to understand how people do things in reality, as we cannot rely on people to accurately report to us what they do. However, we must also understand that this act of observation may feel invasive to the observed, regardless of the nature of their activities. We also cannot always know in advance which activities or topics of discussion will seem sensitive or private to someone else.

To engage in ethical research, then, we must treat our human subjects with dignity and autonomy by recognizing their freedom to stake out the boundaries of what is open to our probing and what is not. To do this we inform them about the forms of research we intend to subject them to, the risks and benefits for them of participating in this research, and the fact that we will not proceed unless they provide us with their **informed consent.** That is, we must assure them that there will be no negative consequences if they refuse to be researched, withdraw from the research at any point, or request that any data be erased. Further, we need to assess if they are members of a **vulnerable population**—vulnerable in any ways that would make it impossible for them to give their autonomous, informed consent to this research. Various countries have enacted regulations and created organizations or committees who oversee research on human subjects, such as the institutional review boards (IRBs) housed at many American universities. They play a role in ensuring that ethical research methods are used in order to protect human subjects from physical, psychological, or other harm.

To clarify these points, we begin by probing the notion of informed consent in a little more detail. Consent is considered informed when and only when a potential participant has fully understood how researchers will be asking them to participate and what the researchers hope to do with the data generated from the research. In particular, they need to understand the risks and benefits for them of participating. The benefits are frequently minimal, but not non-existent. For example, anthropologists' funding proposals are frequently designed to offer some financial remuneration for the time our participants spend with us, such as helping with the tedious work of transcribing the recordings we make. Sometimes bringing food to share is a culturally acceptable form of exchange with those who are willing to invite us into their lives in less formal ways. Alternatively, many anthropologists, especially those referred to as **engaged anthropologists**, attempt to design their research to be relevant and useful for their participants.

By contrast, the list of possible risks to participants may be long, and worse, they are frequently unpredictable. That is, we cannot know in advance all of the effects that our research presence in certain settings will produce. However, over a century of research in this field has shown us that we need to be careful with the information our participants provide to us, thinking about how we will safeguard the data and how we will represent it to others through the publication of our findings. That is, we need to be sure our participants do not suffer from having shared information with us that ought to have stayed private.

The issues of risks, benefits, privacy, and consent are most salient for vulnerable populations. Severable vulnerable populations that researchers might wish to study while engaging with food and language research include children, prisoners, and semi-literate peoples. A lot of food-and-language socialization research works with children from birth on up. Different societies consider adulthood to begin at different ages; however, in many Western societies, 18 years old is the usual age when individuals are considered to be able to make decisions for themselves, including voting, marrying, and enlisting in the military. Until that age, researchers are bound by law to ask the parents' permission to engage in such research. However, many anthropologists request not only the parents' official consent but also the children's assent from as early an age as seems reasonable. We attempt to make our research comprehensible to the children so that they feel comfortable with our presence in their social spaces.

For example, Paugh has worked closely with children in both the United States and Dominica in settings where adult caregivers were present and others where they were not; she is thus familiar with how the presence of adults may influence how children understand the experience of being researched. In Dominica, the children came to enjoy her presence as she recorded them while they played with peers. As they became more comfortable, many used some Patwa, the Afro-French creole that parents typically forbade children from speaking because they feared negative influence on children's English (Paugh 2012). Though they were informed at the start of the research, the children may not have fully understood the implications of the recordings in that Paugh would be sitting down with their parents to transcribe their words afterwards. Fortunately, the parents did not take any real offense at how the children behaved in mildly illicit ways outside their purview, but this was a risk that Paugh stumbled into and could not have anticipated, especially since the children hardly used Patwa in adult-controlled settings. To help with this dilemma, she transcribed video data with older children in the family who had participated during recordings, instead of parents, when possible. The younger children were often present during transcriptions sessions with adults as well.

In Riley's research with Marquesans, few of whom are fully literate, she discovered many well-grounded suspicions concerning the implications of signing her informed consent documents. First of all, her participants do not perceive that writing imparts credible knowledge, and secondly they do not trust that protections promised to them in writing will come true. To the contrary, they are aware that signing documents whose contents they only vaguely understood have been the means by which they lost title to their family lands, were locked into labor contracts with less than favorable working conditions, or were made liable for actions they were not aware were illegal. Thus, asking them to sign such forms has presented difficulties over the years as it is hard for them to believe that the form is designed not to make them give up their rights but to acknowledge that they understand that they have rights and may act on them if they feel the need to.[6]

Finally, there are several vulnerable populations who may feel that their well-being is contingent on their consent and therefore feel obliged to sign such a consent form. While neither Paugh nor Riley has worked with such populations, we recognize the challenges that would arise in, for example, asking for the consent of incarcerated individuals who work on farms or in kitchens as part of their (underpaid) labor while in prison. While access to the prison could only be arranged by going through the state system, the consent of the prisoners would need to be acquired in a non-policed context in which they could be made to understand that they were at liberty to give or withhold their consent. It is difficult to know how easy it would be to attain this level of privacy or this degree of willing consent.

Next, we consider the types of topics that are "sensitive" for our subjects—both those that are obviously delicate and those that on the surface seem innocuous enough but turn out to be fraught with emotion. As an example of the former, consider research with families and schools on the topic of "eating disorders." Body size and shape is a source of sensitivity for many adolescents and adults in the United States and elsewhere (Nichter 2000; Shohet 2007). Debate and accusations abound as to whether "disorders" such as obesity and anorexia are the result of genetics, structural inequities in the food system, and/or the result of "bad" parenting and "poor choices" by individuals. Given the psychological tensions prompted by such discourses, researchers interested in such a topic would need to tread lightly there.

Another set of topics dealing with food and parenting that turned out to be sensitive for subjects arose for Riley while conducting research in the Marquesas. While working with a mother in 1993 on transcribing her family's meal discussions, Riley discovered that her assistant believed in a range of traditional in utero food taboos, such as specific fish that ought not to be eaten while pregnant lest one's children be born with various ailments. She also realized that her assistant feared discussing these with Riley lest she be reported for poor parenting. At the time it seemed easy to assure the mother that this information would never reach the ears of the French authorities. Then, 20 years later, while working with a different mother on transcribing, Riley discovered that this woman too was concerned over the fact that several adults in her family had been caught on tape pre-chewing some tough fish for her 16-month-old child to eat. She said that French nurses had instructed her on the lack of hygiene this traditional practice entailed, and she wanted to know Riley's opinion. By now sensitized to the fact that her role as an American anthropologist could be easily confused with that of a French social worker, Riley was quick to explain that she had no special medical knowledge about such matters but that this was not the first time she had witnessed this activity (and not only in the Marquesas) and that, so long as no one was sick in the family, she had always thought of it as a sensible way to make various healthy foods digestible for small children. The mother seemed somewhat relieved by this explanation.

How to Handle Research Data Ethically Afterwards

Our food-and-language research subjects sometimes discover that their foodways and discourses are being observed, recorded, and discussed in surprising and unanticipated ways; for instance, the Marquesan mothers who realized that they were feeding their children in ways that outsiders might think of as "uncivilized" or at least unhealthy or the Dominican mothers who discovered that their children were talking in Patwa when role-playing farmers and pig hunters. What becomes of these data after we collect them? Can we publish them? Should we destroy them?

In public settings, it is difficult to not infringe on the privacy of others. While in some research cases, controversial information is already on the public or semi-public record (for instance, if quoting newspapers or public figures), in other cases, the sensitive information is only revealed because of the researchers' analytic tools. When reflecting on the use of recording

Figure 3.6 Market in Fuengirola, Spain
Credit: Photo by Caleb Stokes on Unsplash

devices for her research on food and language in Italy, Cavanaugh points out that there can be logistical issues involving where to put the device in a location like a slaughterhouse, as well as ethical issues involved in ensuring participant privacy when recording in a public setting like an open-air market (Cavanaugh et al. 2014:87). Thus, the question becomes whether, when, where, and how to make these data and analyses public.

One approach is to keep some of the information wholly confidential, or to protect the privacy of subjects by disassociating data from their sources and masking the identities of individuals and whole communities so they will not be subject to injurious or humiliating consequences outside of the researcher's control. This approach is far more feasible in large-scale studies with huge pools of participants whose names and other identifying data are never collected to begin with. An additional problem for personalized ethnographic research is that the project's trajectory, the consequences for the participants, and the fate of the data we collect cannot always be predicted. Nonetheless, there are some possibilities that we can attempt to know and account for.

First, the raw data. Researchers make every attempt to keep our notes and recordings, survey information and transcriptions under lock and key, whether in real filing cabinets or on virtually locked hard drives. Secondly, by whatever means possible, we keep our subjects' real names and contact information separated from any data that might incriminate them. Finally, we conscientiously destroy any data that our subjects have objected to.

Even more complex than managing the raw data, however, is the issue of how we analyze these data and publish our findings. Here we continue to confront the problem of how, and how well, we can or should protect our subjects' identities from public view. And perhaps more importantly, given the near impossibility of hiding the subjects of ethnographic study from the prying eyes of any really interested party, is the question of how much to say about them.

First, there are the difficulties of wholly cloaking identities. As we have seen, anthropologists make a specialty out of learning about humans by getting to know small communities and individuals quite intimately. Though we may use impersonal surveys to collect quantitative information about the larger background setting, what we really make of human culture is what we learn through breaking bread and chatting with individuals in an everyday way for months on end. Thus, much of the evidence we use to make our analytic arguments takes the form of evocative descriptions of places meaningful to local inhabitants, well-told narratives involving events and characters with unique personal histories, and idiosyncratic conversations displaying tell-tale details among individuals whose identities would be obvious to anyone in the immediate community. Is it possible to cloak these stories by changing lots of specifics, from the name and location of the community to the words and features of the individuals? Should we avoid or constrain the ways in which we publish these if we cannot? Is the best approach to collaborate actively with our subjects in order to be sure that everyone is on board with what comes out?

Anthropologists have sought out diverse and ever-evolving resolutions to these problems. Riley, for instance, asked her Marquesan subjects' opinion about whether or not to use their actual names in her publications, and having been told that they would prefer to be named, proceeded to do so. However, she has constrained much of what she includes. There are many interactions, personalities, and events that she will never publish, or only very circumspectly, by way of respect not only for the individuals whom she knew best but also out of respect for the community as a whole. Note how in the descriptions above, for instance, the references to the parental food taboos and pre-chewed food are presented without any identifying features.

In the more usual practice, pseudonyms were assigned in both of Paugh's research projects in the United States and Caribbean, but she has also chosen to not publish child-rearing interactions that could be misinterpreted or not fully grasped by outsiders. This has meant leaving out some very rich moments of language use, eating practices, and language socialization that could enhance a publication or presentation. While such interactions inform a researcher's overall interpretations, it is important to consider how the dissemination of specific information could put people at risk, whether in terms of identification and confidentiality or misinterpretation and false generalization.

Summary

In this chapter, we have explored a range of fruitful methods for studying food and language. From participant observation to audio/video recording of food talk in context to elicited foodways discourses in focus groups and interviews, researchers have developed numerous techniques for learning about people's food-and-language practices and beliefs. We have also touched on various ethical issues and provided suggestions for engaging in ethical food talk while procuring food-and-language data in the field, processing it through writing and analysis, and disseminating it via public presentations and publications. Readers may refer to the eResources page for resources to expand their understanding of these issues, exercises for trying out some of these research methods, and examples of how our students undertook these exercises.

Now, we turn to the meat of the matter and look at some intriguing findings about how food and language interact in contemporary cultures. We investigate how different discourses are associated with different ways of producing and consuming food within specific settings, such as at ritual feasts versus domestic meals. We provide illustrations of how the methods discussed in this chapter can be used to analyze how discourses contribute to the semiotic mediation of foodways while foodways constrain the semiotic mediation of discourses in the world. Specifically, in the next chapter, we focus on how humans fill food with meaning and use food as a kind of language to communicate within and across cultures.

Notes

1. See Chrzan and Brett (2017) for anthropological methods used to study food and foodways, and see Gerhardt (2013); Szatrowski (2014); Cavanaugh et al. (2014); and Riley and Cavanaugh (2017) for more about specific approaches to studying food and language.
2. Cultural relativism is a complicated concept in anthropology. While attempting to understand foreign social norms from another culture's perspective is an ideal to be promoted up to a point, we cannot expect ourselves to accept all of the beliefs and practices of every society. We must also be willing to draw the line at times. For instance, Riley refused to take communion at the village church in the Marquesas despite the urgings of her friends to do so; she is not a Catholic and felt it would be disrespectful toward the institution as it is practiced around the world. Many other anthropologists encounter far more difficult situations of belief and practice, such as those that may potentially infringe on human rights.
3. Haines and Sammells (2010) and Colman (2011) provide rich accounts of the moral and practical gustatory difficulties encountered by ethnographers in the field.
4. See Riley (2009) for an example of learning alimentary competence while on the job as an anthropologist in France.
5. These researchers deserve thanks for their hard work and many insights: Amber Brookmire, Carolina Carvajal, Seth Cipriano, Sesaley Graciani, Jackson Kuang, Esther Liu, Kristen Policastro, Brittany Schuler, Yexenia Vanegas, Keishla Santana, Geraldine Then, Brooke Vermillion, and Gabrielle Williams.
6. Then again, how many of us understand the real import and provisions of the forms we sign on various occasions, such as each time we visit a doctor? While the first function of these forms is to advise us of our rights, the secondary function is to avoid liability in case anything goes wrong—the doctor can claim to have apprised the patient, who signed something stating that she was informed.

References

Austin, J. L. 1962. *How to Do Things with Words*. Cambridge, MA: Harvard University Press.

Barker, John. 2016. *Ancestral Lines: The Maisin of Papua New Guinea and the Fate of the Rainforest*. Toronto: University of Toronto Press.

Blommaert, Jan. 2013. *Ethnography, Superdiversity and Linguistic Landscapes: Chronicles of Complexity*. Bristol: Multilingual Matters

Cavanaugh, Jillian R., Kathleen C. Riley, Alexandra Jaffe, Christine Jourdan, Martha Karrebæk, and Amy Paugh. 2014. "What Words Bring to the Table: The Linguistic Anthropological Toolkit as Applied to the Study of Food." *Journal of Linguistic Anthropology* 24(1): 87–88.

Chrzan, Janet, and John Brett. 2017. *Food Research: Nutritional Anthropology and Archaeological Methods*. New York and Oxford: Berghahn.

Colman, Leo, ed. 2011. *Food: Ethnographic Encounters*. Oxford: Berg.

Cosgriff-Hernández, Kevin-Khristián, Amanda R. Martinez, Barbara F. Sharf, and Joseph R. Sharkey. 2010. "'We Still Had to Have Tortillas': Negotiating Health, Culture, and Change in the Mexican American Diet." In *Food as Communication/Communication as Food*, edited by Janet M. Cramer, Carlnita P. Greene, and Lynn M. Walters, 115–135. New York: Peter Lang.

Counihan, Carole M. 2004. *Around the Tuscan Table: Food, Family, and Gender in Twentieth-Century Florence*. New York: Routledge.

Counihan, Carole M. 2009. *A Tortilla Is Like Life: Food and Culture in the San Luis Valley of Colorado*. Austin: University of Texas Press.

Duranti, Alessandro, and Charles Goodwin, eds. 1992. *Rethinking Context: Language as an Interactive Phenomenon*. New York: Cambridge University Press.

Duranti, Alessandro, Elinor Ochs, and Bambi B. Schieffelin, eds. 2012. *The Handbook of Language Socialization*. Malden, MA: Wiley-Blackwell.

Frake, Charles O. 1964. "How to Ask for a Drink in Subanun." *American Anthropologist* 66(6, pt. 2): 127–132.

Gerhardt, Cornelia. 2013. "Food and Language: Language and Food." In *Culinary Linguistics: The Chef's Special*, edited by Cornelia Gerhardt, Maximiliane Frobenius, and Susanne Ley, 3–49. Amsterdam: John Benjamins.

Haines, Helen R., and Clare A. Sammells, eds. 2010. *Adventures in Eating: Anthropological Experiences in Dining from Around the World*. Boulder: University of Colorado Press.

Hymes, Dell. 1964. "Introduction: Toward Ethnographies of Communication." *American Anthropologist* 66(6–2): 1–34.

Johansson, Barbara, Joanna Mäkelä, Gun Roos, Sandra Hillén, Gitte Laub Hansen, Tine Mark Jensen, and Anna Huotilainen. 2009. "Nordic Children's Foodscapes: Images and Reflections." *Food, Culture, and Society* 12(1): 25–51.

Jourdan, Christine. 2010. "The Cultural Localization of Rice in Solomon Islands." *Ethnology* 49(4): 263–282.

Jourdan, Christine, and Sylvain Poirier. 2012. "Le Goût en Héritage: Exploration des Transformations Alimentaires dans quelques Familles Montréalaises." *Anthropologica* 54(2): 281–292.

Knauft, Bruce. 2016. *The Gebusi: Lives Transformed in a Rainforest World*, 4th edition. Long Grove, IL: Waveland Press.

Malinowski, Bronislaw. 1935. *Coral Gardens and Their Magic: A Study of the Methods of Tilling the Soil and in Agricultural Rites in the Trobriand Islands, Vol. 2: The Language of Magic and Gardening*. New York: American Book Company.

Nichter, Mimi. 2000. *Fat Talk: What Girls and Their Parents Say about Dieting*. Cambridge: Harvard University Press.

Ochs, Elinor, and Tamar Kremer-Sadlik. 2013. *Fast-Forward Family: Home, Work, and Relationships in Middle-Class America*. Berkeley and Los Angeles: University of California Press.

Ochs, Elinor, and Bambi Schieffelin. 2012. "The Theory of Language Socialization." In *The Handbook of Language Socialization*, edited by Alessandro Duranti, Elinor Ochs, and Bambi Schieffelin, 1–22. Malden, MA: Wiley-Blackwell.

Ochs, Elinor, and Merav Shohet. 2006. "The Cultural Structuring of Mealtime Socialization." *New Directions for Child and Adolescent Development* 111: 35–49.

Paugh, Amy L. 2012. *Playing with Languages: Children and Change in a Caribbean Village*. New York: Berghahn Books.

Paugh, Amy, and Carolina Izquierdo. 2009. "Why Is This a Battle Every Night?: Negotiating Food and Eating in American Dinnertime Interaction." *Journal of Linguistic Anthropology* 19(2): 185–204.

Riley, Kathleen C. 2009. "Who Made the Soup? Socializing the Researcher and Cooking Her Data." *Language and Communication* 29(3): 254–270.

Riley, Kathleen C. Forthcoming. "'Don't Yuck My Yum': Semiotics and the Socialization of Food Ideologies at an Elite Elementary School." *Semiotic Review* 5: *The Semiotics of Food and Language*.

Riley, Kathleen C., and Jillian R. Cavanaugh. 2017. "Food Talk: Studying Foodways and Language in Use Together." In *Food Culture: Anthropology, Linguistics and Food Studies*, edited by Janet Chrzan and John Brett, 143–158. New York and Oxford: Berghahn.

Salazar, Melissa, Gail Feenstra, and Jeri Ohmart. 2008. "Salad Days: A Visual Study of Children's Food Culture." In *Food and Culture: A Reader*, 2nd edition, edited by Carole Counihan and Penny Van Esterik, 423–437. New York: Routledge.

Shohet, Merav. 2007. "Narrating Anorexia: 'Full' and 'Struggling' Genres of Recovery." *Ethos* 35(3): 344–382.

Szatrowski, Polly E. 2014. "Introduction." In *Language and Food: Verbal and Nonverbal Experiences*, edited by Polly E. Szatrowski, 3–28. Philadelphia and Amsterdam: John Benjamins.

Chapter 4

Language Through Food

For most humans in most cultures, producing and consuming food is not only a means of funneling nutrients into the body. Instead, foodways operate as a meaningful set of symbols, practices, and beliefs through which we express who we are, how we relate to others, and how we feel about the world we live in. These semiotic values are constructed partly through discourses about food (the focus of Chapter 5) and partly through social interactions while growing, cooking, and eating food (the focus of Chapter 6). But in this chapter, we focus on the forms, meanings, and functions of foodways and on the larger forces that forge these. To use our shorthand, here we look at language *through* food, that is, how food operates somewhat like language as a medium of communication because of how we invest it with significance and use it to do meaningful things in our lives.

We use the semiotic terminology developed in previous chapters to focus first on how foodways can sometimes *iconically* look like and be decoded like a language or read as a text. Second, we consider how foodways are *indexically* associated with meaning in various social settings, cultural contexts, and historical moments. And third, we explore how foodways are used as conventionalized *symbols* by people in a variety of ways. As we will see, some scholars focus more on the cross-cultural similarities of these food signs due to regularities in human cognition or the physical world. Others work to deconstruct the political-economic soup out of which they emerge at specific times and places. In this chapter we introduce both approaches to the meanings of food and foodways.

Interpreting Foodways: The Iconic Mirror

Some theorists think of food as operating, in and of itself, as a communicating agent. For instance, in an essay from 1947, Howard (2012) reads nature as a system of communicative exchange: plants make food out of sun, water, oxygen, minerals, and other organisms that participate by eating and dying. For Howard, food imparts life via this intricate cycle of give and take. It is a product of natural semiosis and thus an illustration of how food communicates meaning as a form of language.[1] By now this iconic relationship between food and language has become a mainstay not only for semioticians and anthropologists, but also for a growing number of historians, linguists, and food studies scholars. We begin by considering several classic approaches to this topic.

Levi-Strauss: Culinary Contrasts

Claude Levi-Strauss (1909–2009), the founder of what is known as **structural anthropology**, spent his career seeking to understand the universal structures of human cognition that underlie similarities across all human languages and cultures. In this quest, he frequently focused on parallels between language and foodways (Lévi-Strauss 1966, 1969, 1973, 1978). First, he noted, all humans have both language and cuisine. Second, cuisine, like language, is based on meanings conventionally associated with specific contrasts, primarily the contrast between nature and culture. In terms of foodways, cooked is to culture as raw is to nature because humans, unlike other animals, apply culture and cooking to mediate and elaborate upon nature and raw foods.

4.1   To make this clear, he borrowed the **vowel triangle** from linguistics in which consonants and vowels are seen to be distinguished by the way the tongue moves in the mouth. In order to grasp the contrasts between high/front, low, and high/back, try noting where your tongue is in your mouth as you say the vowels in 'hit,' 'hot,' and 'hoot.' Languages rely on distinctive vowel sounds found along this triangle to form a huge vocabulary of words. Similarly, Levi-Strauss (see Fig. 4.1) suggested that human cuisines could be mapped onto culinary triangles to model how humans prepare food using a few universal modalities to form a panoply of distinctive cultural dishes.

The triangle bounded by 'raw,' 'cooked,' and 'rotten' illustrates how raw food is transformed by culture into cooked food and how both of these can be transformed by nature into rotten food. Although Levi-Strauss himself grew up in a culture (French) that valued fermented (aka rotten) products (e.g., cheese and wine) as well as raw veggies in the form of crudités, he nonetheless considered cooking as the pinnacle of human food intervention and further broke down this form of "cultured" food preparation into

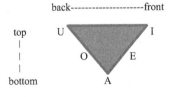
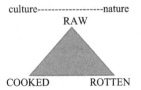

Figure 4.1 Vowel and culinary triangles

another triangle: 'roasted,' 'boiled,' and 'smoked.' Here roasting represents the unmediated application of fire to raw food, while smoking entails the mediation of air and boiling the mediation of water.[2]

Additionally, Levi-Strauss held that humans use these structural contrasts as homologues for other cultural structures, such as kinship. Symbols derived from these structures are used in myths and rituals to give voice to cultural assumptions and to resolve contradictions when apparent facts do not fit the cultural paradigm. Thus, language and food are linked in two ways: food communicates like language—language *through* food—and foodways show up in linguistic genres such as myths—language *about* food. For Levi-Strauss, food's meanings within these myths is also part of what is read, that is, language *through* food within language *about* food.

Barthes and Douglas: Culinary Grammars

Similarly, for the French semiotician and literary critic, Roland Barthes (1915–1980), both food and language are signifying systems to be read. Foodways, Barthes claimed, could be compared to linguistic grammar in that just as changing one word can change the significance of a whole sentence, so can changing one aspect of a meal transform the whole meal—changing the type of bread, for example, can transform an everyday dinner into a holiday meal. He also likened how sentences take on significance due to our intonation, or **suprasegmental prosody** as he called it, to how certain sensual aspects of food come in associative clumps depending on the culture. For instance, he described how "[t]he ancient Greeks unified in a single (euphoric) notion the ideas of succulence, brightness, and moistness, and they called it *yávos*. Honey had *yávos*, and wine was the *yávos* of the vineyard" (2008[1961]:31). Americans, he said, appreciate two contrasting forms of food pleasure, each one identified with clumps of non-overlapping aesthetic qualities: crisp/sour/cold versus sweet/soft/soothing.

4.2

While Lévi-Strauss sought universals, Barthes tried to read the mythological significance of various foods and foodways for particular cultures. For him, wine and steak illustrated the life blood of the French (Barthes 1972) whereas chopsticks and sukiyaki—a stew served as raw ingredients and cooked communally at the table—exemplified the delicacy of the Japanese (Barthes 1982). He also set the stage for studying how foods, settings, and social values become semiotically linked. For example, a "business lunch" is marked by conviviality and fine dining whereas "snack bar" food is understood to be efficient and energizing (2008[1961]). Additionally, he identified the ways in which foods and foodways become systematically attached to particular social values because of the symbols used in discourses about them—in advertising, the Brandy of Napoleon is indicative of French identity (2008[1961]).[3]

Figure 4.2 Sukiyaki in a hot pot in a Japanese restaurant (© Shutterstock)

Mary Douglas (1921–2007), a British symbolic anthropologist, also published influential work (1966, 1972) on decoding our foodways much as we do languages. By contrast with Barthes's focus on meaning, she focused on the forms and functions of foodways. But, like Barthes (and unlike Lévi-Strauss), she was less interested in the universal binary contrasts through which cultural meanings are displayed and more interested in the culture-specific ordering of these contrasts in ways that are recognized in particular cultures as appropriate. In other words, just as we recognize grammatical sentences in our own language, so do we recognize the appropriate ingredients and sequencing of dishes at meals in our own culture.[4]

In her best-known article on the subject, "Deciphering a Meal" (1972), Douglas first looked at what her own family of bourgeois Brits expected from a meal, including both essential elements and their proper arrangement, whether in the form of a canape or a celebratory feast. The "meal," she noted, was something one shared only with friends and family while the "drink" was something one might invite less intimate others to share. The contrast between the two operated as a marker of social difference. She then went on to explain how the kosher food regulations of Moses were structured according to symbolic categories to do with purity and taboo—how only some animals could be eaten, how those that may be eaten must be bloodless, and how this bloodless meat must be kept separate from dairy. Such categories are related to the notion of pollution that results

4.3

from broken taxonomies when things are out of symbolic place, rather than from actual dirt as material stuff out of place. Finally, according to Douglas's food-language system, a meal is like a poem in that both must be deciphered according to patterned rules.

The Language Metaphor Applied

Levi-Strauss, Barthes, and Douglas all used language as an explicit model for food. Levi-Strauss employed a phonological metaphor: just as language relies on sound (phonemic) contrasts to form meaningful words, so do foodways rely on technical cooking contrasts to form meaningful cuisines. Similarly, Barthes and Douglas traced semantic and syntactic parallels: just as languages present speakers with lexical options for constructing meaningful utterances, so do foodways create meaningful cuisines out of variously categorized dishes and food characteristics. And just as language uses rules of grammar to order words in ways that make sentences comprehensible, so do diners use culture-specific alimentary rules to create and enjoy a properly assembled meal. Other scholars have taken these ideas and run with them!

Douglas's model has been much borrowed to analyze how humans use food and language to organize meals into several ritual stages from entrance through departure. For instance, Beeman (2014) uses data from four cultures (American, German, Japanese, and Middle Eastern, including Persian, Turkish, and Arabic) to hypothesize that the goal of staged meals in these cultures, and perhaps universally, is to create sociality and a sense of **communitas** during the central space of the meal—that is, through meals, hierarchical barriers may be both respected and momentarily dissolved.

An example of applying Levi-Strauss's culinary triangle to the interpretation of a whole eating venue can be found in Clark's study (2004) of the Black Cat Café, a punk culture hangout in Seattle in the 1990s. Here the mostly young, white, middle-class, and vegan clientele used the notion of "raw" and "rotten" foodways to resist mainstream American culture. The 4.4 1990s saw the rise in the United States of various branches of punk ideology and practice that focalized foodways; they preferred their food "raw" or "rotten," either wild or as organically produced as possible but washed of all cultural mediation/cooking by being stolen from yuppie stores or rotten from dumpsters. The décor of the café broke normative rules about how restaurants should look and feel clean, orderly, and tasteful by being haphazardly furnished with stolen, broken, out-of-place objects. In this safe space for homeless activists, the food further symbolized their anti-sexist, anti-racist, and anti-classist concerns about corporate capitalism and environmental collapse; they did not want to let their food be mediated by unjust human systems.

Food rules, contrasts, and categories take on iconic fixity for culturally imbued human beings. As such, they can be used like language to transmit meanings to those who share our cultural assumptions. In the next section, we see how these food meanings emerge out of human interaction within specific foodscapes or sociocultural **food social spaces** (Poulain 2017). Once filled with personal, social, and cultural meanings, foods and foodways may then continue to operate as indexes of those meanings even beyond the spatial and temporal contexts in which the food meanings were originally forged.

Vignette 4.1   Christine Jourdan: Communicating Through and Around Food in France and the Solomon Islands

Christine Jourdan is a Professor of Anthropology at Concordia University, and researches food and language in Quebec, France, and the Solomon Islands.

I do not know exactly when I started to be interested in the anthropological study of food. But I know that this interest was hidden behind the one I had for an anthropological study of language, which led me progressively to reflect on how people used language to refer to food and how food serves to index personal relationships. Over time language and food merged together naturally in my research.

4.5

In the Solomon Islands, an archipelago in the Pacific Ocean, I work in a society where food anchors social relationships: exchanges of food serve to initiate or feed kinship, friendship, marriage, and so on. A gift of food is a gift of oneself; a pledge that one is in earnest in the relationship that the gift celebrates. No formal ceremony can take place without food being offered. The local languages of the Solomon Islands (about 74 of them) are laden with food metaphors about life and belonging. For instance, if I want to say that I have adopted a child, I say that I feed it. No explanation is needed: people know the importance of the food tie. Feeding is the metaphor for adoption, but more importantly it symbolizes the essence of Solomon Islands society: kinship. No observer of language could miss the cultural underlay that food is.

Being of French descent, I was early on surprised that my Solomon Islands interlocutors did not choose to speak when they ate. People gathered once a day around the evening meal, ate it quickly without speaking, and started to speak only when the food was all gone. The contrast between my society of origin (French) and my society of immersion (Solomon Islands) could not have been stronger. For French people, conversations during meals are as essential to the success of the meal as is the quality of the food one eats. Food without talk does not make sense and French people go so far as to talk about previous meals while eating another one. It was the absence of speech during meals in the Solomon Islands that led me to reflect on the importance of food and how language indexed it. In France, food is so important that people equate it to speech: if one eats, one speaks. Eating alone, without speaking, is tantamount to discipline and punishment. No wonder that in very strict boarding schools like the ones I attended, children were not allowed to speak while eating. By contrast, in the Solomon Islands, food is equally important to social relationships. Yet, talk during meals is not welcome: one needs to concentrate on the food, reflect on the day, and appreciate the moment. These are two different ways of doing food and language: the first one mingles food with speech, the second one with silence. My Solomon Islands friends know of my taste for mixing the two. Out of kindness, they sometimes humor me and speak to me during meals, for they know that I am starved for a good conversation. Most of the time, though, we eat in silence while I take the scene in and take mental notes.

Since beginning my research in villages in South West France, I am also paying attention to the way people mix food and language during the outdoors evening meals that they organize in the summer months. People in these villages are often linked through marriage and friendship. Eating local food, raised and grown in the vicinity and cooked with local recipes, is essential to the success of the meal. But it is just as essential to diners that they be gathered around the meal with friends or family, and catch up on news, argue about politics, or comment on the food. The conversation makes the meal, and so are the comments people make on the quality of the food. When I study these meals, and how people use language to prepare and enjoy them, I am able to understand why they come to the meal; how they situate themselves socially in the crowd of diners; what social network they belong to; and what relationships they entertain with the food itself. The crowd around the dinner table is more than a collection of individuals having a good time. It is clear to me that language and food binds them in a way that food alone could not.

Identifying Food Meanings: The Indexical Link

Very few early anthropologists focused much on the cultural meanings of food for social actors.[5] Explorers' reports and early ethnographies regularly included information about food production and exchange as well as taboos and sacrificial practices, especially eye-popping ones such as cannibalism. These authors focused especially on the ways in which spiritual rules about who could and couldn't eat certain forms of foods when, where, and how appeared to correlate with age, gender, and status differences. Early sociologists such as Emile Durkheim (1982) and Marcel Mauss (2000) were also interested in how food functioned as a kind of social glue for bonding and regulating communities. But a real interest in tracing *what* food meant across cultural contexts and *how* these meanings came to be attached and transformed over time awaited the work of later anthropologists.[6] In this section, we look at how food can be read not only *like* language, but how food, like language, performs as an index—both pointing out and constructing identities and relationships.

For some researchers, this aspect of food meaning can be best explored based on a parallel with the linguistic concept of **linguistic registers**, or the ways of speaking associated with particular activities or contexts of use, such as sports or cooking. These ways of speaking become in a sense enregistered (Agha 2005) at the level of language ideology for community members and as such can be used as an index both to reflect and construct the context. For instance, soccer players switch into using their sports register when they step out onto the soccer field because it allows them to facilitate team communication; however, soccer fans may also transform any other social situation by switching to their sports register, thus excluding anyone present who does not share this register or the cultural knowledge that it encodes. Similarly, food anthropologists have begun to speak of **food registers** to discuss the socioculturally and contextually specific variations in people's foodways (e.g., Karrebæk 2013). Like linguistic registers, food registers are socially recognizable ways of growing, preparing, serving, and eating foods that carry significance for those who are enregistered to use them while excluding those who do not share the same food ideologies.

Soup Stories: What Food Sharing Means in Particular Contexts

As mentioned in Chapter 3, for an anthropologist newly arrived in a community it takes time to adapt not only to the new foods being eaten but also to the significance of the new food registers. Through Riley's (2009) research in France, she learned that a simple question such as "Who made the soup?" can be unfortunately misinterpreted yet lead to fascinating findings. In this case, French norms led her hosts to respond to her question as if it were a critique rather than a prelude to a compliment as she, an American, had intended. Not only did Riley learn about the norm from this incident, she was also amazed to see how one of the children, only seven years old, was already "properly" socialized to hear the (unintended) critique and follow up with precise culinary details—in this case, noting how she had observed her mother way over-salting the soup.

In a very different context, Bourke (2001) was puzzled when after helping a family plant maize on one of her first days in Ecuador, the family sat her down alone on the porch and brought her multiple (too many!) bowls of soup while they ate inside. She understood that this was a form of thanking her for her labor but also imagined that they did not think a "white woman" would want to go inside an "Indian" house. It took long-term participant observation for her to learn that the way in which the soup had been presented was indicative of the social distinction typically made between household members, who eat inside the house, and non-members (not just foreigners), who are expected to eat outside the house. Additionally, an Indian household tends to give too much food, especially during festivals. For instance, on *Finados* (the Day of the Dead), food is prepared and left overnight for the deceased, who ingest only the smells, and is then redistributed by the plateful to other households who have helped the giving-household in the fields producing maize. The circulation of dishes acts to bind the community, and the capacity to provide more and better dishes signifies a household's standing in the community. Only cooked food is given in this way whereas raw foods are given in exchange for nontraditional services, such as offering eggs to the doctor.

Bourke found that in these situations, communication through food gifts was also accompanied by commentary about how much food was received from other households and how good it was. Similarly, the dead were believed to circulate between the households, discussing and comparing the offerings in order to decide whose fields to bless next year in return. In other words, the communicative value of the food depended on its quality and quantity. Additionally, differences between Indians and *mestizos* (people of mixed Indian and European descent) were marked by foodways differences—for example, whether mestizos would eat guinea pig and, if so, whether or not they would pick them up and eat them with their hands like Indians. Visiting mestizo officials would politely eat in this way at public feasts to garner the Indians' votes in future elections whereas village mestizos used foodways to emphasize their differences, lest they be mistaken for Indians. For instance, instead of leaving food offerings for the dead and distributing it afterwards by the plateful, mestizos would cook a big meal for *Finados* and invite their kin over to eat together. It took Bourke time to develop the communicative-alimentary competence needed to make sense of these food events—that is, to read what the food and its circulation indicated about her hosts' identities and social connections. In the process, she also eventually developed the social ties she needed to be invited to eat inside some households.

Figure 4.3 Day of the Dead offering in Oaxaca, Mexico (© Shutterstock)

One more soup story further elucidates the ways in which food is used in particular settings to index social identities and relationships. Among the Chambri in Papua New Guinea, Gewertz (1984) found that a soup made from sago palm starch, coconut milk, and meat stood iconically for procreation, with women represented by the sago (a pink substance resembling mother's blood) and men represented by the coconut (white stuff resembling semen). However, during one particular incident, sago soup took on another level of significance based on the identities of the participants and the context. Before Australian colonialism, a neighboring group had been militarily inferior to the Chambri and as a result had supplied the Chambri with their staple sago. However, since the Australians had halted warfare and given all residents equal voting rights, their neighbors had begun to resist Chambri dominance, and the Chambri were having trouble accessing the sago on which they were dependent. When one of the neighboring leaders then committed an affront against the Chambri leader by killing a crocodile—considered his totem—the leader was able to use food to get out of the double bind of having to react to the affront without acknowledging that the neighboring leader was no longer subservient. The way out was to invite the crocodile-killer to a ceremony and attempt to serve him sago soup in which the male coconut indexed the strong Chambri and the female sago indexed the weak neighbors. If the crocodile killer had eaten the soup, he would have been acknowledging his subservience. As it turned out, he claimed that his stomach was not feeling well and left without eating. Nonetheless, the Chambri leader had successfully resolved his double bind as no one could say that he had not confronted the crocodile-killer using appropriate food messaging that displayed his continued dominance. Gewertz shows here how the culturally specified significance of the food being exchanged, the identities of those participating in the exchange, and the context in which the exchange takes place all indexically influence the communicative act and its message.

Culture and Class: How Food Speaks With Distinction Over Space and Time

One of the first scholars to attempt a comparative examination of how food indexes sociocultural meanings was the British social anthropologist Jack Goody (1919–2015). In *Cooking, Cuisine and Class*, Goody (1982) sought to explain how differences in the way food is produced, distributed, and prepared across cultures—due in part to environmental and technical constraints—results in differences in the ways foods are consumed. He focused first on how meaningful consumption patterns were shaped by the processes of food production and exchange among two groups in Ghana, one a small-scale, agrarian people (the LoDagaba) and one a kingdom of warriors, traders, craftspeople, and slaves (the Gonja). He correlated divisions of labor based on age, gender, and status (e.g., slave, farmer, merchant, chief, or religious leader) with divisions in what and how people ate. For instance, men hunted and grilled meat, and ate more of this prized part of the diet, while women gardened, ground flour, boiled vegetable sauces, and made beer to serve to guests, and ate less meat. Chiefs lived off the labor of slaves and retained their power by storing and distributing crops to commoners in times of need and by marketing delicacies such as kola nuts; their power was displayed not by the diversity of what they ate or complexity of how it was prepared, but only by the quantity (more) and by the fact that they ate alone.

Goody then compared these African foodways to the larger-scale, class-stratified societies of Europe and Asia. He claimed that the complexity of foodways found in many Eurasian societies in terms of diversity of foods and preparations, number of courses and dishes, and general dining regalia reflected and confirmed the elaborated division of labor, accumulation of wealth, and consolidation of power into more rigid class structures. Writing intersected with these new foodways, particularly in the form of recipes and cookbooks, a topic to which we return in the next chapter on language about food. Suffice it to say here that he saw a correlation between writing, complex cuisines, and social stratification, with non-literate, non-stratified societies tending to have far less elaborated forms of cuisine.

This relationship between social hierarchy and culinary messaging is also found in Appadurai's (1981) examination of the **gastro-politics** of Tamil Brahmins in India. According to Appadurai, food carries significance for Indians not only because of their long and literate history of social stratification organized around the exchange of food between peasants and elites, but also because of the religious significance attached to food as a medium of communication between humans and their gods. The resulting culinary rules are not only standardized but also fully rationalized in terms of this religious ideology and govern who cooks and serves whom, when, what, and how—with this mostly determined by social factors of age, gender, kinship, and caste.

For instance, within a Brahman family, these rules make clear not only when meals are to be held and what is to be eaten (strictly vegetarian), but also that older men related to the eldest male in a household are to be served more of the choice foods first whereas the younger women, newly married into a family, are expected to cook for everyone else first and then make do with their husbands' leftovers. However, when social realities create ambiguity in how to interpret these rules, as frequently happens because of the complexities of these extended, intermarrying families, individuals find numerous ways to use food to express their personal displeasure with

Figure 4.4 Family in a Hindu temple in Jaipur, Rajasthan, India (© Shutterstock)

other individuals—cooking poorly or slowly, withholding valued foods, or switching who is served first.

In Appadurai's analysis, gastro-politics also shows up in more public settings. Wedding feasts provide a venue for the enactment of many of the same hierarchical conflicts and ambiguities found in the domestic sphere but here involving non-family guests as well, sometimes even from other castes, all through foodways: cooking roles, assigned seating, order of service, solicitation of guests' well-being, and so on. Similarly, temples also operate as a public stage for using food to negotiate social standing. Offerings to the gods index the status of the donors and the gods to whom the food is offered—as gods too vary in their spiritual rank and their individual tastes—as well as the status of those to whom the left-over foods are redistributed, with the shifting meaning of caste being one key factor negotiated via food. Overall, Appadurai interprets food as a means to resolve structural contradictions in a society that insists on marking intimacy and solidarity on the one hand and hierarchy and relative status on the other.

Dispositions, Habitus, and Haute Cuisine: How Meanings Attach to Foods Across Sociocultural Contexts

Similar to age, gender, kinship, and caste, socioeconomic class operates as a feature of contrast to highlight the social categories around which unequal social structures are forged and marked by food. This notion is codified in the term **haute cuisine**, the form of cooking first associated with the upper classes of France and then spread to other corners of the globe.[7] Trubek (2000) explains how French cuisine came to signify haute-ness (that is, the high or upper class) and serve as a model for what cuisine itself could be, specifically the transformation of natural stuff by trained artisans into exquisitely cultural stuff and commodities people would pay for. Following Goody, the tale she tells has much to do with writing through recipes and cookbooks, and the codification of culinary rules in much the same way that **standard** languages (especially French) were being codified via classic texts written by experts and legitimized by authoritative institutions beginning around the 17th century.[8]

4.6

It is a French sociologist, Pierre Bourdieu (1930–2002), who is best known for putting class on the menu by establishing how our aesthetic dispositions, including both our ways of consuming food and our ways of speaking, can be read and linked to the political economic marketplace. In *Distinction* (1984), Bourdieu explored how tastes and table manners both mirror and help bolster the class system in France. That is, the "proper" ways of sitting, holding cutlery, serving food in courses, and speaking at table, are a kind of **symbolic capital** minted by the elite, transmitted to their children, and used as a form of semiotic currency to identify and exclude commoners from the upper echelons of society. He then went on in *Language and Symbolic Power* (1991) to apply this model to linguistic formations. That is, he formulated the notion of the linguistic marketplace (discussed in Chapter 1) in which speech varieties are valued in ways that manifest, reinforce, and reproduce status hierarchy in stratified societies. He himself experienced the impact of the language ideology held by Parisians that the southern dialect of French he spoke due to his upbringing in the province of Béarn was considered rude and uncultured.

Dispositions become deeply ingrained as habitus, a word Bourdieu borrowed from Aristotle to refer to all the embodied ways of knowing and dealing with the world that we develop through early patterns of socialization. Because of our dispositions and habitus, most of us tend to assume that the social meanings signified by our foodways simply are as they are. We don't ask how or why they came to be attached in this way or how we came to be attached to them. However, the identification of food meanings is an indexical process—it happens because we experience objects

Figure 4.5 Out-classed pasta in a foodie world

and events in particular contexts of temporal and spatial contiguity. For instance, we read foods and dishes as "traditional" not simply because they *actually* originated long ago in the places we consider home, but because we clothe them in the personal emotions and social myths picked up from the contexts wherein we have personally experienced them. Essentially, these indexical meanings transform into icons of "home," reassuring us as to who we *are* while allowing others to have a sense of this as well. This tendency is reflected in the much-quoted aphorism by the 19th-century French food philosopher Jean Anthelme Brillat-Savarin: "Tell me what you eat, and I shall tell you what you are" (2009[1825]:15).

Sometimes we may not even be aware of the indexical associations our foods had prior to our encountering them. For instance, Stummerer and Hablesreiter (2016) explain that many of the shaped breads of Europe carry false pedigrees. The "French" croissant is the perfect illustration. Invented in Vienna to look like a horn in celebration of the Austrian victory over the Turks in the 1680s, it was much more recently appropriated and transformed into an iconic bit of French cuisine. Similarly, consider the phenomenon of "junk food." According to Danesi (2016), hotdogs, hamburgers, and ice cream have transformed from treats eaten occasionally at fairs in the 1920s, to a form of food associated with fast, consumer, youth culture in the 1950s, and eventually becoming a hallmark of American cuisine eaten at comfortable family restaurants. For many North Americans, these foods are no longer read as "unhealthy" so much as they are appreciated for being easy and affordable, indexes of our American democracy.

Food meanings acquired early in life may be maintained even in the midst of vastly transforming contexts. For example, the older Hungarian women Fischer (2010) worked with retained many of the same meaningful foodways throughout the struggles they experienced during both socialist and post-socialist periods in that country. During the socialist period, women developed a variety of food-procuring strategies to deal with food shortages and low labor morale, including scrounging, food-hoarding, and creating social networks of reciprocity and semi-illegal exchange. Although the socialist regime had instituted a range of policies intended to empower women, such as providing them with industrial wage labor, access to abortions, day care, and communal kitchens, women resisted these collectivizing practices and used their foodways to build a sort of domestic fortress.

Following the fall of socialism, the same strategic foodways retained their pragmatic efficacy for older female pensioners as they faced price inflation and disillusionment with Western modernity. In fact, the women continued to reject modern labor-saving devices that might liberate them because that would mean giving up their old status as heroic fighters capable of providing food to their social intimates in the face of difficulties. Activities that persisted as signs of their heroism included plucking up discarded cabbage leaves from the market floor, buying turkey backs from the vendor, slicing by hand in tiny kitchens, keeping a refrigerator stuffed with free (and rotting) food from social agencies, canning fruit from country homes, and never using the dollars sent by their children living in the United States. In short, as conditions changed, these women continued to derive a sense of power from acting in ways that to some might seem disempowering and lacking in significance.

This example illustrates the topic we turn to in the next section: the many ways in which foods are transformed from icons and indexes into symbols—in other words, signs that cannot be considered "motivated" by natural relationships of resemblance or contiguity. We will see how food meanings, like linguistic meanings, do not grow organically out of "natural" political economic circumstances, but also how they may sometimes be purposefully produced, canned, and marketed. In other words, we look at how foods may be consciously and purposefully filled with cultural meaning in ways that have consequences for human encounters.

Vignette 4.2   Megan Tracy: Constructing Meaningful "Green Food" in China

Megan Tracy is an Associate Professor of Anthropology at James Madison University.

My interests in food, culture, and language predate my anthropological career. In the early 1990s, I served as a Peace Corps volunteer—first in Mongolia and later in the People's Republic of China. My years in both countries provided a non-academic window into the importance of food in everyday sociality, and it was my exposure to pastoralism in Mongolia that left an indelible mark on my personal and academic path. In a country where meat predominates, I faced challenges living as a vegetarian. However, I also encountered an array of unfamiliar but tasty milk-based products: milk tea seasoned with salt and not sugar, cream in different forms, dried curds, and fermented dairy products. I was hooked, and in graduate school was determined to work with Mongolian groups in the region. However, I did not intend to make food the focal point for my dissertation research.

My first project idea was to study cross-border interactions between groups on the Sino-Russo border. While that project never fully took off, the project that did emerge came out of a love for coffee—a product whose ground (and not instant) form was still difficult and expensive to find in northern China in the late 1990s and early 2000s.

A store not too far from where I was studying at Beijing's Minzu University carried a ground coffee brand produced in one of China's southern provinces, Yunnan, which carried a logo for "Green Food,' a national certification scheme that marked food as meeting standards between organic and conventional ones. I became interested in the ways in which Green Food demonstrated new forms of consumption based on corporate and consumer morality. The project examined a broad range of actors who collectively worked to implement, maintain, and promote certification standards that focused on food safety, the environment, and corporate responsibility. Based largely in Beijing and China's Inner Mongolia Autonomous Region, I conducted research with Green Food regulatory and marketing bodies, corporations with registered Green Food products, environmental and poverty reduction activists, representatives of international commercial and other non-governmental entities, and a small number of consumers.

A second vital aspect of this project was a focus on milk, in particular the rapid growth of China's domestic dairy industry and the identification of China's Inner Mongolia Autonomous Region—with its pastoral traditions and minority groups—as a key area for both dairy and Green Food development. The growth of the industry represented a major cuisine shift. China's Han majority has not traditionally consumed dairy products, and Asian populations are commonly considered to be lactose-intolerant. The assumption at the time was that the industry's development was limited. What I found was that the global rhetoric surrounding milk as a "natural" and "pure" product overlapped with similar discourses found within China's Green Food industry. In the context of a Chinese consumer body that largely distrusts its food safety systems, the successful linking of these discourses to an idealized Inner Mongolian landscape and culture created confidence in the quality of these products. My interest in the role of language included and went beyond these rhetorical strategies to explore how place-based characteristics were converted into sensory qualities that were packaged literally and figuratively into their products.

4.7

My most recent project emerged following repeated food safety scandals that led to a restructuring of China's dairy industry. This time I focused on the global governance of food and health risks. My goal was to better understand how food safety regulations and "best practices" are created to meet increasing demands for greater transparency. Calls for regulation are not simply abstract ideals, but are produced within cultural understandings of particular products and services. Here, discussions about translation within linguistic anthropology provided inspiration for documenting and analyzing the circulation of information, materials, and practices. Translating regulations involves more than transferring information through documents. It also includes the movement of technologies across various mediums through the actions of a wide array of participants. For example, although national and international experts develop raw milk standards in often-distant locales, these standards are carried out on dairy farms in the milking practices of the farmers. Farmers have little knowledge of the actual standard and only implement practices to suit the requirements of local dairy processors. If the goal of regulatory and corporate actors is to create a fixed set of notions about food safety and quality, transparency, and accountability, the transference of technoscientific knowledge through these different media makes this less predictable. Because they distrust China's food regulatory system, consumers use their own bodily knowledge when they taste milk to gauge both its quality and safety that unintentionally mirror, but also completely disregard, sensory requirements (the taste, smell, and appearance) in the national standards.

Processing Meaningful Foodways: The Symbolic Transformations

In situations of cross-cultural contact and conflict, food is often translated and reframed, incorporated and rejected, mixed and purified and (re)invented. Sometimes distinctive food meanings are deliberately produced and marketed, but sometimes this happens in slightly less managed ways as salient foods are transformed into symbolic currency for human exchange. Loosed from their iconic and/or indexical moorings, decontextualized and recontextualized, new symbolic values are shaped.

(Re)Creating Food Value

As discussed in Chapter 2, humans regularly devise new technologies for creating new foodways, which may then spread to other locales as people develop a taste for the foods that arrive from afar. Recall, for instance, Mintz's (1985) analysis of how sugar and its meanings were created and globalized. In that case, a complex set of political and economic developments in one particular time and place produced not only the material but also the symbolic value of a particular food item that we tend now to take for granted. Manufactured *elsewhere*, transported globally, and then sold *here*, this symbolic value reflected but also helped feed (literally and figuratively) social inequalities and power relations.

Figure 4.6 Bags of sugar are loaded into a container for export (© Shutterstock)

In a later book, Mintz (1996) continued his exploration of constructed food tastes by looking at how Americans' tastes for both sugar and meat were heightened during World War II because these foods were rationed for women and children at home while their consumption by men in the service was enforced (sugar was supplied to the armed forces in the form of Coca-Cola). At this period, the whiteness of refined sugar was read and valued as an iconic sign of purity whereas a taste for honey, the most ancient source of sweetness in the human diet aside from fruit, only returned to the United States following its re-valuation as a "natural" food in the 1960s. According to Mintz, this natural food movement was inspired by that generation's protest against the Vietnam War and the various forms of American imperialism (both cultural and military) that it represented. Similarly, the recent trend to valorize natural, local, traditional foods and profess a distaste for mass-produced and globally marketed foods such as McDonald's hamburgers and Starbucks coffee seems to be discursively associated with this particular population's political critique of **neocolonial** ideologies and practices—that is, the control of ex-colonies by ex-colonial states via multinational corporations and global trade policies.

Another instance of recreating and revalorizing an old food can be found in Paxson's (2013, 2014) study of artisanal cheesemaking entrepreneurs in the United States. She finds that while they inevitably borrow cheesemaking techniques from Europe, they also have purposely avoided the ideology of tradition and instead deploy innovation as a marketing tool. As she points out, tradition is a somewhat recent invention, even in France. For example, in the origin myth of Camembert, Brie was brought to a Norman peasant family by a fleeing cleric during the French revolution, and this family transformed Brie into Camembert, thus preserving something of the *ancien régime* in the new Republic. In this case, it is the tradition of having a tradition that is important, since the production of Camembert is now highly mechanized and regulated in France. By contrast, in the American cheese narratives, there is always a moment of disjuncture where a food is removed from its "original" context and taken up in a new context with a newly packaged message about innovation, despite evidence of continuity. For instance, the longest-running cheesemaking company in the United States was born when a farmer in San Francisco during the Gold Rush had the brilliant idea that French seamen would gratefully consume little squares of fermented milk with their beer because they were European. Similarly, the craze for artisanal cheeses supposedly began in 1980 when a back-to-the-lander in California who had learned to make goat cheese in France brought her handcrafted *chèvre* to the famous locavore chef Alice Waters, who promptly added it to a salad at Chez Panisse—no need for tradition here!

When new foodways spread via the forces of globalization, they not only take on new meanings in their new contexts, they may also wipe out older local foodways and their meanings. People sometimes react to these changes with a resurgence of interest in "local," "natural," and "traditional" foodways—perhaps particularly those people who have lost the knowledge and skills to produce and prepare foods in their own gardens and kitchens. Given this new taste for locally grown traditions, an array of foodways and their values are (re)claimed and (re)constructed, presenting us with some interesting paradoxes. First, how can *new* tastes take their significance from being *old*? Second, how can *local* foodways gain legitimacy as a result of *global* forces?

(Re)Claiming Authenticity

The semiotic valorization of exotic delicacies arriving from *afar* to be relished *here* probably began even before the ancient spice trade. However, the processes driving the valorization of natural, local, and traditional, or what we will call here **authenticity**, is more recent. Authentic foods are valued because they are presumed to have been produced and consumed according to culturally unique traditions in particular locales for a very long time. The value of authenticity is based in part on time through tradition and in part on place through localness, but also on something we have been referring to as naturalness, the notion that something grew up organically and sustainably out of that particular place and time. As a result, whereas an exotic product might once have been a simple index of the people, place, and time in which it was made, an authentic product has been ingeniously transformed into a slippery symbol of identity that can be traded as currency on the open market. What we mean by this is that the consumer of authenticity cares less about the actual social history of the object or practice and more that it carries the impress of natural and unique authenticity, despite the fact that that impression of authenticity was discursively constructed.

As mentioned above, in a paradoxical reversal, authentic foods are now valorized as special delicacies precisely because the world's foodways appear to be increasingly **homogenized**, or mass-produced, to be always the same no matter where they are made or eaten. In other words, at the same time that colonialism and global capitalism increased our abilities to eat the same foods anywhere in the world and at any season—from fresh asparagus in Alaska in January to fresh Chilean sea bass in Mumbai in July—so have a growing number of people in the world begun to value authentic cuisines from exotic corners of the world precisely because it makes them feel unique.

Let's break this down just a little more. Authenticity in the world of food is frequently presumed to be the result of a natural sociohistoric connection between a food and a specific territory. Thus, authenticity is partly based on topography and the idea that specific minerals, climate, and biota contribute to the specific tastes of the food produced there, and partly based on tradition and the notion that these foods are unique because produced by practices transmitted across time by the people living in this landscape. Both relate to our notion of indexicality, a significance based on social, spatial, and temporal contiguity. *Terroir* is the best-known and most crystallized version of this notion that certain foods can only be produced in particular foodscapes by specific traditional techniques. However, as Trubek (2008) has explored in *A Taste of Place*, even *terroir* is an ideology that was purposefully redesigned in early 20th-century France as a means to preserve and cultivate for sociopolitical and economic reasons the French agrarian "tradition" in its many regional variations. In other words, the value of authenticity became more of a symbol than an index as the meaning was detached from any specific form and locale and was re-packaged as a generalized commodity or currency of value regardless of its original local attachments.[9] Nonetheless, more and more people seem to relish the experience of sampling a wine or cheese or sausage that they have been made to understand is an authentic bit of some exotic yet local landscape and culture. So how is authenticity constructed?

This valuing of authentic cuisine can be found in many parts of the world, even when not driven by the pocketbooks of the cosmopolitan elite. For instance, based on his research in Belize beginning in the 1970s, Wilk (1999) has shown how people from all classes and ethnicities use food to construct national identity, cultural capital, and distinction in the face of homogenizing, globalizing forces. Comparing two meals he was served in 1973 and 1990, he demonstrates how Belizean foodways and consciousness transformed as a result of colonial and post-colonial influences. As in the example of Ghana discussed above, British colonialism as well as migration to the United States for schooling and employment had long spurred local tastes for imported, processed foods in class-structured ways. By contrast, in the post-colonial period, an emerging consciousness of national identity led to a reinvestment in local foods and "Belizean cuisine," something no one knew existed before. Belizean restaurants began to pop up in the capital, and the government promoted eating the local river fish, *pupsi* and *crana*, that were once considered a low-class, outback food. Most telling is the tale of the "royal rat." On the queen's first royal visit to the ex-colony, she was served a tasty indigenous rodent called the gibnut. Although this dish had been appearing on menus for some time as a nationally valued food, its appearance on her plate was transformed by the press into an international, identity-politics juggernaut.

One other fascinating example of an attempt to transform "low-class" local food into an authentic, haute cuisine treat can be found in Patrick, Shaer, and Budach's analysis (2017) of how seal meat was treated and signified differently in two dining events. During the first, a frozen seal was flown into an Inuit community center in Ottawa and eaten in "traditional" ways—raw with knife and hands—the objective being to socialize young Inuits into the significance of their indigenous foodways. The second event, by contrast, was a meal enjoyed by Canadian members of Parliament in a symbolic attempt to confront the European Union's ban on importing seal meat. According to newspaper reports, this seal meat was decidedly *cooked* into *pâté canapé* appetizers to disguise its wildness.

Tensions can also arise over whether authentic foods are organically filled with meaning or artificially stuffed, packaged, and commodified. One instance of this debate can be found in Beriss's (2012) examination of the meaning of red beans and rice for New Orleanians who fled the destruction of Hurricane Katrina. This dish is a creole construction, the result of 400 years of cross-cultural contact between Africans and Europeans in the Caribbean and New Orleans, captured in words such as *gumbo* (meaning 'okra' in some African languages). However, not until New Orleanians became refugees, unable to find the requisite brand of beans anywhere else in the country, did they realize the deep significance of this dish, a comfort food, for their sense of feeling safely settled in some new place. Later, when some inhabitants were able to return home, this dish was re-processed and re-packaged via restaurant reviews, food talk-radio shows, tourist flyers, and political manifestos. These touted New Orleans as an antidote to modern life, a "slow city" that takes the time to cook its beans slowly. The popular discourses reinvested the local dish with local pride as it came to symbolize New Orleans as a cultural stew that combines diverse ingredients (especially black and white) without losing their distinctiveness.

Certifying and Performing Authenticity

Given the uncertainties of market forces driving and undermining the value of authenticity, it is clear that humans might have sought out ways to fix and certify this valuable quality by creating official channels of legitimation. One way first developed in France was the creation of authoritative experts, institutions, and labeling mechanisms, such as the Institut National des Appellations d'Origine (INAO) and its Appellation d'Origine Contrôlée (AOC). Another authenticity-granting institution and program is UNESCO's Intangible Heritage List, which began in 2010 granting recognition to specific food products such as Croatian gingerbread and whole regional cuisines such as the Mediterranean Diet. The anointing of specific listees is based on a range of complex and contradictory factors. For example, Mihuacan cuisine was conflated with Mexican cuisine as a whole and illustrated by reference to chefs working on a global stage with techniques borrowed from many other traditions (Sammells 2014). And certification of this kind can be used to package not only authentic foods, but also environmentally sustainable ones. For instance, in China, a range of local qualities are bundled together to make Mongolian milk into a "green" product (Tracy 2013, and see Vignette 4.2 above).

 4.8

Aside from official means, other ways of accruing authenticity have been developed, especially in the form of **gastrotourism**, that is, tourism that revolves around the search for unique alimentary experiences. Some forms of gastrotourism can be consumed in one's own cosmopolitan backyard. For instance, many high-end restaurants are now devoted to constructing and selling very specific authentic cuisines. One restaurant in Copenhagen has sought to diversify an already crowded, high-end restaurant market by bringing in regional foods and cuisine from the isolated Danish island of Bornholm, populated by people who could never afford to eat at this haute cuisine restaurant (Karrebæk and Maegaard 2017). The servers do a lot of talking, sometimes employing linguistic aspects of the Bornholmian dialect, to introduce the diners to both the Bornholmian origins of the raw ingredients and the relationship of the recipes to the island. Furthermore, photos of pigs in the wild on the restaurant walls index the idea that the pork served in this restaurant is made from Bornholm pigs.

Other forms of gastrotourism allow one to travel and consume the food (supposedly) in situ. In Italy, the specificity of foods are **heritagized**, or transformed into regional patrimony, by **ecomuseums**. Here tourists may visit and learn about cheesemaking in the Italian Alps through re-enactments of

4.9

Figure 4.7 Gastrotourism in the Bavarian Alps (© Shutterstock)

traditional processes (Grasseni 2014). In Corsica, tourists are offered the chance to get even closer to the authentic people and places responsible for producing authentic foods. One may take a hike into the mountains to taste Corsican cheese made by shepherds at their remote huts in ways that have been practiced for centuries . . . or so the tour guide claims (Pietikäinen et al. 2016:125–149). The tour guide, shepherds, and tourists all collude in enacting the authenticity of these foodways in these settings. The shepherds invite the tourists to sample sausage, while the tour guide explains how they were made in traditional ways from pigs who have been raised semi-free-range on local chestnuts. Once a lowly peasant food, the chestnut has become valuable due to its scarcity and its small-scale production in local places such as Corsica, information that the tourists can access from educational TV programs. Performances such as these create value for the foodways, which is clearly not the same as the value these foods had for Corsican shepherds in the past. Foodways are more or less consciously transformed for the sake of increasing their symbolic and frequently material value.[10]

Let us look in a little more detail at how spatial and temporal authenticity is proven by persons and objects by looking at an example of gastrotourism from Riley's fieldwork in the Marquesas. Tourists usually arrive by cruise boat and are fed local feasts at several village sites. To supply the appropriately authentic cuisine, local meats and seafood (pig, goat, cow, lobsters, fish, and shrimp) and root and tree crops (taro, sweet potato, breadfruit, and bananas) are collected, prepared, and served using local recipes and techniques. Pigs and bananas are steamed in earth ovens, tuna is prepared raw with lemon and coconut milk, and breadfruit is fermented and pounded together with fresh breadfruit roasted on open fires. The symbolic value for the tourists and material value for the Marquesans who benefit from the tourist trade rest in the potentiality of these foods, dishes, and feasts to be understood as both authentically Marquesan and tasty. Yet, non-local ingredients from flour and sugar to mayonnaise and ketchup are incorporated in the dishes, and non-traditional tools and techniques, such as steel knives, pans, electric stoves, and graters, are used to cook and serve the dishes. Modernized situations are constructed to make the diners comfortable as they eat in dining halls with tiled floors and are provided with cutlery, glasses, chairs, and tables. All of this seems to do nothing to erase the legitimacy of the experience. If the diners even notice these details, what they take away from the experience is that they watched the pig be unearthed from a steaming hole in the ground by tattooed young men while graceful Polynesian women taught them to pour fermented coconut milk over their boiled taro. This exoticized meal is punctuated by the coconut-frond roof of the dining hut, the traditional drumming and *haka* dances performed in traditional grass skirts, and the music of "Polynesian" ukuleles accompanying the feast.

Figure 4.8 Opening the earth oven (*umu*) for a Marquesan tourist feast, with pork, plantains, and breadfruit

Credit: Photo by Kathleen C. Riley

In other words, the evidence of authenticity is constructed through the process of providing materials that index spatial presence (this stuff is from here) and temporal rootedness (this stuff has been developing here for a very long time). The setting, the food, the people, and their ways of doing food are all multisensual proof that you, the tourist, have been allowed to pay for the right to transform a unique there-and-then Other into a here-and-now commodity through situational contact and the illusion of immediacy. Of course, none of this would work if the food had not been hybridized with modern products and thus made palatable for tourist taste buds and if the experience not been mediated by prior romanticized understandings of exotic Polynesian peoples and their relaxed way of life. The facts of how all of this came to pass—beginning with European colonialism followed by the global traffic in goods, peoples, and ideas across the Pacific since World War II—are irrelevant to this highly valued experience of authenticity and presence, indexically established and symbolically transformed.

Summary

By way of concluding this chapter, we look at two universal "foods," salt and fat, whose meanings have been read as icons, indexes, and symbols. Salt has been universally understood as an icon of taste. As a necessity of life, it is also the element that, when placed on the tongue, has the physical effect of enhancing the taste of any food it accompanies. Fat, by contrast, comes in many forms, from animal fat to olive oil, but is also universally understood to transform in the human body into the thing it appears to be: that is, fat. According to Kulick and Meneley (2005:7): "It exists in food, and it accumulates on bodies. But it isn't just a chemical or biological fact. It is also a supremely cultural fact." That is, salt and fat (the food) operate to some degree as icons of taste and fat (on the human body) but have also been used in various sociocultural times and places as indexes of wealth or poverty.

Salt began its human history as a scarce resource, valued for its indexical properties as a food preservative and currency of exchange, once used for salaries, taxes, and ritual commensality. It has since been transformed through technological innovation into the cheapest and most easily accessed spice in any culinary cabinet, and now becomes a symbol of death by hypertension (Laszlo 2002). Similarly, fat was for millennia treasured as an indexical sign of riches, health, and power, beginning with the male hunter's prerogative to the greasiest flesh and turning up most recently with the elite's consumption of whipped cream and extra virgin olive oil (Meneley 2005) or elegantly served as local *lardo*, precisely carved and presented raw animal fat (Cavanaugh 2005). But, this same "fat" has been transformed over the last century into a symbol of lower-class cuisine in the form of deep-fried foods and of the obesity pandemic.[11]

Fat and salt, like most other foods and foodways, are produced, consumed, and exchanged not only as icons and indexes, but also as symbols by communicating humans. Like language, we use food to express who we are and what we want and interpret the foodways of others in much the same ways. Just as language includes words that sound like their meanings and others that take on specific significance from the immediate contexts of their use (for instance, the shifters "I" and "you" or "here" and "there"), so do foodways sometimes look or taste like what we're trying to express or index about the place they were first encountered. But in the case of both food and language, many of the meanings we understand from these semiotic systems take the form of conventional, culturally inflected symbols. That is, these signs take on values and are used to communicate about things that cannot be interpreted as a consequence of similitude or co-presence. Loosed from their "natural" bearings, these symbols may have a material impact on our lives. We turn in the next chapter to exploring how we use language to communicate *about* these powerful alimentary symbols.

Notes

1. This understanding relies on Peirce's 19th-century theory of semiotics that can be used to understand not only human semiosis but also the ways in which all elements of the universe are transmitting and receiving signs all the time, a notion that is suggested by models of quantum physics (Baker 2015).
2. Others have elaborated on this food-language parallel, for instance, Adrianne Lehrer (1969, 1972) modeled the notion of "gustemes," tastes particular to individual cultures, on the phonemes or sounds of a language.
3. Barthes's use of semiotics to critique modern consumer culture has been adopted and applied by a number of food researchers. See for instance the special issue of *Semiotica* (Stano 2016).
4. An interesting extension of this parallel (which she did not make) would be to say that people learn the appropriate ways to share a meal and with whom just as we learn to know how to speak with whom.
5. One exception was Audrey Richards (1899–1984), who devoted two books (1932, 1939) to the study of food—its production, exchange, consumption, and social significance—among the Bemba of Northern Rhodesia (now Zambia).
6. For a recent overview of the field of food and anthropology, see Watson and Klein (2016).
7. Consider also the widespread use by Americans of the term *gourmet*, a word borrowed from the French language to capture the notion of high-class foods eaten by those with cultivated tastes prior to our borrowing of the term *haute cuisine*.
8. These "experts" and their texts came out of the French court: for language, the experts were convened by Cardinal Richelieu in 1635 as L'académie française and they produced *Le Dictionnaire de l'académie française* (beginning in 1687 and now available in its 9th edition online). Similarly, La Varenne's *Le Cuisinier françois* (published in 1651) emerged from the kitchens of the French court and made way for the grand restaurants of France.

9. And yet for the French, the Discourse of 'terroir' is so naturalized that it operates as an icon. For example, a Bourdeaux looks, smells, and tastes to those with this habitus like the landscape of that vineyard where it was grown, fermented, and bottled. As Trubek writes, "In France, food and drink from a certain place are thought to possess unique tastes. Thus, more than words, *terroir* and *goût du terroir* are categories that frame perceptions and practices—a worldview, or should we say a foodview?" (Trubek 2008:18).

10. Brulotte and Di Giovine (2014) is full of specific examples of how indexical foods are transformed into symbols via the commodifying trope of "cultural heritage." The particular economic, political, and psycho-social rationales for heritagizing each of these foodways are fascinating.

11. See Kulick and Meneley (2005) for a compilation of essays on the various forms and meanings of fat.

References

Agha, Asif. 2005. "Voice, Footing, Enregisterment." *Journal of Linguistic Anthropology* 15(1): 38–59.

Appadurai, Arjun. 1981. "Gastro-Politics in Hindu South Asia." *American Ethnologist* 8(3): 494–511.

Baker, Baranna. 2015. "Signs of Probability: A Semiotic Perspective on the Heisenberg Principle." *Semiotica* 2015(205): 87–93.

Barthes, Roland. 1972. *Mythologies*. Translated by Annette Lavers. New York: Hill and Wang.

Barthes, Roland. 1982. *Empire of Signs*. Translated by Richard Howard. New York: Farrar, Strauss and Giroux.

Barthes, Roland. 2008(1961). "Toward a Psychosociology of Contemporary Food Consumption." In *Food and Culture: A Reader*, 2nd edition, edited by Carole Counihan and Penny Van Esterik, 28–35. New York: Routledge.

Beeman, William O. 2014. "Negotiating a Passage to the Meal in Four Cultures." In *Language and Food: Verbal and Non-Verbal Experiences*, edited by Polly E. Szatrowski, 31–52. Amsterdam: John Benjamins.

Beriss, David. 2012. "Red Beans and Rebuilding: An Iconic Dish, Memory and Culture in New Orleans." In *Rice and Beans: A Unique Dish in a Hundred Places*, edited by Richard Wilk and Livia Barbosa, 241–263. Oxford: Berg.

Bourdieu, Pierre. 1984. *Distinction: A Social Critique of the Judgement of Taste*. Translated by Richard Nice. Cambridge, MA: Harvard University Press.

Bourdieu, Pierre. 1991. *Language and Symbolic Power*. Translated by Gino Raymond. Cambridge, MA: Harvard University Press.

Bourke, Nicole. 2001. "Eating Your Words: Communicating with Food in the Ecuadorian Andes." In *An Anthropology of Indirect Communication*, edited by Joy Hendry and C. W. Watson, 85–100. London: Routledge.

Brillat-Savarin, Jean Anthelme. 2009(1825). *The Physiology of Taste, or Meditations on Transcendental Gastronomy*. Translated by M. F. K. Fisher. New York: Everyman's Library (Knopf).

Brulotte, Ronda L., and Michael A. Di Giovine, eds. 2014. *Edible Identities: Food as Cultural Heritage*. Burlington, VT: Ashgate.

Cavanaugh, Jillian R. 2005. "Lard." In *Fat: The Anthropology of an Obsession*, edited by Don Kulick and Anne Meneley, 139-151. New York: Penguin Books.

Clark, Dylan. 2004. "The Raw and the Rotten: Punk Cuisine." *Ethnology* 43(1): 19–31.

Danesi, Marcel. 2016. "A Note on the Meanings of Junk Food." *Semiotica* 211: 127–137.

Douglas, Mary. 1966. *Purity and Danger: An Analysis of Concepts of Pollution and Taboo.* London: Routledge & Kegan Paul.

Douglas, Mary. 1972. "Deciphering a Meal." *Daedalus* 101(1): 61–81.

Durkheim, Emile. 1982. *The Rules of Sociological Method.* Translated by W. D. Halls. New York: The Free Press.Fischer, Lisa Pope. 2010. "Turkey Backbones and Chicken Gizzards: Women's Food Roles in Post-Socialist Hungary." *Food and Foodways* 18: 233–260.

Gewertz, Deborah. 1984. "Of Symbolic Anchors and Sago Soup: The Rhetoric of Exchange among the Chambri of Papua New Guinea." In *Dangerous Words: Language and Politics in the Pacific,* edited by Donald Brenneis and Fred R. Myers, 192–213. New York: New York University Press.

Goody, Jack. 1982. *Cooking, Cuisine and Class: A Study in Comparative Sociology.* New York: Cambridge University Press.

Grasseni, Cristina. 2014. "Of Cheese and Ecomuseums: Food as Cultural Heritage in the Northern Italian Alps." In *Edible Identities: Food as Cultural Heritage,* edited by Ronda L. Brulotte and Michael A. Di Giovine, 55–66. Burlington, VT: Ashgate.

Howard, Sir Albert. 2012. "The Operations of Nature." In *The Rhetoric of Food: Discourse, Materiality, and Power,* edited by Joshua J. Frye and Michael S. Bruner, 7–21. New York: Routledge.

Karrebæk, Martha Sif. 2013. "Rye Bread and Halal: Enregisterment of Food Practices in the Primary Classroom." *Language and Communication* 34: 17–34.

Karrebæk, Martha Sif, and Marie Maegaard. 2017. "Pigs, Herring and Bornholm on a Table: A High-End Restaurant's Construction of Authenticity." *Semiotic Review* 5: *The Semiotics of Food and Language.*

Kulick, Don, and Anne Meneley, eds. 2005. *Fat: The Anthropology of an Obsession.* New York: Penguin Books.

Laszlo, Pierre. 2002. *Salt: Grain of Life.* Translated by Mary Beth Mader. New York: Ecco.

La Varenne, François Pierre. 1983(1651). *Le Cuisinier François.* Montalba: Bibliothèque Bleue.

Lehrer, Adrianne. 1969. "Semantic Cuisine." *Journal of Linguistics* 5: 39–56.

Lehrer, Adrianne. 1972. "Cooking Vocabularies and the Culinary Triangle of Levi-Strauss." *Anthropological Linguistics* 14: 155–171.

Lévi-Strauss, Claude. 1966. "The Culinary Triangle." Translated by Peter Brooks. *Partisan Review* 33(4): 586–595.

Lévi-Strauss, Claude. 1969. *The Raw and the Cooked.* Translated by John Weightman and Doreen Weightman. New York: Harper & Row.

Lévi-Strauss, Claude. 1973. *From Honey to Ashes.* Translated by John Weightman and Doreen Weightman. New York: Harper & Row.

Lévi-Strauss, Claude. 1978. *The Origin of Table Manners.* Translated by John Weightman and Doreen Weightman. New York: Harper & Row.

Mauss, Marcel. 2000. *The Gift: The Form and Reason for Exchange in Archaic Societies.* Translated by W. D. Halls. New York: W. W. Norton & Co.

Meneley, Anne. 2005. "Oil." In *Fat: The Anthropology of an Obsession*, edited by Don Kulick and Anne Meneley, 29-43. New York: Penguin Books.

Mintz, Sidney W. 1985. *Sweetness and Power: The Place of Sugar in Modern History*. New York: Penguin Books.

Mintz, Sidney W. 1996. *Tasting Food, Tasting Freedom: Excursions into Eating, Culture, and the Past*. Boston: Beacon Press.

Patrick, Donna, Benjamin Shaer, and Gabriele Budach. 2017. "Language and Territorialization: Food Consumption and the Creation of Urban Indigenous Space." *Semiotic Review 5: The Semiotics of Food and Language*.

Paxson, Heather. 2013. *The Life of Cheese: Crafting Food and Value in America*. Berkeley: University of California Press.

Paxson, Heather. 2014. "Re-Inventing a Tradition of Invention: Entrepreneurialism as Heritage in American Artisanal Cheesemaking." In *Edible Identities: Food as Cultural Heritage*, edited by Ronda L. Brulotte and Michael A. Di Giovine, 29–38. Burlington, VT: Ashgate.

Pietikäinen, Sari, Helen Kelly-Holmes, Nikolas Coupland, and Alexandra Jaffe. 2016. *Sociolinguistics from the Periphery: Small Languages in New Circumstances*. Cambridge: Cambridge University Press.

Poulain, Jean-Pierre. 2017. *The Sociology of Food: Eating and the Place of Food in Society*. Translated by Augusta Dörr. London: Bloomsbury Academic.

Richards, Audrey I. 1932. *Hunger and Work in a Savage Tribe: A Functional Study of Nutrition among the Southern Bantu*. London: Routledge and Kegan Paul.

Richards, Audrey I. 1939. *Land, Labour, and Diet in Northern Rhodesia: An Economic Study of the Bemba Tribe*. New York and London: Oxford University Press.

Riley, Kathleen C. 2009. "Who Made the Soup? Socializing the Researcher and Cooking Her Data." *Language & Communication* 29(3): 254–270.

Sammells, Clare A. 2014. "Haute Traditional Cuisines: How UNESCO's List of Intangible Heritage Links the Cosmopolitan to the Local." In *Edible Identities: Food as Cultural Heritage*, edited by Ronda L. Brulotte and Michael A. Di Giovine, 141–158. Burlington, VT: Ashgate.

Stano, Simona, ed. 2016. "Special Issue: Semiotics of Food." *Semiotica* 211.

Stummerer, Sonja, and Martin Hablesreiter. 2016. "Food Design: Symbols of Our Daily Nutrition." *Semiotica* 211: 355–369.

Tracy, Megan. 2013. "Pasteurizing China's Grasslands and Sealing in Terroir." *American Anthropologist* 115(3): 437–451.

Trubek, Amy B. 2000. *Haute Cuisine: How the French Invented the Culinary Profession*. Philadelphia: University of Pennsylvania Press.

Trubek, Amy B. 2008. *The Taste of Place: A Cultural Journey into Terroir*. Berkeley and Los Angeles: University of California Press.

Watson, James L., and Jakob A. Klein. 2016. "Introduction: Anthropology, Food and Modern Life." In *The Handbook of Food and Anthropology*, edited by Jakob A. Klein and James L. Watson, 1–27. New York: Bloomsbury Academic.

Wilk, Richard R. 1999. "'Real Belizean Food': Building Local Identity in the Transnational Caribbean." *American Anthropologist* 101(2): 244–255.

Chapter 5

Language About Food

"No, I don't know if the Gingerbread man was gluten-free."

Figure 5.1 New questions about an old story

Humans communicate not only through our food, but also about it. Via talk, text, or pictures, language *about* food comes in a wide range of recognizable forms from recipes and restaurant reviews to gardening books and food films. It also slips in under our radar in the form of pointed nose-wrinkles, grocery lists, and farm bills. In fact, if you pay attention you may begin to notice discourses about foodways, or **food talk** for short, everywhere you wander or interact with others.

This particular food-language relationship may seem like simple **referentiality**—just an example of us conveying information about food as we would about any other object. What's so interesting about that? Yet, when we communicate about food and foodways, we are rarely discussing only the material stuff that fuels our bodies. Because food is in and of itself a weighty semiotic media, fraught with ideologies as we saw in the last chapter, we are also frequently indexing a panoply of sometimes personal, sometimes political matters. Thus, we may be using not only the referential but also the performative potential of language to make an impact on the world as we talk about food. Food talk can be simultaneously **multivalent** (full of multiple meanings), multimodal (carried by multiple channels), and multifunctional (used for multiple purposes).

To analyze the range of forms, meanings, and effects of food talk, we begin by considering how food crops up as a topic of discussion in everyday interactions, whether face-to-face or more mediated. We then look at less interactive representations of food, including forms that are written, graphic, or both (for example, cartoons) as well as forms that rely on audio and visual input (for example, films).[1] Finally, we consider why food chatter has become so prevalent in society today.

Food Talk in Everyday Life

While some of us seem obsessed with talking about food, all humans discuss food sometimes and in various ways if only to figure out how to grow it, buy it, or put it into edible form. Here we first look at how these more immediate, embodied, and situated forms of food talk operate in face-to-face interactions, such as through conversations at home and in the market. Then, we focus on how we have come to engage more and more in mediated, disembodied, or decontextualized forms of food talk, such as through interactive texts including letters and online communication.

Face-to-Face Food Talk

Language about food comes in many face-to-face forms of interaction. There are the practical gestures and non-verbal signals used for this purpose: some impromptu and indexical such as pointing at the ice cream flavor you want to try at the ice cream store. Others are conventionalized, such as the Italian gesture of screwing your finger into your cheek to signify "delicious!" Certain gestures are emotional, such as expressing disgust through a "sour face" or delectation through lip-licking. Others are signals of social stance: the host at a formal dinner party takes their seat and raises their spoon, which means everyone may now begin to eat.

5.1

There are also aural forms of communication: stomach growls and burps that are (somewhat) out of our control and considered more or less rude ways of expressing our state of satiation, depending on cultural norms.

Some gestures are culturally meaningful while others are not: a belly rub after a big meal may be an attempt to communicate to the chef that the meal was enjoyable and filling, or it may just be an attempt to soothe the pain. And there are more or less voluntary expressions and yelps, sometimes translated as semi-words (known as **vocal gestures**) such as *yuck* and *yum* in English.

And then there are the actual words for what we eat. Some were imported along with the foods: for example, the English term 'orange' seems to have arrived in England around the 13th century, a borrowing of the Persian *nārang*, which speaks to that fruit's historical trajectory from Asia to Great Britain. Other terms can be traced back to the proto-languages from which our present-day languages originated and were produced along with the original means of procuring or preparing those foods. For instance, English 'hunt' is derived from Proto-Indo-European **kend*, meaning 'grasp, seize,' and 'bread' can be traced to the Proto-Indo-European *bʰrew* for 'boil, seethe.'

Scholars have long been interested in investigating the etymological roots of food terms, idioms, and expressions, the intrigue being with how our words reflect our cultural notions and obsessions.[2] One early ethnographic study of food terms and the concepts underlying them can be found in Conklin's (1955) work on botany, agriculture, and color categories among the Hunanóo in the Philippines. More recently, Silverstein (2006) has analyzed **oinoglossia,** or wine talk, looking at the semantic content and a range of indexical values involved in using these terms in specific contexts. For instance, connoisseurs use their distinctive jargon to elevate their social status in the eyes of their fellow diners. Similarly, coffee producers in Rwanda have developed a specialized vocabulary and way of speaking about their "specialty coffee" in order to increase its taste and therefore value in the eyes (and tongues) of their first-world coffee buyers (Goldstein 2011).

5.2

Some food talk takes place differently when in the presence of actual food. For example, Noda (2014) compares the expressions Japanese speakers say they use to describe and evaluate food as collected from surveys with instances of expressions used in situ while eating food at a university potluck party in an East Asian language department. The decontextualized surveys revealed lots of onomatopoeic terms for texture (*motimoti* 'elastic' and *sakusaku* 'crusty') whereas the party small talk was about flavor, ingredients, past food experiences, and food evaluations. In that naturalistic context, the positive descriptor *oisii* 'it's tasty' was usually accompanied by rationales based on preferred qualities, while negative judgments were expressed through mention of excess rather than statements of dislike.[3]

We further detail many other examples of talk about and in the presence of food in this book, such as how Trobriand Islanders cast yam spells while gardening (in Chapter 3), how vendors discuss sausages and other products with their customers at Italian farmers markets (in Chapter 6), how Andean women recount myths about supernatural cooks and deathly foodways while processing food (in Chapter 7), and how middle-class parents and children in Los Angeles, California, negotiate who must eat what at the dinner table (in Chapter 7). In these cases, both the food and talk about it are integral features of the communicative context and goals at hand.

However, food does not have to be actually or virtually present on the chopping board or in the grocery store, depicted on billboards or computer screens, for us to find things to say to each other about it. The ease with which researchers have been able to elicit foodways discourses through interviews speaks to the juiciness of the topic. As described in Chapter 3, Counihan (2004, 2009) was able to establish the **food voices** of her participants, Italians in the region of Florence and Mexican-Americans in Colorado, because they were happy to discuss their foodways even when not actually engaged in gardening, cooking, or eating.

The fact that food talk is ubiquitous in daily life may be because it likely emerged long ago in human history as a form of semiotic mediation, at least in part, to share information about where the next meal could be found—the herd of gazelle, the tree of ripe nuts—or how it would be prepared and distributed for consumption by whom. Just think of the talk that goes into planning food and drink for a special celebration, deciding what to order for takeout, or designing the backyard vegetable garden. Iskut hunters in British Columbia return from the trail telling tales that ennoble the moose and downplay the hunter's skill so that the Meat-Mother will look kindly on future hunts (McIlwraith 2008); and food talk, assumed to be casual *small talk*, is used in a New Zealand workplace to do humor, salve tensions, and mark the boundary between formal and informal interactions (Holmes, Marra, and King 2013).

Yet food is not always treated as a lighthearted topic and can indicate or contribute to social tensions and inequities. Praying and singing to the gods for food when it is absent is found in many cultures. Discussions of what you ought not to eat for health and fitness reasons can lead to serious food disorders (Nichter 2000). The United States Food and Farm Bill that apportions subsidies to farmers for growing certain types of crops (especially corn and soy) is one of the most regularly and hotly debated forms
5.3   of legislation in the United States Congress (Imhoff 2007). In Botswana, the sorts of global aid provided to AIDS orphans inspires gossip in the community as the children become "too fat" to be considered orphans (Dahl 2014). Situations such as these are discussed at more length in other chapters. For now, we will turn to specific forms of food talk that are not discussed elsewhere.

Vignette 5.1   Gwynne Mapes: Constructing "Elite Authenticity" Through Food Discourses

5.4

Gwynne Mapes is living, eating, and finishing her doctorate in Language and Communication at the University of Bern in Switzerland.

From an early age I was fascinated with language, and with food. I grew up in a family that adored cooking, eating, and talking—we were the type that "lived to eat," if you will, and we still spend most of our time together chatting around the dinner table. As I became an adult, I found myself seeking out food experiences as one of the primary contexts for spending time with people I love, and because my sister moved to Brooklyn, New York, many of my most memorable food moments ended up being located there. One day as we drove down Atlantic Avenue in Brooklyn she mentioned a Jewish deli around the corner, and told me how delicious it was. She said the owner had done what many Brooklyn restaurateurs do: take a classic cuisine and make it gourmet. Years later, this simple statement would become the focus of my doctoral research.

My initial foray into studying food discourse was prompted by a paper that was, interestingly, not about food at all, but rather about elitist stancetaking in travel writing (Jaworski and Thurlow 2009). I noticed that similar discursive patterns could be detected in a food magazine I subscribed to, *Bon Appétit*. I ended up writing my Master's thesis on the "Editor's Letter" columns from the magazine, demonstrating how a number of linguistic features across these articles work in unison to contribute to an overall normalizing (and consequent concealing) of privilege in food writing. And of course, what I started to realize was that the patterns I'd identified in *Bon Appétit* were actually everywhere in contemporary food discourse: posted on food blogs and Instagram, in restaurants' marketing materials and menus, in newspaper articles and restaurant reviews, and in spoken conversations about food. I became interested in understanding not only how food is represented in media discourse, but also how these ideologies and discourses are picked up, and (re)circulated. How they become embodied by speakers and eaters, and how they in turn contribute to, and reflect, widespread class inequalities.

After deciding to pursue my PhD, I naturally oriented to elite discourse studies, a field in which my food and language interests fit perfectly. I developed a project that allowed me to examine the construction of "elite authenticity" across various genres of elite food discourse: these include *The New York Times* food section articles and reviews of Brooklyn restaurants (and corresponding Instagram posts); ethnographic fieldwork in four renowned Brooklyn restaurants (including the Jewish deli my sister mentioned to me years before); and a recorded dinner conversation with Brooklyn residents—all of whom love food, and love eating out in Brooklyn. I almost immediately identified "authenticity" as the connecting principle between these varied, mediatized food representations and spoken language about and around food. Ultimately, I found that it is via a number of conveniently non-elite-sounding rhetorical strategies (e.g., historicity, simplicity, lowbrow appreciation, pioneer spirit, and locality/sustainability) that authenticity is problematically commodified in food discourse, and is subsequently used as a means for producing status and distinction in contemporary society—albeit in ways that are not traditionally elitist.

Thus, while my research began with an interest in institutionally produced language about food, it has expanded to account for evolving genres of mediatized food discourse (like Instagram and restaurant websites), as well as material texts (like food and restaurants themselves), and, of course, the everyday talk produced in these restaurants, and around the dinner table. It is my hope to continue exploring the complicated ways in which language and food intersect not only in Brooklyn, but also across the world, as a means of contributing to an understanding of what it is to eat and speak "elitely" on a global scale.

Interactive Food Texts

In addition to immediate and situated instances of food talk, humans have for millennia been figuring out ways to interact with each other in mediated, decontextualized, and therefore disembodied ways across spatial and temporal divides. We have used writing systems in part to record our thoughts about food in ways that others elsewhere in the world would be able to make sense of and respond to even at some later point in time. One evocative instance of food texts of this kind can be found in a manuscript of recipes written by women imprisoned in the Nazi concentration camp of Theresienstadt (German 2011). In the absence of actual food, they sustained themselves by re-membering and re-presenting dishes that signified their past lives. The acts of writing, discussing, circulating, and preserving the recipes apparently helped sustain them and provide some means of resistance. And although the woman who collected the recipes in the camp died there before the end of the war, the handwritten cookbook

5.5

was delivered to her daughter decades later to be decoded for all its tragic meaning.

5.6

In the last century, humans also discovered the means to project our actual voices in the form of long-distance phone calls, followed most recently by the transmission of our visual selves via video chat, such that we now almost feel that we are there, co-present again. Given these technological transformations, our interpersonal communications about food have taken on a flurry of forms as evidenced by the recent rage for sending Instagram images of particularly voluptuous dishes we are about to devour at a friend's house or a restaurant while traveling on another continent. Or we shoot off a "like" to a "friend" who posted a plea for famine aid on their Facebook feed. Or we text an office mate: "Stopping at Starbucks? Grab me one pleeeease" to indicate our wish for the usual café latte.

These disembodied and decontextualized forms of food talk, whether mediated by telegram or Skype, are still interpersonal in the sense that we are attempting to communicate with others and hoping for a response either immediately or in the imagined future. For example, even the 19th-century missionaries from New England who went to Hawai'i, mentioned in the previous chapter, eventually received answers from home to their letters about hungering for bread or watching the "natives" eat dog (Kashay

Figure 5.2 Snapping a photo of a meal in Toronto, Canada

Credit: Eaters Collective on Unsplash

2009). By contrast, many forms of food representation are clearly designed and crafted to have some intentional impact on an audience with whom we may have no personal relationship.

This difference between mediated but interpersonal forms of food talk and the public discourses about food that we will explore in the next section can be illustrated by Owens's (2011) study of two types of food texts written by Spanish Capucin nuns traveling to the New World. In the late 17th century, nuns voyaging from Toledo to Mexico City wrote letters to their sisters that focused on their hardships—seasickness, hunger, and the strangeness of the foods encountered. In this case, the traveling nuns were seeking sympathy from intimates for their real-life struggles in this new place. By contrast, in the early 18th century, the nuns wrote a foundational narrative to glorify the founding of their nunnery in Lima, Peru. Here, the authors shaped their text to impress some imagined future audience, so food was primarily discussed to prove the ascetic integrity of the founding mothers and to inspire future generations of nuns to follow in their footsteps. They critiqued the gluttony of Portuguese nuns they encountered and sought ways to continue to abstain from meat even when the only foods available in the pampas were chicken and beef. This case shows how the audience and function of the communication greatly influences what and how the food is discussed even when we have no idea if and how our intended communications will be received.

Public Food Talk

Food has perhaps always been a topic of representation in whatever form of media humans created, from cave art mastodons to the Bible story of the apple in Eden. While these forms may emerge out of actual interpersonal situations and may receive actual personalized responses from the intended (or unintended) audience, they do not generally seek to create anything but virtual communities of interaction. That is, even in the interactive, design culture we presently live in, in which food talk may be generated and sent out on the web to garner users as viewers and consumers, the responses are generally collected as data and statistics rather than as the stuff of ongoing face-to-face relationships. In other words, the primary role of the audience is to receive and consume these forms of language *about* food within situations that are only minimally or virtually interactive or social. To explore this world of food representations, we focus first on textual genres that feature written verbal material and perform a range of functions from aesthetic to informative through poetry, recipes, labels, and laws. We then examine texts that feature graphic material, from paintings and sculptures to cartoons and websites. Finally, we bring our gaze to the rapidly expanding world of audio-visualized food, including films and TV programs.

Written Texts

Writing about food comes in so many forms from cookbooks to sacred books (the Upanishads, Old Testament, etc.), and etiquette manuals to urban gardening guides. We will sample just a few of these many food texts, from literature and labels to recipes and laws, exploring their aesthetic and instrumental, identity-indexing and rhetorical functions.

Literature

English prose and poetry has been steeped in food from the *Canterbury Tales* to Virginia Woolf's *Mrs. Dalloway* (Wiedenmayer 2016). To demonstrate how food can be cooked into literature, we briefly analyze two poems. In "Blackberry Eating" by Galway Kinnell (1993), we see how the form and content of both food and poem take a parallel course.

5.7

> I love to go out in late September
> among the fat, overripe, icy, black blackberries
> to eat blackberries for breakfast,
> the stalks very prickly, a penalty
> they earn for knowing the black art
> of blackberry making; and as I stand among them
> lifting the stalks to my mouth, the ripest berries
> fall almost unbidden to my tongue,
> as words sometimes do, certain peculiar words
> like *strengths* or *squinched* or *broughamed*,
> many-lettered, one-syllabled lumps,
> which I squeeze, squinch open, and splurge well
> in the silent, startled, icy, black language
> of blackberry eating in late September.
>
> *Figure 5.3* "Blackberry Eating" from *Three Books* by Galway Kinnell
>

The poem is framed by the multisensuousness of blackberries at the start—*fat, overripe, icy, black, prickly*—and the multisensuousness of language at the end—*silent, startled, icy, black*. In the middle, we learn that both blackberries and words "fall almost unbidden to my tongue," especially the "peculiar words," the "many-lettered, one-syllabled lumps" that resemble the lumpy form of blackberries (aggregates of drupelets) such as *strengths* and *squinched*.[4] In fact, the other verbs for what we do with these words and berries in our mouths—squeeze, squinch, and splurge—also work according to the phonemic possibilities of English that allow us to put multiple-consonant clusters, including s-t-r and s-k-w and ŋ-Θ-s and n-č-t, on either side of a single vowel, which is the juicy center. Additionally, this blackberry-shaped poem explores the dark underside of late September when some "black arts" allow prickly blackberry stalks to bear overripe fruit with which to break our fast, splurging and startled even as the rest of the harvest is dying out and going quiet.

By contrast, Naomi Shihab Nye in "Olive Jar" (2002) uses the form and content of food poetry to bring our focus to social and emotional, cultural, and political matters.

In the corner of every Arab kitchen,
    an enormous plastic container
of olives is waiting for another meal.
    Green tight-skinned olives,
planets with slightly pointed ends—
    after breakfast, lunch, each plate
hosts a pyramid of pits in one corner.
    Hands cross in the center
of the table over the olive bowl.
    If there are any left they go back to
the olive jar to soak again with sliced lemon and oil.
    Everyone says
it was a good year for the trees.

At the border an Israeli crossing-guard asked
    where I was going in Israel.
To the West Bank, I said. To a village of
    olives and almonds.
To see my people.

What kind of people? Arab people?

Uncles and aunts, grandmother, first and second
cousins. Olive-gatherers.

Do you plan to speak with anyone? he said.
    His voice was harder
and harder, bitten between the teeth.

I wanted to say, No, I have come all this way
    for a silent reunion.
But he held my passport in his hands.

Figure 5.4 "Olive Jar" from *19 Varieties of Gazelle: Poems of the Middle East* by Naomi Shihab Nye

Yes, I said, We will talk a little bit. Families and
   weddings,
my father's preference in shoes, our grandmother's
love for sweaters.
We will share steaming glasses of tea,
the sweetness filling our throats.
Someone will laugh long and loosely,
so tears cloud my voice: O space of ocean waves,
how long you tumble between us, how little you
   dissolve!

We will eat cabbage rolls, rice with sugar and milk,
crisply sizzled eggplant. When the olives come
   sailing past
in their little white boat, we will line them
   on our plates
like punctuation. What do governments have to do
with such pleasure? Question mark.
YES I love you! Swooping exclamation.
Or the indelible thesis statement:
   it is with great dignity
we press you to our lips.

Figure 5.4 (Continued)

Here we almost see, touch, and smell the green, tight-skinned, pointed
olives, grown on the trees, then jar-soaked in lemon and oil, finally served
and passed in a white bowl. We also nearly taste and hear the meals of
sweet tea, cabbage rolls, rice-sugar-milk, crisply sizzled eggplant, as the
family enjoys long, loose laughs. This contrasts with the *harder, bitten*
words that border guards produce. Olives (and almonds) index ocean-
crossing connections—the extended family, the *we*—by contrast with the
violent, political borders. The poetic form, wherein the end-stop lines
reflect rather than break the grammatical unit (a sentence or prepositional
phrase), facilitates the narrative flow. The visual food imagery—olives like
planets, pits a pyramid, the bowl a boat—contributes to the underlying
meanings to do with crossing oceans, reaching new worlds, yet keeping
sight of ancient monuments. And finally, the taste of olives, to which we
pay homage with our lips, becomes the punctuation—question marks and
exclamation points—through which this poet expresses the pleasure of
communion by way of resistance to the pain of political disjuncture.
   This figurative language about blackberries and olives, about picking
and eating, sharing and reminiscing, reflects through both form and content the communicative power of the food itself and the power of language
to capture and express emotional and social meanings. Whether these food

Figure 5.5 A bowl of olives (© Shutterstock)

texts are read for entertainment or insight into the experiences of others, they nourish us as only language can do (a topic we return to in Chapter 7), even when decontextualized from any social setting as writing.

Gastrotourism Texts

Many of us are drawn to literature that provides an entrée into other cultural worlds, and much of that literature includes the topic of food, thus allowing us to enjoy a form of virtual gastrotourism. Gastrotourism texts may take the form of travel writing, as exemplified by Elizabeth Gilbert's (2006) bestseller *Eat Pray Love* (see Bernoussi 2016 for a review of such texts), or it may take the form of nostalgic culinary books that allow us to sample the lives of others in terms of their food memories. For example, the authors of four such books examined by Karaosmanoglu (2011) use a mix of their own memories and the oral histories of others to delineate the urban geography, smells, and markets of Istanbul. They look at the temporal divide between an idealized past and the degenerate present as well as between separate ethnic identities (Turkish, Greek, Armenian, and Jewish) and their shared cosmopolitanism. Additionally, their memories are filled with information about how people used foods and food names to identify their ethnic differences and similarities (for example, same ingredients and different cuisine or vice versa) and to engage in cross-cultural exchange. These texts *about* food are as much about the meanings produced and consumed via food, that is, as language *through* food.

Another body of literature filled with culinary nostalgia provides a way to explore multi-ethnic foodways. For instance, Fellner (2013) examines three ethnic culinary texts: two short stories by Canadian Caribbean and Asian authors and a novel by a Puerto Rican in the United States. She seeks to understand how writing about food becomes for these writers a way to establish a sense of home and cultural (culinary) citizenship, even when these no longer map onto easily identified political territories (such as Puerto Rico, India, Fiji, Trinidad, Malaysia, and China) or "authentic" identities. These works are set against an identity-politics backdrop in which ethnic culinary literature feeds the hungry ghost of the North American commodity culture on two fronts: it satisfies our taste both for ethnic foods and for multicultural literature. However, Fellner warns against the desire to extract and consume simple messages from these narratives about food and citizenship.

Recipes and Cookbooks

An interest in expressing one's own or tasting another's cultural identity can also be fulfilled by recipes and cookbooks. Of course, many texts of this type were probably written and circulated with the instrumental intent of remembering for oneself or instructing someone else in the proper preparation of a particular dish or meal. But how they are interpreted by subsequent consumers is a far more complicated affair.

Several studies focus on how the style of writing recipes has transformed over time. For instance, Diemer (2013) looks at changes in the lexical, syntactic, and pragmatic forms found in food writing from Old English through Modern English. Focusing mostly on recipes, but also on menus and books on etiquette, he finds that, over time, these food genres have displayed less specific lexicons, more precise ingredient amounts, more detailed directions about techniques, and more personalized, lifestyle commentary. From this he concludes that food writing has become increasingly directed toward non-professionals. In a similar analysis, Arendholz et al. (2013) compare two recipes for beef stew: a manuscript from the 1400s and a recent online recipe from British celebrity chef Jamie Oliver's website. Based on formal similarities such as simple syntax, 'and/then' conjunctions, non-standard punctuation, and the prevalence of 'you,' the authors claim that the **text type** (type of food text—in this case, the recipe) has not greatly changed for over 600 years. However, they conjecture that the pragmatic functions have transformed from a medium for the transmission of referential information *about* cooking

5.8

in a medieval kitchen into a way to connect socially *through* food via contemporary social media.

In the process of tracing the history of the vast exchange networks inspired by the taste for spice, Nabhan (2014) looks at cross-cultural connections demonstrated through a range of food talk, from specific food words to specific food texts such as recipes. For example, he explains how the English terms *spice* and *species* sprung from the same Latin root *spec* meaning 'form, kind.' He also considers a recipe for lamb stew that was found with only minor variations on opposite ends of the earth in the 21st century. The first version was discovered as part of a healthy diet manual compiled by a doctor of Muslim heritage for a 14th-century Mongolian emperor. The other version appeared in a Spanish-language cookbook, dated 1939, that was found in a used bookstore in New Mexico. It is fascinating to imagine the globalizing force of food and food interactions that transmitted these food texts of such similarity across continents and centuries.

The significance of the food itself in these texts, what we call language *through* food, is part of what has made recipes and cookbooks into vehicles for the expression of regional, national, and ethnic identities. For instance, O'Connor (2013) has written a culinary biography of the "English Breakfast" as a national symbol of England. Appadurai (1988) has traced the development of a national cuisine in India via cookbooks, analyzing their role in the construction of class-inflected national identities. And Jurado (2016) explores the meaning of "spicy meals" in several cultures from Italy to Mexico and Texas.

Labels and Laws

Other more utilitarian types of food texts range from shopping lists to school food policies. Consider for example food labels, which many school children in the United States are taught to read in elementary school health classes, partly as a literacy exercise and partly to teach them how to assess the nutritional value of the foods. For instance, the label in Figure 5.6 would be dissected for the high fat, sodium, and cholesterol content of the food. In addition, as the cartoon at the start of this chapter indicates, some children are being primed by both the media and their health-conscious parents to keep track of various food-sensitivity issues to do with gluten, lactose, nuts, and so on, which are also indicated on labels.[5]

5.9

5.10

Labels have become a topic of intense debate for consumers interested in knowing whether their foods are organic or genetically modified.[6] Fair Trade labels mark whether they were processed with chemicals or produced with the health and economic interests of the laborers in mind. And in Europe, labels are used to identify where foods come from and how they were processed. To be considered *appellation d'origine contrôlée*, the

Nutrition Facts

Serving Size 5 oz. (144g)
Servings Per Container 4

Amount Per Serving

Calories 310   **Calories** from Fat 100

	% Daily Value*
Total Fat 15g	**21%**
Saturated Fat 2.6g	**17%**
Trans Fat 1g	
Cholesterol 118mg	**39%**
Sodium 560mg	**28%**
Total Carbohydrate 12g	**4%**
Dietary Fiber 1g	**4%**
Sugars 1g	
Protein 24g	

Vitamin A 1% • **Vitamin C** 2%

Calcium 2% • **Iron** 5%

*Percent Daily Values are based on a 2,000 calorie diet. Your daily values may be higher or lower depending on your calorie needs:

	Calories	2,000	2,500
Total Fat	Less Than	65g	80g
Saturated Fat	Less Than	20g	25g
Cholesterol	Less Than	300mg	300mg
Sodium	Less Than	2,400mg	2,400mg
Total Carbohydrate		300g	375g
Dietary Fiber		25g	30g

Calories per gram:
Fat 9 • Carbohydrate 4 • Protein 4

Figure 5.6 Food label with "Nutrition Facts" (or not so nutritious, in this case) (© Shutterstock)

ingredients (such as grapes for wine or milk for cheese) must have been grown in a particular *terroir* and processed according to methods developed in that region—these labels become a highly valued (and expensive to acquire) form of trademark for this "intangible heritage" some of which has been assigned UNESCO status (Brulotte and Di Giovine 2014). As discussed in Chapter 4, the production of this heritage food has become big business and is heavily policed by national and international trade policies. Additionally, all food labeling is subject to national laws, and what is considered valuable (and legitimate) information to report in one country may be censored in another. For example, due to new food labeling laws in Hong Kong, the packaging on imported American foods have been redacted beginning in 2010 to remove any health claims (Jones 2014), but in ways that impede legibility. For instance, nearly a third of the words on the bottom of a Paul Newman's popcorn box were simply blocked out in black, leaving phrases such as: "fresh tasting popcorn . . . and hydrogenated oils" (Jones 2014:478).

However, long before food is packaged and distributed to venues where consumers can assess the printed labels, food is being produced and mediated by written text. Cavanaugh (2016) finds in her work with sausage producers in northern Italy that concepts like *food safety* require as much linguistic as material labor, since products must not only be made safe but must be also textually documented as such. For instance, the kinds and amounts of ingredients are tabulated and signed off on in office documents. The audience for these texts are employees' bosses as well as various inspectors and government officials, who become central in making the sausage marketable. Here, written language is performative in that it produces not only the food but also the idea of food safety.

Persuasive Food Texts on the Net

Discourses about food on the internet can be specifically analyzed for their rhetorical impact. Many of these employ evocative graphics, photographs, and written text and thus can be used as an interesting segue into the next section on visual imagery. However, it is worth looking first specifically at the impact of the verbal material in these virtual contexts. For instance, charity websites circulate persuasive success story narratives to demonstrate the benefits of donating, many of which include a lot of textual material about foodways. Let's look at such a narrative on the Heifer International website (Bailey 2017).

5.11   Heifer International specializes in offering donors a chance to send specific animals to peoples in particular regions of the world where raising these animals will hopefully help them feed their families and make a living. The idiom they use for this form of charity is: "the food gift that keeps giving." In this article, we find the narrative of Panna Devi, along with some alluring photographs that show Panna Devi interacting with her gift animals (goats in this case). According to the narrative, Panna Devi's first goat not only gave birth to other goats, but also provided subsistence food in the form of milk and cash by way of selling meat to neighboring Muslims for the religious holiday Eid. Secondly, education provided through Heifer-inspired self-help groups gave her husbandry and bookkeeping skills. In particular, she learned to feed her goats an easily grown garden crop (*azolla*), which increased their milk production. And she used her improved marketing abilities to recycle capital into a little store selling potato chips and candy, vegetables, and grains. Additionally, both stigma and structural oppression based on caste and gender are overcome through persistence and entrepreneurial spirit as Panna Devi transforms from an untouchable underpaid worker, a "manual scavenger" cleaning the latrines of higher-caste people, into a successful store owner, trained animal health worker, and respected *sethani* (person able to give money to others in need). Finally, both her own access to food and education are re-circulated as Panna Devi is able to feed her extended family (her sister's handicapped son, his wife, and their child) while also teaching other community members through ever-expanding self-help groups. Finally, and most remarkable of all is how nourishing discourses such as these foodways narratives of overcoming deprivation through hard work and a helping hand feed the hearts of donors so they keep giving, thereby sustaining sustainable giving.

However, many researchers and activists suggest that reaching the hearts of generous donors via narratives such as Panna Devi's is not enough due to some fundamental flaws in how the global food system is structured by corporate forces, some of which can be revealed by discourse analysis of online corporate documents. As Singer (2011) argues, CSR (corporate social responsibility) discourses can colonize our minds and close off discussion of alternatives. In this case, despite widespread critique of GMOs and other products (PCBs, dioxins in Agent Orange, bovine growth hormones, etc.), the multinational company Monsanto has shut down debate about the utility of using biotechnology to solve **food insecurity**, that is the lack of dependable sources of food in many sectors of society and many parts of the world. Effectively this stance works to protect their market share control over global agriculture. Their corporate reports display three strategies: through *legitimation* they highlight their success stories, through *naturalization* they make their narrative about curing world hunger sound like the only reasonable one, and through *disqualification* they target any stakeholders who would contradict their scientists.

It is also important to compare and contextualize online foodways texts with everyday talk. For example, Dutta (2012) juxtaposes the rhetoric of international financial institutions and government trade agreements with the narratives of poverty, hunger, and pain that she "co-constructed" during fieldwork in West Bengal, India. By doing this, she manages to capture the absurd disjuncture between the Discourses of development and the face-to-face food stories of men and women on the ground who have experienced the disappearance of the commons (where mangos could once be foraged for free), the rising price of rice and dahl, and the deep shame at being unable to feed their children. The powerless who share these narratives *about* food are hopeful that their words may nurture new discourses among those in power (language *as* food). The struggle to draft the right message for the right audience, in this case those who hold the purse strings and reins of power of the international food system, is ongoing, and will be explored at more length in our final chapter on food (inter)activism.

5.12

Vignette 5.2   Susan D. Blum: Signs of Eating Local

Susan D. Blum is a cultural and linguistic anthropologist and local food activist who teaches at the University of Notre Dame.

For decades I kept my work on language and my work on food separate. I wrote about food in an academic way: China and the WTO, women in sustainable farming, and reviews of food books. I was a member of the American Anthropological Association's Society for the Study of Food and Nutrition and loved going to their meetings and conference sessions. But I had other interests too: education, childhood, notions of the self, China, deception, plagiarism, ethnicity and nationalism, naming practices, authorship. I tried to combine everything in a couple of talks, but felt my writing had become random, my research interests just a collection of tongs and spatulas and whisks getting all tangled up. Could there be a pattern somewhere? Could I tug on the clump and end up with neatly arranged tools?

Meanwhile, back in the real world, I'd become president of the board of directors of a local food co-op during the period when we were trying to open a physical store, and I became interested in the question of what "local" means. This had practical implications. Could we convince people in our small, non-affluent, non-coastal city that "local" mattered? Could we entice enough shoppers to pay prices that would support our local farmers? How could we tell this story? Why was it hard?

So, I gave a talk at the American Anthropological Association about local food. I pulled together other co-ops' and other people's portrayals—especially in websites and posters and infographics—of "local" food and saw that there was no single unified approach. Some people emphasized the environmental or physical benefits of local food, and others the moral and aesthetic benefits. I had assumed that the more benefits we showed from buying and eating local food, the better. We could appeal to some people's concern about economic justice and returning more of the money to local farmers, and to others' obsession with "food miles," and others' appreciation the idea of *"terroir"* and eating food picked that morning that retained the flavors of the place. But what to me seemed like beautiful multiple flavors ended up something of a kitchen sink to others. Was local a brand? A scientific formula? A gestalt feeling?

At this time, I was also teaching graduate students in linguistic anthropology and was delving deeply into semiotic theory, where the notion of indexicality was central. Surely "local" was an index. How could I use this idea to challenge myself to integrate these things? The idea of "indexicality" was helping me understand which aspect was important in which context. And at the same time semiotics theorists were writing of materiality. Surely food was material but not only material? It was always a sign, but it also had weight and cost and calories.

In a recent semester I taught two of my courses that previously had seemed entirely unrelated: Food and Culture, and Orientations to Linguistic Anthropology. It became clear for the first time that eating and talking are two of the most ordinary, ubiquitous things that humans do, and that there is an endless amount that has been written about both, but not enough about their interrelationships.

In the end, it is the very ordinariness, the ubiquity, of both food and language, that demands an anthropological analysis. To me, it is only with anthropological tools, putting our entire evolutionary history in conversation with political and economic and psychological and social factors that we can begin to understand the ways our talking and eating vary and have such power. They define who we are; we fight over words and we fight over food. Good words and good food define the good life. We fall in love over words and we fall in love and celebrate our love regularly with food. We can't really go a day without language or food—even if we refrain occasionally for all kinds of cultural reasons.

As someone fascinated beyond measure by our human (and increasingly beyond-human) ways of being, it has come to seem absolutely obvious that these two domains are intertwined and that their relationships must be made understandable to us. So, I've tried to offer a few tidbits, a few aphorisms, a word, a flavor . . . Besides, the food puns are irresistible.

Visual Imagery: From Sculptures to Cartoons and Ads

Many food texts, such as paintings and sculptures, rely primarily on visual images to portray and say something about food. In other food texts, such as signage, ads, and cartoons, the messages about food depend on an interplay between visuals and words.

Visual Art

One study (Calefato, La Fortuna, and Scelzi 2016) of the contemporary obsession with **foodography**, or the melding of food and photography, traces the fad back to the Italian Renaissance artist Giuseppe Arcimboldo,

Figure 5.7 "Avocaboats" in a sea of guacamole
Copyright © Emily Leary. Reproduced with permission.

5.13

5.14

who painted human portraits made of food. His work has now inspired a range of recent artists, as exemplified by Carl Warner's photographic foodscapes, in this case, photographed landscapes populated by and constructed out of food. Calefato and colleagues suggest that this present-day ubiquitous, almost **orthorexic**, fixation with food is an attempt to grapple with our food desires in relation to a particular social order shaped by ideologies about health and morality.

This interest in visual food art can be found in a recent special exhibit at the Art Institute of Chicago in which American paintings about food are "read" for their cultural significance (Barter 2013). But one food sculpture we would like to spend some time unpacking is Kara Walker's *A Subtlety, or the Marvelous Sugar Baby*. Walker was commissioned to make a piece

5.15

of art in the Domino sugar plant in Brooklyn prior to its dismantling in 2014. What resulted was a mammoth sculpture coated in sugar of an African-American woman positioned in sphinx form. Many features speak to Walker's artistic reflections on the slave and sugar trade—from the sugar itself, to the reformulation of the Aunt Jemima caricature, to the dark molasses carriage boy figures surrounding her. All are intended to revise our understanding of the slave and sugar trade of the 18th and 19th centuries (discussed in Chapter 2) and to provide a kind of monumental respect to this figure that was otherwise treated by Euro-Americans as an object of comedy, scorn, and sexual fixation.

Cartoons

Cartoons tend to employ a spartan mix of simply drawn situations and the short utterances presumed to be spoken by one of the participants in the event. Their humor depends in part on shared cultural knowledge, which sets up expectations that are in turn broken and realigned in new and surprising ways. In fact, several of the cartoons reproduced in this book rely on shared understandings of the food ideologies that are prevalent in our society at present and make us laugh because of the new off-kilter perspectives they provide. For instance, to understand the cartoon in Chapter 1 (Figure 1.2 "Caffeinated cave art"), one needs to know several things: that Paleolithic humans, popularly caricatured as *cavemen*, made self-referential art, such as inscribing their handprints next to the animals they hunted. Further, one must recognize that coffee is a stimulant and may make one perhaps overly self-involved. Also, coffee was not always imbibed by humans but was discovered at some particular moment in history, probably long after the cave artists were making their art.[7] Additionally, comedy depends on some shared sense of who or what can be appropriately targeted for a laugh. In this case, the object of mockery is ourselves, or at least those of us who not only share the requisite cultural knowledge but also sometimes become overly taken with our own not too terribly creative productions when "under the influence." Part of what makes this funny is some feeling that this may well be an age-old issue.

An understanding of the cartoon in Chapter 2 (Figure 2.1 "Having Reservations") relies on our shared knowledge about the origin myth of the American Thanksgiving tradition: that the Pilgrims wanted to thank the local Indians for helping them through their first harsh winter in New England. In this case, the humor derives from looking askew at this "tradition" from the perspective of the Native Americans who are using American norms to discuss this potluck exchange of (valued) meat for (devalued) "rabbit food" or veggies in terms that could be used by any contemporary couple to discuss the strategies of an unwanted guest who attempts to regularize the hospitality of the unwitting host. The multivalence of the word *reservations* (second thoughts, restaurant reservations, and Indian reservations) also contributes to the humor here.

The two noodles (whether macaroni or rigatoni) in Chapter 4 (Figure 4.5 "Out-classed pasta in a foodie world") are voicing their sense of being out-classed by the newer, classier kinds of pasta. At the simplest level, we do not expect pasta to speak (or wear spectacles or sit on a shelf), and at the next level, we laugh at the idea that they would have a sense of class consciousness or indeed any form of consciousness. That, we assume, is the prerogative of "complex" human beings rather than "complex carbohydrates," a phrase that also speaks to a relatively recent food Discourse concerning the health benefits of eating carbs made from whole foods rather than highly processed carbs that will transform too quickly into sugar. Similarly, the child who has asked if the gingerbread man was gluten-free in the cartoon in the present chapter (Figure 5.1 "New questions about an old story") is clearly sensitized to gluten-free discourses, but it is not clear if the child has celiac disease, is gluten-intolerant, or is caught up in this diet as a kind of fad. What makes the situation comical is that this level of sensitivity impels the child to inquire during the bedtime reading ritual about the identity of the gingerbread man. In this case, the adult is responding somewhat quizzically we feel, as our commonsense understanding tells us that most children would only subliminally even notice that this familiar storybook character is a form of food, much less subject to the properties and constraints of food.

Other familiar ideologies may bring a smile to the face of the properly initiated. For the cartoon in Chapter 6 (Figure 6.6 "Break time chat"), where one co-worker informs the other that there is only sugar for the coffee because "Someone decided that the pink and blue sweetener packets are sexist," one needs to know that pink and blue are commonly associated with girls and boys in American society, that the sweetener publicists probably had no intention of indexing gender with their packaging colors (any more than sugar in white and brown packets is meant to index anything to do with race), and that accusations of sexism are not uncommon in the workplace. Thus, the response to the disappearance of the packets at the coffee station is not only comprehensible but humorous to those who mock political correctness especially when taken too far by someone (in this case the "someone" who deemed the sugar packets sexist).

Similarly, the parental scold, "Stop loafing around! Your brain will turn to toast!", in the cartoon in Chapter 7 (Figure 7.1 "Feeding our brains") is comical not only because of the visual food puns (loaf and toast), but also because it points to a relatively recent moral panic about the health risks of children spending too much time inside sitting in front of computer screens (turning into *couch potatoes* as we used to say in the early era of television watching) and interacting with non-human participants. In other words, their minds, bodies, and social selves are suffering (turning to toast) according to the mother bread loaf. Finally, the cartoon in Chapter 8 (Figure 8.1 "Finish your peas!") plays with a parental discourse found in many Western households over the past 50 or so years—namely the need to finish your plate, especially your healthy vegetables, because children are starving elsewhere in the world—along with an also familiar reaction on the part of children who resist not only the Discourse, but also peas in particular. Here the humor gains a lot from the sideways glance at the child's adult-like sense of scale and reasoning about real global issues by contrast with the adult assumption that children lack any sense of proportion and act as if they are the center of everything.

Ads and Other Forms of Signage

Food ads represent another way in which text and images are conjoined in somewhat predictable, even formalized ways, not unlike the poetry we analyzed above. Here we pause to consider several recent ad campaigns found on the subways in New York City.[8] These ad campaigns were run by several different food delivery companies and used a variety of techniques to hook the captive commuter's attention by offering a spectrum of desirable food values. The companies range in their services from offering groceries (Peapod) to fully cooked meals (Seamless), as well as some that offer the exact ingredients and recipes needed to cook a precise meal (Hello Fresh).

As with many ads, they rely on an interplay between clever graphics and text, as in one from Hello Fresh that portrays a wild mushroom and asks if we are looking for a new way to *forage* for our meals. Similarly, a number of these ads use eye-catching poetic devices such as rhyme (*store/door*), alliteration (*fishery* and *fifth floor*), and parallelism (aligning the terms *cage-free* and *schlep-free*). They also employ specific linguistic forms that speak to specific populations, such as how the word *schlep* appeals to New Yorkers or texting lingo (*mins* for minutes) calls out to the young and hip.

5.16

Finally, a variety of food values are indexed in these ads as well as on their websites. Perhaps most highlighted is the notion of convenience (having the food appear at your door without schlepping or even putting on your pants), but just as important, and not always shared, are the sorts of desirable qualities of the food to be delivered. Choice is a major factor, the idea being that consumers can have whatever they want and that some of these choices can be hugely idiosyncratic. For instance, the ad campaign for Seamless makes use of the many special (and humorous) requests that supposed customers have included with their orders; for instance, one has asked for organic mayo because yes, it tastes different, and another asked for light breading on the chicken, but specified it isn't because of an actual case of gluten-sensitivity. Additionally, many ads sport terms such as *fresh*, *organic*, *gluten-sensitive*, *cage-free*, and others that signal a concern with local, healthy, and environmentally correct food, a kind of **orthopraxia**, or correct practice, assumed to exist among New York commuters. Deeply embedded in the ads for the ready-to-prepare meals is something about commensality and the importance of slowing life down, learning to cook again, and enjoying the iconic family meal. One recent set of ads for a pizza delivery service (Slice) appeals to the New Yorker's assumed desire to protect small entrepreneurs by charging them nearly nothing so that these local pizza makers can continue to use the freshest ingredients and preserve their traditional recipes.

5.17

Focusing on the particular quality of sustainability, Blum (2017) looks at flyers, bumper stickers, and websites that promote and inform viewers about the moral good of "eating local." She explores what "local" actually means, particularly how its use is meant to be an index of "here" and "now" and of less mediated forms of relationships between food producers and food consumers. She looks especially at how various iconic visuals and graphs, ranging from pictures of farms and cows to mileage maps and charts, are meant to convince us through both **pathos** (appealing to the emotions) and **logos** (appealing to rationality) of the need to change the food system in this way. By contrast, ad analyses can also show how foreign foods are made to seem local through language choice, as in Jourdan's (2010) examination (discussed in Chapter 4) of how Pijin, the lingua franca of the Solomon Islands, was used there in early advertising to help promote rice as local and on par with the traditional diet.

Labels, ads, and other promotional materials have been used to semiotically brand several drinks in the country of Georgia: water, sodas, gin, vodka, beer, and wine. As Manning (2012) analyzes, the advertising for these can be read not only for the significance of the drinks themselves for Georgians (language *through* food), but also for the ways in which these types of food texts are used to index Georgian identity during socialist and post-socialist times. Following the breakup of the Soviet Union, the Georgian economy was left in tatters as the state production of basic commodities such as bottled drinks went under. Eventually new private companies emerged with commodities based on adulterated ingredients, low-quality production techniques, and falsifying advertising to sell them. For instance, bottled water companies attempted to valorize their ability to produce a "natural" resource by tapping and mixing waters with different amounts of mineralization and carbonation, the assumption being that this so-called (paradoxical) "natural product" would appeal to the old Soviet love of minerals on the one hand and the perceived love of carbonation by Europeans on the other.

According to Manning, the goals and efficacy of the new advertising depended on indexing a mix of European-style entrepreneurial capitalist ideologies and the newly aroused Georgian nationalism. Some of this was based on "wild nature" and some was based on the pre-Soviet culture of the aristocratic elite. For example, the labels on these water bottles showed a drawing of the pre-Soviet spa, symbolizing a traditional elite lifestyle, embedded within a simple graphic of mountains, iconically indexing the wild, natural landscape. Many of the newly produced and branded beers depended on what Manning calls a "dual lineage," relying on the twin association between Georgian nature via the natural spring waters used as the essential ingredient and European culture via the technologies used to craft the beer. However, some beer companies sought to establish a more specific semiotic heritage, using ethnographic narratives and iconic graphics, such as of castles, in their promotional materials to identify their beer with some traditional mountain people's brewing methods.

Marketing can also be examined as it circulates signs across media from print to product to television to internet, deftly mixing genres in playful ways to sell people on ideas and commodities. For instance, Thomson (2011) explores how advertisers brand child consumers via immersion in online advergaming and performative food play. Following the interactive game on the back of a cereal box (Froot Loops), through a magazine

5.18

(*National Geographic*), and onto the web (Millsberry.com), she immerses herself as a child would in the performative play and branded commodities (General Mills cereals in this case). Noting how this food genre (language *about* food) turns children into sedentary online players and real-life consumers of highly sweetened cereal brands, both of which activities put them at risk of obesity, she also analyzes how this ploy works: the brand becomes associated with fun (language *through* food) while communicative play becomes a kind of sustenance (language *as* food), all of which subverts the parental proscription: "Don't play with your food."

Adding Lights, Sounds, and Action: Films and Television

Finally, we turn to food texts that incorporate audio-visual material in the form of spectacle and entertainment such as food films and TV cooking shows. We explore a few of these below for their messages and implications.

One of the best-known early food films is *Babette's Feast* (1987). According to Marrone (2016), this film represents the meeting of two ethnic groups and two cultural approaches to taste: the gastro-aesthetic gourmandizing of the French and the religious asceticism of the Danish. That is, this film portrays the French as having raised food to a high art while the Danish protestants are seen to repress all discussion of the experience of gastronomic pleasure. However, because of a particular set of circumstances, a French chef, Babette, introduces a group of Danish diners to an experience of flavors that are outside their cultural purview and allows them to dine, talk, and enjoy in a new and syncretic way. According to Marrone, the story relies upon the treatment of food as a form of language and on a distinction between "tasty" and "flavorful." The former is our aesthetic reactions to foods that are based on cultural knowledge and socialization whereas the latter is the form our reactions take to aesthetic experiences that cannot be classified or articulated using our known food vocabulary. Babette moves her Danish hosts with her culinary arts beyond their notions of taste and into the unknown world of the flavorful.

5.19

As Lindenfeld (2011) explores, adults have had no problem turning food into a "feast for the eyes" in the burgeoning genre of food films, in which food is character and plot mover, sensually (even erotically) loved by the camera. Sometimes this is even referred to as "food pornography." Lindenfeld has three critiques of this new genre. First, viewers are enticed to become consumers of "classy" foodways in a world where food of this kind can be afforded only by the elite. Second, food and women are sexualized for mutual consumption—for example, Penelope Cruz as a "hot chili" in *Women on Top*. And third, the ethnic Other is exoticized and stereotyped for palatable consumption by middle Americans, as in *What's Cooking?*.

5.20

This film depicts Thanksgiving in four ethnic households: Jewish, African-American, Latin@, and Vietnamese. In other words, this food discourse feeds us ideas that are not necessarily healthy, a topic we return to again in Chapter 7.

Looking at food in films but from a different angle, Parasecoli (2011) asks: how do global blockbuster films (explicitly not food films) use food to represent and construct variable forms of masculinity? The author claims that very few food scenes are found in movies associated with hegemonic masculinity, such as action films with powerful male heroes like *Star Wars*, where no food ever appears (except as alcohol in the bar at the margins of the galaxy). Where food is found, it is frequently a tool for men to express their dominance over women, as in *Titanic*, where the man expresses ownership of his fiancée by ordering her food for her. Or food serves as a channel for men's destructive powers, such as when food poisoning is used in *Se7en, Casino Royale*, and *Harry Potter*. By contrast, in films with more romantic themes (e.g., *Pretty Woman, Forrest Gump*, and *Body Guard*), the male protagonists may cook or express emotions about food, embodying alternative masculinities. Thus, gendered food associations are ingested and incorporated by the performance of food in these films (language *about* food produces language *through* food via language *as* food).

Food on TV is another fruitful place to look not only at how food is represented but also how it is used to mean other things. Based on a thematic analysis of 30 hours of Food Network programming, Cramer (2011) identifies which themes and values are privileged by cooking shows (*Easy Entertaining, Barefoot Contessa, Paula's Homecooking*, etc.). The least circulated themes were those celebrating humans' sustainable relationship to the earth: small-scale civic agriculture represented by gardens and farmers markets, seasonality marked by mentions of freshness and canning, vegetarianism by showcasing only one vegetarian meal, and sensuality with gustatory 'mmms' highlighting the immediate relationship between cultural eater and eaten nature. By contrast, consumption themes were prevalent, resting as they do on **speciesism**, the ideology that the human species has the right to use up earth's resources, including all other species. These include: *gluttony* through the assumption that we all want huge servings of sweet and fatty foods, *competition* in that cooking well makes us look good, and *meat-eating* as if we all want and need it. An unrelated, but celebrated, theme was that of human bonding via food, for instance, the idea that cooking at home is a simple, pleasurable, tasty, affordable way to connect with friends and family.

Chiaro (2013) examines how two British TV "celebrity chefs"—Jamie Oliver and Nigella Lawson—use contrasting communicative tactics for presenting a fantasy of simple cooking that anyone can do at home, noting in particular several performance contrasts based on class and gender. While Oliver presents himself as a working-class man by using fast,

5.21

scattered, Essex "mate" talk (including more slang and informal discourse markers such as *right*, *like*, and *yeah*), Lawson performs her upper-crust, sexy female persona by speaking slowly in standard British English, using "refined" syntax, and employing "poetic" word choices. Yet overall, both are familiar characters and use "fresh talk," apparently impromptu performances of their actual selves, to engage the audience. They keep their directions vague and stay expressive, using endearments and 'mmms.' Both fashion social identities that appeal to their audiences through this highly scripted form of language about and around food preparation.

However, language about food on TV does not only take the form of cooking shows, as illustrated by Freeman and Leventi-Perez's (2012) deconstruction of a televised American ritual: the presidential pardon of two turkeys on Thanksgiving Day. By analyzing two decades of media and presidential discourse about and around the turkeys, the authors expose the unexamined cultural assumptions fed by this spectacle: both speciesism and **carnism**, that is, the anthropocentric ideology that human animals have the right to raise, slaughter, and consume other animals. Any guilt humans may once have felt for this act and expressed through non-human animal sacrifices to the gods is inverted through this ceremony that allows two turkeys, selected and donated by the National Turkey Federation, to be retired from their lifelong labor of transforming themselves into meat. Bred to be all breast, and no legs, they arrive beakless, overweight, and shuffling, and are mocked for pooping and gobbling in the White House. Rather than be sacrificed or "pardoned," since their only crime against the state is the public enactment of the fact that meat comes from sentient beings, they are granted the right to live, though their lifespan tends to be shortened by the ordeal. They are not eaten by the head of state, who makes jokes about the other delicious turkey he will enjoy later, or by any of the other thousands of viewers who will now turn to eating the millions of pounds of meat awaiting them in their own kitchens. Rather than critiquing this display of carnism, however, the media sometimes fault the president for not having pardoned more deserving humans this year and sometimes save a few belittling asides for the animal rights activists demonstrating outside the White House.

5.22

Summary

This chapter has explored how food talk comes in multisensual, multimodal, multivalent, and multifunctional forms and has many intended and unintended effects. It also raises the question of whether or not face-to-face (immediate and embodied) communication is the source material for the other discourse forms and to what degree they are stimulated by them. That is, do disembodied representations of food, whether Instagram posts, cartoons, or films, simply reproduce the talk about food that has always occurred among humans, or have they in fact transformed the ways in which we talk about and experience food? In asking this, we are also thinking about the role foodways discourses play in the world today as well as why and how they have become so prevalent and meaningful.

In fact, by way of conclusion, we draw attention to Thompson's (2012) analysis of the proliferation of food talk in the 21st century, from food activist books and blogs to foodie films and cooking shows. Likening it to the "rights talk" of the 20th century, he claims that it is this era's response to globalization, especially to the breakdown of the nation-state's ability to promise fundamental citizenship and the attendant rights. Instead, as we struggle to find a new identity that will function for our transnational lives, he proposes that the universal identity of *eater* is one we should all embrace. While the *eat local* slogan tells us to be an eater in a particular locale, the message is global and the action available to all—a new form of agency in making sense of changing times. While on the surface an analysis of language *about* food, this article is also a discussion of how we talk both locally and globally *around* food, the topic of the next chapter. It is also a plea to find new discourses with which to feed the destabilized masses (language *as* food), in effect proposing the food (inter)activism that we will explore further in Chapter 8.

5.23

Notes

1. See Riley (2017a) for an overview of the many kinds of food texts and methods for analyzing them.
2. For words and their etymologies, see Ayto (2012) and for aphorisms, see Brillat-Savarin (2009[1825]). For a recent exploration by a linguist, see Jurafsky (2014).
3. Interestingly, the goal of Noda's analysis was to consider how best to teach the communicative competence language learners would need to perform food talk, presumed to be a culturally important form of talk in context.
4. In earlier published versions of this poem, Kinnell did not include the word *broughamed*. Despite its spelling, *brougham*, meaning a kind of carriage and later a type of Cadillac, is pronounced in one syllable like *broom*, so adding '-ed' puts another consonant on the end, as would happen if *broom* became *broomed*. Thus, the word fits the pattern of words with consonant clusters on either side of a vowel, but the meaning of *broughamed* is less than transparent.
5. Riley (forthcoming) explores how these sorts of sensitivities are consumed and digested by children, parents, and teachers.
6. For more on political discourses about the dangers of industrial agriculture, including GMOs, see Cook (2004) and Heller (2013).
7. Some (e.g., Lewis-Williams 2002) believe that early cave art was related to practices of altering consciousness, possibly through the consumption of psychotropic substances.
8. This research was presented (Riley 2017b) at an AAA roundtable entitled "Food Talk Matters: How Health, Wealth, and Security Are Semiotically Produced, Consumed and Unequally Distributed." Unfortunately, images from the subway campaign are not available on the web, and Riley has not succeeded in acquiring

permission to use the photographs she took of the ads while the campaigns were running. As a result, this analysis also avoids using any full quotes from the ads.

References

Appadurai, Arjun. 1988. "How to Make a National Cuisine: Cookbooks in Contemporary India." *Comparative Studies in Society and History* 30(1): 3–24.

Arendholz, Jenny, Wolfram Bublitz, Monika Kirner, and Iris Zimmermann. 2013. "Food for Thought: Or, What's (in) a Recipe? A Diachronic Analysis of Cooking Instructions." In *Culinary Linguistics: The Chef's Special*, edited by Cornelia Gerhardt, Maximiliane Frobenius, and Susanne Ley, 119–138. Amsterdam: John Benjamins.

Ayto, John. 2012. *The Diner's Dictionary: Word Origins of Food and Drink*. Oxford: Oxford University Press.

Bailey, Austin. 2017. "A Way Out of Misery." *World Ark Magazine*, Heifer International, fall. www.heifer.org/join-the-conversation/magazine/2017/fall/way-out-of-misery.html, accessed February 4, 2018.

Barter, Judith A., ed. 2013. *Art and Appetite: American Painting, Culture, and Cuisine*. Chicago: The Art Institute of Chicago.

Bernoussi, Mohamed. 2016. "Semiosis of Intercultural Cooking: The Nineteenth Century Travel Literature as a Case Study." *Semiotica* 211: 45–57.

Blum, Susan D. 2017. "Eat Food from [Here]: The Talismanic Semiotics of Local Food." *Semiotic Review* 5: *The Semiotics of Food and Language*.

Brillat-Savarin, Jean Anthelme. 2009(1825). *The Physiology of Taste, or Meditations on Transcendental Gastronomy*. Translated by M. F. K. Fisher. New York: Everyman's Library (Knopf).

Brulotte, Ronda L., and Michael A. Di Giovine, eds. 2014. *Edible Identities: Food as Cultural Heritage*. Burlington, VT: Ashgate.

Calefato, Patrizia, Loredana La Fortuna, and Raffaella Scelzi. 2016. "Food-Ography: Food and New Media." *Semiotica* 211: 371–388.

Cavanaugh, Jillian R. 2016. "Documenting Subjects: Performativity and Audit Culture in Food Production in Northern Italy." *American Ethnologist* 43(4): 691–703.

Chiaro, Delia. 2013. "Passionate about Food: Jaimie and Nigella and the Performance of Food-Talk." In *Culinary Linguistics: The Chef's Special*, edited by Cornelia Gerhardt, Maximiliane Frobenius, and Susanne Ley, 83–102. Amsterdam: John Benjamins.

Conklin, Harold C. 1955. "Hanunóo Color Categories." *Southwestern Journal of Anthropology* 11(4): 339–344.

Cook, Guy. 2004. *Genetically Modified Language: The Discourse of Arguments for GM Crops and Foods*. New York: Routledge.

Counihan, Carole M. 2004. *Around the Tuscan Table: Food, Family, and Gender in Twentieth-Century Florence*. New York: Routledge.

Counihan, Carole M. 2009. *A Tortilla Is Like Life: Food and Culture in the San Luis Valley of Colorado*. Austin: University of Texas Press.

Cramer, Janet M. 2011. "Discourses of Consumption and Sustainability on the Food Network." In *Food as Communication/Communication as Food*, edited by Janet M. Cramer, Carlnita P. Greene, and Lynn M. Walters, 317–333. New York: Peter Lang.

Dahl, Bianca. 2014. "'Too Fat to Be an Orphan': The Moral Semiotics of Food Aid in Botswana." *Cultural Anthropology* 29(4): 626–647.

Diemer, Stefan. 2013. "Recipes and Food Discourse in English: A Historical Menu." In *Culinary Linguistics: The Chef's Special*, edited by Cornelia Gerhardt, Maximiliane Frobenius, and Susanne Ley, 139–156. Amsterdam: John Benjamins.

Dutta, Mohan J. 2012. "Narratives of Hunger: Voices at the Margins of Neoliberal Development." In *The Rhetoric of Food: Discourse, Materiality, and Power*, edited by Joshua J. Frye and Michael S. Bruner, 238–253. New York: Routledge.

Fellner, Astrid M. 2013. "The Flavors of Multi-Ethnic North American Literatures." In *Culinary Linguistics: The Chef's Special*, edited by Cornelia Gerhardt, Maximiliane Frobenius, and Susanne Ley, 241–260. Amsterdam: John Benjamins.

Freeman, Carrie Packwood, and Oana Leventi-Perez. 2012. "Pardon Your Turkey and Eat Him Too: Antagonism over Meat Eating in the Discourse of the Presidential Pardoning of the Thanksgiving Turkey." In *The Rhetoric of Food: Discourse, Materiality, and Power*, edited by Joshua J. Frye and Michael S. Bruner, 103–120. New York: Routledge.

German, Kathleen M. 2011. "Memory, Identity, and Resistance: Recipes from the Women of Theresienstadt." In *Food as Communication/Communication as Food*, edited by Janet M. Cramer, Carlnita P. Greene, and Lynn M. Walters, 137–154. New York: Peter Lang.

Gilbert, Elizabeth. 2006. *Eat Pray Love: One Woman's Search for Everything across Italy, India and Indonesia*. New York: Riverhead Books.

Goldstein, Jenny E. 2011. "The 'Coffee Doctors': The Language of Taste and the Rise of Rwanda's Specialty Bean Value." *Food and Foodways* 19: 135–159.

Heller, Chaia. 2013. *Food, Farms, & Solidarity: French Farmers Challenge Industrial Agriculture and Genetically Modified Crops*. Durham, NC: Duke University Press.

Holmes, Janet, Meredith Marra, and Brian W. King. 2013. "How Permeable Is the Formal-Informal Boundary at Work? An Ethnographic Account of the Role of Food in Workplace Discourse." In *Culinary Linguistics: The Chef's Special*, edited by Cornelia Gerhardt, Maximiliane Frobenius, and Susanne Ley, 191–209. Amsterdam: John Benjamins.

Imhoff, Daniel. 2007. *Food Fight: The Citizen's Guide to the Food and Farm Bill*. Healdsburg, CA: Watershed Media.

Jaworski, Adam, and Crispin Thurlow. 2009. "Taking an Elitist Stance: Ideology and the Discursive Production of Social Distinction." In *Stance: Sociolinguistic Perspectives*, edited by Alexandra Jaffe, 195–226. New York: Oxford University Press.

Jones, Rodney H. 2014. "Unwriting Food Labels: Discursive Challenges in the Regulation of Package Claims." *Journal of Business and Technical Communication* 28(4): 477–508.

Jourdan, Christine. 2010. "The Cultural Localization of Rice in the Solomon Islands." *Ethnology* 49(4): 263–282.

Jurado, Alfredo Tenoch Cid. 2016. "The Culinary and Social-Semiotic Meaning of Food: Spicy Meals and Their Significance in Mexico, Italy, and Texas." *Semiotica* 211: 247–269.

Jurafsky, Dan. 2014. *The Language of Food: A Linguist Reads the Menu*. New York: W. W. Norton & Co.

Karaosmanoglu, Defne. 2011. "Remembering Past(s): The Construction of Cosmopolitan Istanbul through Nostalgic Flavors." In *Food as Communication/Communication as Food*, edited by Janet M. Cramer, Carlnita P. Greene, and Lynn M. Walters, 39–55. New York: Peter Lang.

Kashay, Jennifer Fish. 2009. "Missionaries and Foodways in Early 19th-Century Hawai'i." *Food and Foodways* 17(3): 159–180.

Kinnell, Galway. 1993. "Blackberry Eating." In *Three Books*, 92. New York: Houghton Mifflin Harcourt.

Lewis-Williams, David. 2002. *The Mind in the Cave: Consciousness and the Origins of Art Reprint Edition*. London: Thames & Hudson.

Lindenfeld, Laura A. 2011. "Feasts for Our Eyes: Viewing Films on Food through New Lenses." In *Food as Communication/Communication as Food*, edited by Janet M. Cramer, Carlnita P. Greene, and Lynn M. Walters, 3–21. New York: Peter Lang.

Manning, Paul. 2012. *The Semiotics of Drink and Drinking*. New York: Bloomsbury Academic.

Marrone, Gianfranco. 2016. "Food Meaning: From Tasty to Flavorful." *Semiotica* 211: 187–201.

McIlwraith, Thomas. 2008. "'The Bloody Moose Got up and Took off': Talking Carefully about Food Animals in a Northern Athabaskan Village." *Anthropological Linguistics* 50(2): 125–147.

Nabhan, Gary Paul. 2014. *Cumin, Camels, and Caravans: A Spice Odyssey*. Berkeley: University of California Press.

Nichter, Mimi. 2000. *Fat Talk: What Girls and Their Parents Say about Dieting*. Cambridge: Harvard University Press.

Noda, Mari. 2014. "It's Delicious!: How Japanese Speakers Describe Food at a Social Event." In *Language and Food: Verbal and Nonverbal Experiences*, edited by Polly E. Szatrowski, 79–102. Philadelphia: John Benjamins.

Nye, Naomi Shihab. 2002. "Olive Jar." In *19 Varieties of Gazelle: Poems of the Middle East*, 80–82. New York: Greenwillow Books.

O'Connor, Kaori. 2013. *The English Breakfast: The Biography of a National Meal with Recipes*. London and New York: Bloomsbury.

Owens, Sarah E. 2011. "Food, Fasting, and Itinerant Nuns." *Food and Foodways* 19: 274–293.

Parasecoli, Fabio. 2011. "Looking at Men's Tables: Food and Masculinities in Blockbuster Movies." In *Food as Communication/Communication as Food*, edited by Janet M. Cramer, Carlnita P. Greene, and Lynn M. Walters, 155–175. New York: Peter Lang.

Riley, Kathleen C. 2017a. "Food and Text(ual) Analysis." In *Research Methods for Anthropological Studies of Food and Nutrition*, Volume 2, edited by John Brett and Janet Chrzan, 170–182. New York: Berghahn.

Riley, Kathleen C. 2017b. "Circulating Food Talk." Roundtable presentation at the American Anthropological Association Meeting, Washington, DC.

Riley, Kathleen C. Forthcoming. "'Don't Yuck My Yum': Semiotics and the Socialization of Food Ideologies at an Elite Elementary School." *Semiotic Review* 5: *The Semiotics of Food and Language*.

Silverstein, Michael. 2006. "Old Wine, New Ethnographic Lexicography." *Annual Review of Anthropology* 35(1): 481–496.

Singer, Ross. 2011. "The Corporate Colonization of Communication about Global Hunger: Development, Biotechnology, and Discursive Closure in the Monsanto Pledge." In *Food as Communication/Communication as Food*, edited by Janet M. Cramer, Carlnita P. Greene, and Lynn M. Walters, 405–427. New York: Peter Lang.

Thompson, John R. 2012. "'Food Talk': Bridging Power in a Globalizing World." In *The Rhetoric of Food: Discourse, Materiality, and Power*, edited by Joshua J. Frye and Michael S. Bruner, 58–70. New York: Routledge.

Thomson, Deborah Morrison. 2011. "Play with Your Food: The Performativity of Online Breakfast Cereal Marketing." In *Food as Communication/Communication as Food*, edited by Janet M. Cramer, Carlnita P. Greene, and Lynn M. Walters, 23–37. New York: Peter Lang.

Wiedenmayer, Anthi. 2016. "The Translation of Food in Literature: A Culinary Journey through Time and Genres." *Semiotica* 211: 27–43.

Chapter 6

Language Around Food

Discourses arise in the presence of food in social contexts around the world: in dining rooms and cafeterias, on farms and in the bush, in kitchens and over open fires, at farmers markets and convenience stores, and in factories and artisanal workshops. In such contexts, discussion about the food helps construct the significance of the co-present food as an iconic object of pleasure or disgust, an indexical means of shoring up or stigmatizing social identities, or a symbolic mode of evaluating cultural authenticity. However, it is also possible for the food in these settings to be neither a topic of discourse nor a communicating element. Instead, the food provides a pretext—and therefore context—for social interaction. In this chapter, we consider language *around* food.

We explore the many ways in which communication shapes and is shaped by food-related activities, especially while consuming it, but also while producing and distributing it. Social interactions around food are ordered by cultural expectations and conventions, both verbal and non-verbal, that may partly relate to the process of dealing with food as a material object in ways that differ from non-food settings. We also consider how language around food reflects and even contributes to larger issues of social change. We never forget that social interaction around food is facilitated in part because humans tend to do so much communicating through and about it as well.

The Social Organization of Language Around Food: Context, Genre, and Participation

Linguistic anthropologists have long highlighted the importance of attending to the context in which social interaction occurs in order to understand the social organization of groups and societies, and their communicative patterns. As discussed in Chapter 3, context is generated materially and linguistically through the co-present physical space and objects, participants, communicative modes, and discourse genres that emerge through situated social interaction.

Food-Situated Discourse Genres

We first consider genre, a term borrowed from literary studies where it is used to identify forms of verbal artistry: poetry, plays, and fiction. Mikhail Bakhtin (1895–1975), a Russian literary theorist, expanded the term's meaning to cover the many ways in which people communicate in everyday life as well; the term he proposed was "speech genres" (Bakhtin 1986). As described in Chapter 3, Dell Hymes used genre, the 'G' in his ethnography of SPEAKING mnemonic, to refer to the many culturally recognized ways of speaking: joking, storytelling, gossiping, lecturing, sermonizing, etc. The term communicative genres broadens this to encompass the ways in which these genres involve both verbal and non-verbal features and come in a variety of modes: not only spoken, but also signed and written. Finally, in addition to focusing on the multimodality of genres, the term discourse genres, which we employ here, captures the notion that communicative genres are frequently associated with and/or transmit specific ideological messages, a topic we will further probe in the next chapter.

A wide range of discourse genres are inspired and organized by food-related activities, such as growing, processing, marketing, preparing, exchanging, serving, and consuming food. These activities are in turn shaped by and become integral to the interactional context. In fact, in many cultures, the communication that happens around food, even when not explicitly about or through it, may come to be socially recognized, conventionalized, and named as specific food-related genres, for example, *coffee talk*, *dinner conversation*, and *gardening spells*.

As Gaudio (2003) explores, for many Westerners, an invitation to have coffee is tantamount to a proposal to chat, gossip, or more generally discuss something of interest to both parties. This type of social interaction is scheduled within the commercialized context of the coffeehouse (such as Starbucks) or other similar establishment where casual conversation is naturalized and conflated with the consumption of the coffee in that space. Similarly, Croegaert (2011) explores how refugee Bosnian women in Chicago engaged in *ćejf*, a coffee-based food genre that nourished them with memories of home while also providing them with a mediational onramp into their lives as American immigrants. Here, whether in the context of home, community center, or café, slow coffee-drinking practices facilitated talk about lives past and present among the women and with the researcher. In some cultures, the drinking of stimulants such as coffee and tea become a medium for the interactive genre of fortune-telling.

6.1 These food-situated discourse genres may carry moral messages of deep significance to cultural insiders, which are opaque to the anthropologist who only learns through long participatory immersion and sometimes challenging experiences. For instance, Lee (1969) learned through experience the appropriate discourse genre associated with food-sharing and meat-provisioning among the Ju/'hoansi (referred to as the !Kung at the time) in the Kalahari Desert in southern Africa. Because Lee was research-ing their hunting-gathering subsistence economy, he chose for most of his fieldwork period not to share his food supplies with them so as to obtain accurate data about how much food they foraged. This, however, was viewed as miserly by the egalitarian Ju/'hoansi, who shared their resources amongst all group members. Realizing that he had been behaving in an anti-social way according to local standards and wanting to thank his hosts as he concluded his fieldwork, Lee planned to provide the largest ox pos-sible for their Christmas feast.

6.2

News spread quickly when Lee purchased what he believed was the meatiest ox available, one that could easily feed the 150 people that would attend the feast. But people soon began to make disparaging comments about the animal. One complained, "That ox is thin to the point of death." Another queried, "What did you expect us to eat off it, the horns?" (Lee 1969:31–32). He was told that everyone would remain hungry, no one would dance, and fighting would likely break out at the feast. Despite the talk, the ox provided more than enough food for everyone and the event was a success. Only then did Lee suspect that he was the butt of a joke, the meaning of which he pondered for days. After questioning those who had been most critical, Lee came to understand that the Ju/'hoansi were

Figure 6.1 Children watch as a woman separates grain in Burkina Faso (© Shutterstock)

engaging in a discourse genre known as **ritual insults**, which in this case were commonly used with one another after a kill—insults meant to curb arrogance and enforce humility. Lee could not make up for a year of not sharing with one disproportionate contribution, nor should he think himself better than others because he could provide an animal of that size. Here, the language about and around food provided the ethnographer with a humbling lesson and rich glimpse into another worldview.

Although discourse genres, such as insults and gossip, are not restricted solely to food-focused contexts, these settings clearly inspire and often provide a culturally recognized opportunity for such interaction. That is, social interaction around food while hunting, cooking, or dining is so commonplace that even researchers who did not plan to study food seek out these settings to examine how people use language for negotiating relationships, identities, and social meanings.

Finding Discourse Data in the Kitchen

Social interaction in food-related contexts is frequently examined through the methods discussed in Chapter 3, including participant observation, situated interviewing, and recorded discourse. Researchers using such naturalistic data analyze not only *what* is discussed, but also *how* these discussions are shaped. That is the focus of analysis may be on the content—with topics ranging from the taste of a dish or practicalities about food service to personal moral dilemmas or world news—as well as the forms and functions of the communicative acts and genres—such as storytelling, joking, praying, gossiping, insulting, and assessing. Sometimes it is the food-related context that facilitates anthropological research.

Abarca (2006, 2007) developed what she refers to as *charlas culinarias*, or 'culinary chats,' as a technique for eliciting rich stories, testimonial autobiographies, and culinary memoirs from working-class Mexican and Mexican-American women. Frustrated with her initial attempts at conducting interviews using more formal academic speech, she found that encouraging casual participant-directed talk provided a way to understand how women organize their lives around preparing food for their kin and social networks. Approximately 90 percent of the *charlas culinarias* emerged in the kitchen over a meal prepared by the interviewees for the occasion without Abarca's prompting (Abarca 2006:9). Sharing food in the kitchen space, or at some women's public food stands known as *puestecitos*, contextualized the social interaction and prompted rich storytelling by participants in ways that had not occurred in her earlier interview attempts. The culinary chat format helped create an appropriate context for the researcher to explore the deeper meanings of women's entrepreneurship.

What she found was that the women in her study were empowered by moving out of the domestic sphere into the public sphere. This allowed them to make money, a productive goal usually associated with male labor, while also achieving some of the reproductive goals usually associated with females, such as nurturing children, maintaining family ties and extended social networks, and exchanging social and emotional meanings. In this way, women earned both material wealth (financial resources) but also familial wealth (kinship bonds) by operating public kitchens, food stands or bakeries. Through analysis of the transcribed narratives, Abarca began to challenge the notion of a public/private distinction in which women's labor is limited to the private sphere.

Within the narratives themselves, women also described to Abarca how the public kitchen as a food-focused context served other social functions—as a meeting place where people discussed politics, fell in love, offered advice on marriage and child rearing, and engaged in other meaningful communication. Further, the annual ritual of making tamales for the Christmas–New Year holiday season, known as the *tamalada*, served as a key gathering for the women in one bakery. Coming together and working all night to produce hundreds of tamales prompted conversation and 6.3 *convivencia* (co-sharing or co-living) among the women. Upon purchasing and consuming the tamales, Abarca speculated, customers then experienced *convivencia* as well, particularly during the holidays. While Abarca did not document language use in these particular contexts, her research

Figure 6.2 Street food market in Shanghai, China

Credit: Photo by Hanny Naibaho on Unsplash

methodology around food elicited women's affect-laden memories of such experiences and highlights the potential of food to generate social interaction and communion, even in an interview situation.

How Communication Around Food Is Shaped by Food Practices

While activities around the pervasive human concern with food prompt much communication, how that unfolds depends to some degree on the setting, participants, and types of food-related activities engaged in. In short, social interactions and the topics that are discussed are frequently shaped not only by the food and implements at hand but also by the activities and contexts, including when, where, and how one eats, gardens, or cooks, and the social organization of the situation, including how one engages with others while doing these food-related things.

Linguistic anthropologists have used the terms **participant structure** (Philips 1983) or **participation framework** (Goffman 1981) to refer to the configuration of actors in a communicative event, including whether they act as speakers or interlocutors and the various roles that the latter may take as **ratified** or **unratified participants**—that is, as listeners who are directly addressed by speakers or those who merely act as overhearers, respectively. Participants in talk are not simply influenced by the overall context, but also contribute to its production. As Marjorie Goodwin (2000:178, emphasis in original) states, "The concept of participation shifts the focus from the *structure* of speech activities to forms of *social organization* made possible for talk." Frequently, specific roles related to food are culturally defined, such as host, guest, server, shopkeeper, or consumer, and these are socially differentiated by such factors as age, gender, social status, class, and ethnicity. Thus, it is just as important to examine how people organize speech activities through the regulation of turn-taking, introduction of topics, and who gets to contribute as it is to examine the physical setting, spatial configuration, activity underway, and forms of language usage. This attention to participant framework is clearly applicable to the analysis of food-oriented contexts.

For example, Ochs and Taylor's (1995) study of suppertime storytelling among middle-class American families in Los Angeles, California, elucidates how both the context and participant structure can impact the roles taken up by participants in rehashing the day's events. The dinnertime context and configuration of family members sitting around a table spurred extensive narrative activity in the households they video-recorded. Asymmetrical narrative practices emerged during this multiparty talk that Ochs and Taylor suggest help to create and reinforce gendered family roles and identities (also see Kendall 2008). They demonstrate this by teasing apart key interactional roles in family narration that contribute to the interactional establishing of gender- and age-based family hierarchies: protagonist, introducer, primary recipient, problematizer, and problematizee.

The researchers found that most story introducers were parents, with mothers more frequently eliciting or initiating narratives, and that the stories were often about others, particularly the children, rather than themselves. Children were frequently portrayed as protagonists, the principal characters in a narrative, which subjected them to evaluation by others. This, then, became an assertion of parental narrative control over children. Parents also assumed the role of primary recipient in most cases, with fathers more frequently positioned in this role than mothers—and often *by* mothers. Children most often found themselves in the position of problematizees and participated less often than parents in dinnertime narration. The researchers further suggested that women's introducing of narratives prompted men to act as problematizers, particularly of mothers themselves and their competence. All of this, Ochs and Taylor (1995:108) claimed, positioned the father "to be the ultimate purveyor and judge of other family members' actions, conditions, thoughts, and feelings" during conversation around food at the dinner table. This "father knows best" dynamic fueled unequal gendered dynamics that were continually reenacted in front of and socialized to children during the habitual activity of food and story sharing. The ways in which food genres "feed" our understandings of social hierarchy and other forms of cultural knowledge will be discussed at more length in the next chapter.

6.4

How Language Around Food Organizes Eating and Drinking Practices

Communicative genres and speech acts both shape and are shaped by social interactions involving food and drink. Food production may be orchestrated by work songs, food processing organized by employer commands, market exchanges facilitated by pleasantries, cooking mediated by recipes, and dining triggered by saying grace. Each of these discursive forms gives shape to the food-related practices.

Celebratory toasts, whether in everyday settings or at ritual feasts, provide a clear illustration of how a specific speech act can be used to coordinate not only the ensuing food talk but also food consumption and the social roles of those involved in these activities. Kotthoff (2013) looked at drinking toasts across a narrow band of historically connected but culturally distinctive regions, including Georgia, Russia, Sweden, Germany, and the Netherlands. By comparing the forms, meanings, and functions of toasting, Kotthoff examines how this speech act represents different ways of "doing culture" across these societies, as well as how non-natives predictably get it wrong. None of the drinking toasts are *about* the alcohol, but the alcohol consumption is structured by the toasts. Kotthoff attends to how this happens and to how the ever-changing and culture-specific, gendered and health-related meanings of the alcohol are constructed and comprehended by toasting in this way. In particular, she examines how Georgians use toasts to co-construct pathos, interdependence, and nationalism. Tuite's (2010) study of the Georgian *supra* (banquet) shows that this elaborate system of ritual feasting and toasting has been in existence for centuries, with varying forms and meanings, but at present indexes the notion of hospitality between host and guest (all men, although the women do the "shadow work" of preparing and serving the meal). As a form of reciprocity, it is assumed to be needed in Georgia to fend off traditional savagery on the one hand and state intrusions on the other. The content, artistry, and sequencing of toasts all contribute to expressing and instantiating the power of the host to give (too much) food and alcohol and the powerlessness of the guest to say no.

6.5

Another example of how speech acts orchestrate food events can be found in the act of ordering food at a restaurant. For instance, Kuroshima (2014) analyzes the openings, states of incipient talk, and closings involved in ordering sushi at two restaurants in Japan. The collaborative participation of chefs, servers, and customers in these events is meaningfully arranged and the objects topicalized via conversational practices that organize mutual recognition. Shared semiotic resources that mediate the

Figure 6.3 Conviviality in Vitacura, Chile
Credit: Photo by Antenna on Unsplash

exchanges include talk (requests and offers, welcome and thanks), gestures, gaze, body orientation (pointing, bows), and food props (sake, ginger, fish). A meal in a sushi restaurant could clearly be analyzed as an example of language *through* food and the whole event includes talk *about* food, but this is an excellent illustration of how speech is used to organize activity *around* the food—preparing, serving, ordering, and eating it.

Commensality, Conviviality, and Conversation (or Not)

Commensality has existed in many if not all cultures throughout history and has been a long-standing topic of anthropological and archaeological interest (see Kerner, Chou, and Warmind 2015). Examples abound of how commensality contributes to establishing and reaffirming relationships and community in contemporary societies: business associates meet for lunch, potential romantic partners get to know each other over dinner, friends shore up relationships or make new connections through coffee or cocktails, study abroad programs use meals to foster a sense of community among strangers, and so on.

   In particular, domestic mealtimes have been highlighted informally and formally as a site of conviviality, the form of lively social interaction associated with commensality. Based on research in a range of Western countries, Fischler (2011) claims that regular meals provide a range of social benefits, including the capacity to address obesity issues in the world at large. In particular, he concludes that the obesity problem in the United States may be a result of the medicalization and individualization of eating habits, including what many lament as the loss of the "family meal," compared to the French, whose lower obesity rates correlate with the main-   6.6 tenance of eating together. This widespread idealization of French patterns of consumption is reflected in the fact that UNESCO has added the French "gastronomic meal" to their listing of the Intangible Cultural Heritage of Humanity, noting that this customary celebratory repast "draws circles of   6.7 family and friends closer together and, more generally, strengthens social ties" (UNESCO). The nourishing aspects of food-situated genres, both real and presumed, will be discussed at more length in the next chapter on lan-   guage *as* food.

   And yet mealtimes are not always a time to engage in actual conversa-   6.8 tion or conviviality. As we all may have experienced at some time in our lives, collective meals can provoke anxieties over who we are in relation to others, and thus may not always be an occasion of conviviality. In other words, although sometimes a site of coming together, these meals may also be a site of pulling apart. Think of heated political discussions between diners with conflicting views, rehashing of old arguments or pulling skeletons out of closets at holiday gatherings and family reunions, parent-child conflicts over table manners and eating norms, and cultural clashes when people from different social backgrounds come together in a restaurant, market, festival, or other public food event. In fact, talk around food can serve as a way to bring some people together while limiting interactions with others. Sometimes talk is suppressed, and silence may be the preferred form of expression. Commensality can be stratified, gendered, and racialized, and is impacted by shifts in regional, national, or global political economies. Who can and cannot share food and language together in the same setting impacts relations of inclusion and exclusion, common or contrasting identities, power dynamics, and what can and cannot be shared, learned, and accomplished. Participant structures are related to commensality across the various settings in which it occurs, as well as why it might not occur in other settings.

In a long-term study of village feasts in southern France, Jourdan (forthcoming) explores how these commensal events not only promote solidarity but also **agonism**, or respectful rivalry and non-antagonistic conflict, between villagers and villages. This is expressed during organizational efforts through advertising feasts in advance and debating crowd sizes, personal efforts to ensure someone to eat with at community meals since nothing could be worse than eating alone, and gastronomic discourses evaluating the food's taste, quality, authenticity, and so on. Both seating

Figure 6.4 Sharing a meal and talk in the Netherlands

Credit: Photo by Stella de Smit on Unsplash

arrangements and relations of inclusion/exclusion are forged as people arrive for the meal and save places for their groups by writing on the tables with large felt pens, claiming space in socially marked ways (professionals versus farmers, etc.). Yet residents also try to present themselves in a positive light for visitors from other villagers and vacationers who attend the events. Jourdan's analysis attends to the careful and orchestrated construction of communitas in the feasts.

To Talk or Not to Talk While Eating

Despite the pervasiveness of commensality in many parts of the world, and in particular the Western value placed on mealtime commensality, human cultural variation challenges even the presumed ubiquity of mealtime conversation. In some cultures, conversation during everyday meals is not expected. For instance, in Vignette 4.1, Jourdan discussed the discomfort she felt as a culturally French person having to eat without conversation in the Solomon Islands. In fact, in many parts of the Pacific, it may be less appropriate to talk during meals and more so in the interstices while producing and preparing food.

Indeed, it took Riley (2016) several fieldwork periods in the Marquesas to finally understand that she should not expect to record family conversation around everyday meals. For one thing, there were no set mealtimes and it was rare that more than a couple of family members would show up at once. Secondly, if she did find anything close to a quorum (for instance, early in the morning when the kids would gather before heading off to school), there was not a lot of what she recognized as mealtime discourse. She recorded cries of frustration over the lack of crackers and frantic utterances while searching for a flip-flop, but nothing like the narratives, jokes, and debates found in the mealtime talk that has been collected in the United States and Europe, as in Ochs and Taylor's study described above. Instead, she discovered she would need to be more random about the times and places she recorded children and their caregivers, eventually finding that a better method was to follow them as they picked fruit from the yard, boiled up Thai crackers, grilled fish for the Sunday meal, or baked coconut bread for sale at the church. Indeed, a lot more talk happened while cooking and exchanging food than while sitting down to eat a meal. And even at bigger parties where consumption did sometimes take place at a common table, the talk did not happen while eating but before and after, frequently while drinking. For an upper middle-class American researcher, the food-and-talk patterns initially felt like chaos. They also perplexed the French administrators, teachers, and health workers who have tried to impose their foodways on Marquesans over the years.

Similarly, in some African and Asian cultures, talk is avoided in some contexts of food consumption and encouraged in others. For instance,

Figure 6.5 Children in the Marquesas collecting papayas
Credit: Photo by Kathleen C. Riley

Meneley (2011) found that among the Zabidi of Yemen, the usual meal of boiled lamb, salad, and bread that was eaten from a variety of communal dishes while squatting, was not accompanied by chatting. As in Jourdan's case, her friends in the field did sometimes accommodate her strange Canadian desire for talk while eating. In fact, they used this opportunity to engage in some fascinating critiques of Western foodways norms, such as the insistence on eating from separate plates, taken as indicative of Western individualism by contrast with Yemeni communalism. However, Meneley found another context of sociality to be rife with talk: the evening parties held by women at their homes where only tea was served, no food, and everyone brought their own *qat* (a mild stimulant) to chew.

Talk around food may also be used to mark the difference between mundane and ritual meals. For instance, Hellman (2008) explored a seeming paradox around food and routine eating as compared with the meal rituals occasioned by Ramadan among Muslims in West Java, Indonesia. According to Hellman, food in Java is a major ritual marker as it is shared, exchanged, and offered to ancestors and deities. Yet, during everyday food consumption, families are not required to eat together men and women eat separately, and there are no expected meal gatherings. Even during ceremonial and other occasions when people do eat at the same table, they typically do not talk or even face one another. Chairs for eating at weddings are even set up to face forward in rows to avoid social interaction rather than toward one another to promote it. Minimal conversation during eating allows other participants their privacy, and talk takes place either *before* or *after* eating, as it is polite to *not* interact while consuming food. This applies, Hellman suggests, across different types of meals (lunch, dinner), social events (weddings, lunch breaks, picnics, working in the rice field), and locations (homes, restaurants, rural versus urban contexts), as well as socioeconomic class differences and education levels. There are no specific physical places, like a dining area, for eating in the home. Even during key communal events like circumcisions, weddings, and the ritual meal known as *slametan*, which brings family and friends together to reaffirm their relationships, eating serves primarily as a public performance of accepting one's social obligations rather than a site for creating intimacy or commensality.

During the fasting month of Ramadan, in contrast, there arise occasions for eating to become a collective act with talking being an appropriate mode. People are encouraged to share a morning meal (*sahur*) to signal the beginning of the day's fast, and then in the evening they break the fast together with another communal meal (*buka puasa*). Hellman details prayer routines, recitations from the Qur'an, explanations of Islamic principles and practices, and "a relaxed atmosphere with men and women, old and young, sitting in a circle passing food around while taking time to eat together" (2008:211) during these meals. So why isn't interaction during mundane eating times and social gatherings encouraged, as it appears to be during Ramadan and in so many other societies? Drawing on his ethnographic observations as well as interviews and analysis of passages from the Qur'an, Hellman contextualizes the practice of eating within cultural and religious understandings of *nafsu* (desire, also hunger, lust, or passion) and how to control it. In local interpretations of Islamic principles, eating, with the individual pleasure it offers, is viewed as an anti-social and potentially threatening behavior. Silence during regular food consumption is therefore appropriate. As *nafsu* is a key part of Ramadan—one is fasting to control *nafsu*—it becomes safe to eat and talk during the morning and evening meals that break the fast. Thus, during the regular flow of life, talking during food consumption could potentially harm family and community ties, while during Ramadan it generates community. It is this ritual occasion that brings about family commensality and talk around food—the time of year and purpose of the event create the context for talk around food more than the particular place or participant structure.

While public meals and ritual feasts marking special occasions are key moments for examining the complex interrelations between food, language, and identity, there is a growing literature examining more mundane mealtime interaction. Though not as recognized as special occasions, religious or otherwise, mealtime in family settings is routine and culturally structured and warrants study as a genre. Where family meals are practiced in domestic settings, habitual acts of commensality interwoven with some conviviality and conversation, help to build relationships, families, and communities.

Food-Situated Genres at Home: The Mealtime Conversation

The routines and rituals of mealtime provide a fruitful context for investigating the constitution of societal structures and sociocultural meanings in the most intimate sphere of family life. In many societies, food consumption creates contexts that bring families together, sometimes for the only moments of the day as parents are otherwise at work and children at school. For many busy working families, dinnertime creates "an opportunity space" for joint activity and interaction (Ochs, Smith, and Taylor 1989:238). For example, researchers at the UCLA Sloan Center on Everyday Lives of Families combined videotaping of everyday American family life with ethnoarchaeological tracking methods that pinpointed the location of each family member at regular 10-minute intervals. They found that family members came together most frequently in the kitchen, often around food and eating (Graesch 2013 and see Vignette 2.2). The researchers even refer to kitchens as "command centers" given their multifunctionality and their pivotal role in facilitating family interaction, child socialization, and "everyday operations for dual-income households" (Arnold et al. 2012:81).

6.9

Family meals bring together a relatively regular cast of characters—with variations according to the presence of guests or absence of some members occupied in other activities—that are united through shared conventions and expectations regarding the activity of food consumption within a temporarily bounded, spatiotemporal frame. Different communicative roles may or may not be available in the given participant structure surrounding the meal. Who prepares and serves food, how one prepares (washing hands, praying), how much is distributed and to whom and in what order (who eats first, last, or with whom), when food is provided and if it is tailored to specific kinds of people (by status, rank, age, gender, etc.), who cleans up—all are shaped by cultural beliefs and practices, and indicate information about the sociocultural order while constructing it. It may be preferred for children to refrain from speaking while adults interact or until spoken to—think of the proverb *children should be seen and not heard*. As Ochs and Shohet (2006:39) point out, "socialization into commensality is also socialization into sociocultural embodiments of generation, gender, and other social positionings." For instance, as discussed in Chapter 4, Appadurai (1981) looked at how age, gender, and caste (as well as ranking among the gods) defined who ate when, where, and what during family meals. Ochs and Shohet (2006) point out other examples of stratified ways of consuming food in China, Samoa, and the Peruvian Amazon.

In a study of dinner talk in two settings, Blum-Kulka (1997) found that among the 34 native and non-native Israeli (in Israel) and Jewish-American (in the United States) families she audio-video-recorded during dinnertime, only about one-fifth of dinner talk across all families was about the dinner itself. This food talk included "instrumental" utterances such as requests for food, expressions of personal food preferences, attention to children's food needs, compliments to those who prepared the meal, and parental directives toward children. The rest of dinnertime conversation was about family concerns—including immediate ones expressed in stories about the day's events and what to do about them, and non-immediate ones described in stories about personal histories, such as those relayed to guests. Children were more likely to participate in the instrumental talk about the meal across the families; however, there was much less verbal participation by children in talk about family concerns among Israeli families, and significantly more among Jewish-American ones, indicating the impact of the surrounding culture on the intimate sphere of family communication. Further, while there was a high-involvement conversational style in all families, there were cultural differences in the extent children could participate. Adults in the Israeli families, for instance, took up more time narrating, thus children were more likely to learn through observation rather than participation, in contrast to Jewish-American families where children often served as storytellers, thus exhibiting Americanization according to Blum-Kulka (1997:138). In both settings, dinner talk was a key context for the socialization of children to use language in socially and culturally appropriate ways, including effectively telling a story, developing an argument, demonstrating culturally appropriate politeness, and engaging in bilingual practices. Cultural identities were thus reflected, shaped, and socialized by these varied interactional styles, a topic to which we return in the next chapter.

Discourses Shaping and Shaped by Food Production and Distribution

As we have seen, communication varies in commensal settings across a range of social groups and cultures, but food consumption is not the only activity that allows for or even inspires social interaction. Contexts and activities related to food production, marketing, and distribution also

"We only have sugar for the coffee. Someone decided
that the pink and blue sweetener packets are sexist."

Figure 6.6 Break time chat

Copyright © Randy Glasbergen. Reproduced with permission.

promote social interaction that both shapes and is shaped by the presence
of food. In settings ranging from farms and production plants to grocery
stores and restaurant kitchens, language used around food can help draw
people together, forge connections, or be used to shore up differences, all
while engaging with food as both material and symbolic object.

From cafes to multinational corporations, language is used to market
food and make it more appealing to customers. Sometimes these commercial enterprises depend on language as a referential medium to transact
business, and sometimes it is the specific language, not one necessarily
known to workers or consumers, that acts as an iconic or indexical sign
 of value. For instance, Toback (2017) argues that Tully's Coffee chain in
Japan garnered commercial success in part through its ability to project
6.10   both "culinary-craft authenticity" through use of Italian discourse tokens
that accompany coffee orders and "egalitarian sociability" through applying the English loanword *ferō* ('fellows') to employees. During service
interactions, Tully's employees are mandated to call out adverbial phrases
drawn from an Italian musical register that convey the way the drink is to
be made: *con amore* ('with love'), *con spirit* ('with spirit or vigor'), *con brio*
('with energy or verve'), *con passione* ('with passion or zeal'), and *con sen-
timent* ('with emotion'). Customers may not understand what is being said,
but the tokens evoke foreign imagery of Europeanness and place-based

legitimacy, lending a coffee craft authenticity associated with Italian cafes. Toback also argues that the use of *ferō* on the company's website helps to erase hierarchical relationships between employer and employee in that it evokes equalized social relations among all employees as colleagues or comrades, regardless of position.

Such tactics have been employed by other corporations, including Tully's competitor, Starbucks, which refers to its employees in a way that seems non-hierarchical as *partners*. Yet, Manning (2008) points out, ordering at Starbucks can produce stress for those not familiar with the "correct" coffee lingo required there, thereby producing distinction (Bourdieu 1984) among patrons and tense encounters between baristas and customers. Manning explores how these encounters are even reported online by baristas through "imaginary conversations" with their "stupid" customers. Their "rants" or "vents" often take the form of "Stupid Customer of the Week" stories and detail the many ways in which customers display a lack of communicative-alimentary competence in ordering, thereby frustrating employees during service transactions.

6.11

Others explore the linked material and linguistic processes involved in food production and marketing. Cavanaugh (2016) shows the importance of language around food being produced or sold in direct marketing contexts, in this case farmers markets in Bergamo, Italy. Using participant

Figure 6.7 Coffee transactions in Tel Aviv-Yafo Israel

Credit: Photo by Rob Bye on Unsplash

observation and audio recording at market stands, Cavanaugh collected interactional data including exchange interactions with customers, small talk with officials, and gossip among the vendors themselves. She found that various forms of linguistic labor, such as gossip and everyday conversation, help to generate both social bonds and repeat customers in that setting. Stories about how food sellers prepare the foods they sell, such as sausages, and feed them to their own families reaffirms quality and adds value to market commodities. Such face-to-face banter establishes relationships between the foods, those who produce them, and their consumers. Further, for those producers/sellers from Bergamo, speaking in the local vernacular Bergamasco links them to a particular place and is interpreted as indexing authenticity and trustworthiness. Code choice between Italian and Bergamasco and use of other linguistic devices, such as choice of informal versus formal second-person pronomial address forms, can signal social distance or closeness between customers and vendors. Cavanaugh proposes the concept of "economic sociability" to get at how interaction can be simultaneously social and economic, adding value and meaning for participants while also personalizing economic transactions. Yet Cavanaugh is clear that such interactional work around food in market contexts is just one part of the work, albeit an important one, and that generating profits "requires an integration of verbal with material and documentary labor" (2016:50).

Vignette 6.1   Jillian R. Cavanaugh: Making Food and Talk in Italy

Jillian R. Cavanaugh is Professor of Anthropology at Brooklyn College CUNY and the CUNY Graduate Center. She teaches and writes about language, food, and culture.

I do research in Italy, a country synonymous with "obsessed with food." So it seems inevitable that I would focus on food and people's relationships to it. But I went there originally to study language and how Italians remain connected to their local languages (they call them "dialects"), even as they speak and teach their children Italian. Although speakers value them, local languages like Bergamasco, which I study, seem to be anchored in the past, provoking a compelling question: how do people bring their past into their present? For language, this issue is complicated, as languages must be spoken and taught to children to really survive. Food, however, seems to offer a simpler set of choices. A Bergamasco can search out particular restaurants or food-makers to support their cultural heritage at some times, but also continue to eat pizza and pasta like most other Italians at other times. Everyone can embrace food as heritage, without the effort and risk of being labeled old-fashioned that comes with language. And, unlike language, some people can make a living from food as cultural heritage.

The meaning and value of local food was on display at a salami festival I stumbled into one day in a small town in the province of Bergamo. Most people were at the festival to eat and socialize. Long tables were filled with families and friends eating local food from several stands (polenta with sausages was a popular choice) and chatting in the warm summer evening. In this, it resembled countless community festivals that occur across Italy during the summer.

6.12

But there were other things occurring at this festival. First, there was a "salami-off" happening under a tent in the small central piazza, where two well-known local salami makers were leading teams through butchering, mixing ingredients, encasing, and then tying up salamis. Most families in this area once would have done this together every year, but for many in the audience, this was the first time they had seen it.

Second, there was a salami tasting. A team of local salami experts had been assembled to taste the roughly 70 locally produced salamis entered in the contest, picking the top five. After a brief ceremony where they were introduced to the crowd they retired in their official-looking white coats to a room off the piazza to do their tasting.

Finally, there were local, provincial, and regional government officials assembled in the town council's public meeting hall to hold a public discussion of ongoing efforts to gain European Union recognition for Bergamasco salami. Officials gave speeches on the salami's merits and the economic and cultural advantages to be gained through achieving such recognition. After their speeches, they tasted the top five salamis from the contest to choose the very best. At the ceremony that topped off the night, they announced the winner and runners-up, linking the high quality of the salamis they had tasted to the validity of their efforts toward EU recognition.

As an anthropologist, I was bowled over. There was so much happening around salami: culturally, politically, economically, socially! As a linguistic anthropologist, I noted so much of it was linguistic, from speeches to the cards tasters filled out, friendly talk among friends and family as they ate, and the many documents that would have to be submitted to EU officials in the recognition effort. To look at salami without focusing on the language involved in making it, both spoken and written, would have missed much of the action.

That is the project I undertook: to study the language that surrounds—and, as I eventually learned, is an essential part of—food production. Over the next several years, I spent time with salami producers while they worked, including when they made the food on production floors or small in-home workshops, but also when they sold their foods in farmers markets or to supermarket owners. I observed and sometimes audio-recorded their interactions with customers, food safety inspectors, and local government officials. I interviewed them, their employees, food activists, and the government-employed veterinarians who work with them to ensure what they do with animals and animal-based products is humane and safe. In doing so, I saw how so much of their work to make good, high-quality, safe and culturally valued—heritage—foods happened through language, showing how connected food and language are in the realm of work and production.

Karrebæk (2017) explores how in a small shop selling fruits, vegetables, and other products in Copenhagen, Denmark, ethnolinguistic diversity is expected, and conviviality is a communicative norm, with shop owners using their multicultural products and multilingual skills to cultivate ongoing relationships and reciprocity with customers. For example, the shopkeepers frame their service interactions in terms of hospitality by accommodating customers' language skills, even learning new languages from regular customers and attending to cultural sensitivities, such as providing locally translated written instructions for intimate body products that are interpreted as inappropriate for the shopkeepers to discuss. They offer tastes of items and engage in playful joking discourse to entice customers to buy and return in the future. Further, the types of foods and their origins can become a key piece of the interactional context that connects spaces and people in convivial and cosmopolitan ways while adding value and appeal to the products. For instance, when a Danish woman buys Thai ingredients to prepare a meal for family in another city, the discourse that emerges between her, the shopkeeper, and another customer connects Copenhagen to Thailand through talk about and around the Thai foods she is purchasing, traversing space and time as she explains how she was exposed to them through a recent trip and how she can bring a taste of that trip to her family. Diversity, cosmopolitanism, and conviviality become linked through the global orientation of the foods, multilingual resources, and personal conversations that occur around the foods in this greengrocer, thereby, Karrebæk suggests, smoothing potential tensions that might otherwise arise.

However, economic interactions around food do not always go smoothly any more than they do in domestic settings. For instance, as both Cavanaugh and Karrebæk note, vendors sometimes overstep social boundaries by providing too much private information to customers (Cavanaugh's market transactions) or when sellers and patrons understand the conversational frame differently (serious versus humorous as in Karrebæk's Thai food interaction). Such tensions emerged vividly in Bailey's (1997) study of communicative differences between Korean shop owners and their African-American customers in Los Angeles, California, during a time of significant interethnic violence. Bailey analyzed the role of different strategies for politeness and how they could clash during service encounters in which customers purchased liquor, soda, and other products. Korean-American shop owners leaned toward **restraint politeness**—making indirect requests, being apologetic, and not demanding another's attention—and keeping service encounters socially minimal, while their African-Americans customers demonstrated **involvement politeness**—telling friendly jokes, showing personal interest through narratives, making offers—and attempted to engage in socially expanded service encounters. Bailey found that when things started to go wrong during transactions, participants would try even harder to be polite in their different ways, thus creating even more of a discursive divide, however unintentionally. In this case, we see how interacting around comestibles in settings like convenience stores varies cross-culturally and can lead one group to stereotype another without understanding the different communicative expectations and ways of speaking that shape the other's approach to the situation.

Just as vendors and customers negotiate interpersonal dynamics, intercultural tensions, and salient aspects of their social identities through verbal and non-verbal language in food-related settings, so do such tensions arise among employees and patrons brought together in restaurants, food production plants, and elsewhere. Barrett (2006) was drawn to analyzing social interactions between and among Spanish-speaking Mexican and English-speaking Anglo workers in an Anglo-owned Mexican restaurant in Texas where he was employed and did ethnographic research as he completed his doctorate. Anglo managers, he found, had limited skills in Spanish, and regularly used ungrammatical constructions and pseudo-words (such as *ice-o* for 'ice') in issuing directives and comments to the Spanish kitchen staff, not to mention using explicit epithets, such as *beaners,* about them. While these practices helped to create a jocular persona for English-speakers, it had negative consequences for the Spanish-speaking employees who could lose their jobs if they failed to understand the incomprehensible mock Spanish utterances of their employers. At the same time, in the alternative linguistic marketplace of the kitchen, Spanish became a tool of solidarity and resistance for the

6.13

kitchen staff, who used the code to discuss the racism of the Anglo staff and spread the word about special meals being cooked only for them. Here the communication around and about food perpetuated ethnic tensions and racism.

By contrast, we can also see how language around food in food-related workplaces can serve as a means for building a common workplace culture, as Strangleman (2010) found in a west London Guinness factory that was being shut down after almost 70 years of operation. Strangleman's original goal was not to study food and drink, but it became clear that this was important to understanding the larger workplace culture. Daily ritual tastings of the beer during the research period in the 2000s afforded Strangleman the opportunity to witness the exchange of news and gossip about people in and outside the plant. Workers talked fondly of the use of drink and food at the factory to bring people together in the past, comparing it much more negatively to the restricted contexts for such interaction due to outsourcing and fragmentation of the workforce in the present. They told nostalgic narratives over lunch at the canteen as the imminent closure of the factory neared, describing the full-service canteens of the past when mainly women served the male factory workers, producing a gendered and familial dimension that helped to integrate them into a strong corporate culture. People would gather to eat and drink for rites of passage like retirement parties and apprentice-to-tradesmen initiations, and the preparation for such events employed another whole set of workers. They further related fond stories of alcohol consumption during the workday, as they were given free beer to be consumed at work as part of their agreements. Work groups themselves established and maintained norms of consumption and management of excess. Strangleman thus found that food and drink had helped pull together a vibrant workplace culture and collective identity in the past, one that had gone by the wayside due to contemporary economic changes.

6.14

Language Around Food in Contexts of Sociocultural Change

As seen above, certain food contexts seem to facilitate the sharing of information and personal history that might not easily be obtained in more formal settings, and these in turn shed light on larger sociocultural transformations in these societies. Further, talk around and about food during its obtaining, preparation, and consumption is often about much more than just food, including issues of cultural and linguistic continuity and transformation. Migration, shifting political climates, and socioeconomic change, among other things, can alter the structure of mealtimes and means of obtaining food, and can transform patterns of language use around food. Two case studies help to illustrate this.

6.15

Continuity and Innovation in the Italian Feast of the Seven Fishes

In an exploration of language around and though food, Di Giovine (2010) demonstrates how Italian Americans use ritual foodways in particular contexts—specifically the consumption of various seafood dishes during the annual Christmas Eve feast, *La Vigilia*—to construct and maintain their hyphenated identities. Through an auto-ethnography of his own family and friends, the researcher demonstrates how specific foods and the use of Italian and English mean different things across generations and help to contextualize the feast. For *La Vigilia*, seven kinds of fish are to be eaten, though there are variations across families as they both replicate and innovate in their dishes. There are multiple courses in the meal—antipasti, pasta, fish and sides, dolce, American coffee and dessert—each with their own verbal and non-verbal cues and organization. Further, movement between different contexts signals different ritual phases with different participant structures, including preparing food in kitchens, visiting others to sample their dishes, milling about for the appetizer phase, and sitting down for the formal feast. Much interaction takes place about and around the preparation stage, with remembering and discussion of recipes, talking about how to make the food, and negotiating over traditional and modern practices. This phase represents separation from the profane world: cooks seek the sacred foodstuffs at out-of-the-ordinary places and outside of the normal shopping routine and prepare them in ways that are both traditional/authentic and creative/innovative, though tradition can win out over too much innovation (such as adding hot pepper to a dish) or health concerns (such as adding less oil to a stuffing). Some dishes are erased from the meal because the ingredients are not available in sacred form, such as *zuppa di pesce* (fish soup).

6.16

The verbal and non-verbal communication around the food consumption further helps to accomplish the construction of a hybrid identity, suggesting that the language and other communicative forms used around the feast contribute as significantly as the food. The antipasti stage—which is done standing and allows for more Americanized food items to be brought by younger family members—is the transitional stage before true community members are seated to eat the authentic, sacred dishes in the subsequent courses when communitas is forged. When called to the feast the men, children, and American-born women are seated first, while the cooks, those who were deemed knowledgeable and from the "correct" family lines, serve the meal. There are gender- and age-related seating arrangements at the table that reflect a linguistically marked progression from those who were born in Italy and speak Italian on one end to American-born English-speaking children at the other end. Those in the middle of the table speak both languages. The feast, Di Giovine argues, works to revitalize the identity of Italian Americans in the face of acculturation through emphasis on "traditional" foods and to strengthen family and ethnic bonds (as a "rite of intensification") and socialize new members (as a "rite of incorporation" for those joining the family through marriage) to acquire the tastes and cultural competence of this identity, such as eating hairy anchovies. At the end, American coffee and cookies, with Santa Claus distributing gifts, brings them back to the profane world.

Men, Women, and Change in Chipewyan (Dene) Trailside Meals

Jarvenpa offers insights into shifting contexts of talk and food based on long-term fieldwork among the Chipewyan (Dene) in subarctic Canada. The Chipewyan have faced major societal transformations since the 1950s, including an economic shift from both men and women going to seasonally nomadic family camps to men hunting and fishing on their own while women stay in the village with children. In one study, Jarvenpa (2008) examines the impact of global forces on three types of meals in Chipewyan culture as compared to another subarctic culture, that of Finnish farmers. Using participant observation and note-taking across the different food-contexts—meal breaks during food production work, household meals, and public feasts or ceremonial meals—Jarvenpa explores how particular eating venues have shifted toward expectations of certain indigenous or modern kinds of food and methods of preparation that index gendered and generational change. In both cases, members of the communities prepare and serve more "bush" or nativized foods—lard and bannock for the Dene and coffee for the Finns—in their work groups and to some degree in their family settings. On the other hand, both groups cook and consume more imported foods, served in more "modern" ways, in public settings. Different contexts have different associations with tradition/modernity, and this has created the need for mediating foods as people symbolically negotiate tensions between external market forces, their local ecology, and societal change. Traditional foods represent ecological knowledge and "diets of experience," yet they are missing from larger-scale public performances of identity in the face of shifting political-economic trends, ways of making a living, and influences on local diets.

In a related study, Jarvenpa (2017) used participant observation among men during their food-obtaining expeditions to explore their changing food and language practices without women. One difference is that their meals have become truncated as compared to family meals prepared back at home by women. Yet, sharing the contents of their *ber teli* ('grub boxes'), such as pieces of dried fish and moose meat, around a communal fire while on the trail creates an important context for storytelling, joking, gossip, and advice. Men discuss topics relevant to the practical tasks at hand, such as evaluation of hunting and fishing strategies and the food itself, but also local news and, in particular, women. Jarvenpa suggests that stories of "girling" in other villages index heteronormative masculinity, while tales of missing women (those not there to properly butcher and dry moose meat, or ones who were "lured away" from their home villages by outsiders using "love medicine") index the emotional longing and distress experienced in this changing society.

Through this study of the trailside food break as a particular context of talk around food, Jarvenpa is able to get at larger changes taking place in Dene society. Javernpa even suggests that separate gendered food cultures may be developing, with a female village-household cuisine and male mobile-bush cuisine. Men's talk around food during trailside meals, occasioned by the absence of women, varies from the talk of family groups two generations ago and men's talk in the company of their wives and children back home. Yet through their conversations around food, Jarvenpa suggests that men symbolically bring women back into the ancestral bush landscape that they have withdrawn from in recent times due to increased sedentation. Jarvenpa's analysis demonstrates all four of the constructs we have used to organize this book: how the language *about* food, such as the harvesting and processing of moose and other meats, occurs as language *around* food as they talk while preparing, sharing, and eating those meats, while communicating their ethnic (largely in contrast to neighboring Cree) and gendered identities *through* the foods, and all the while being nourished by this bonding language *as* food while away from their families and unable to protect their loved ones from threats to the community.

Vignette 6.2   Robert Jarvenpa: From Production to Processing and Consumption of Food and Talk

Robert Jarvenpa is Professor Emeritus and a former chair of the Department of Anthropology at the University at Albany, SUNY, and is a research associate at the New York State Museum.

As an ecologically oriented social anthropologist, my interest in food and language developed after a long and circuitous journey through several related areas of research. In the early and mid-1970s my focus was on hunter-gatherer subsistence ecology, mobility, and sociospatial organization. I conducted several years of ethnographic fieldwork with the Kesyehot'ine group of Chipewyan, Dene or Athapaskan-speaking people of northern Canada. As an active participant with teams of hunter-fishermen, I documented their movements on the landscape, trail systems, networks of encampments, work routines, and harvests of moose, caribou, beaver, whitefish, and waterfowl, among other

6.17

animals. While these resources were central to Chipewyan food culture, at that time my approach was focused more on the procurement or production side of food systems, less so on the consumption side.

Along with my colleague Hetty Jo Brumbach, in the late 1970s and early 1980s I began ethnoarchaeological research on historical interactions between Chipewyan, Cree, Métis, and European participants in the fur trade political economy of northern Canada. By analyzing artifactual materials from a network of former encampments and habitation sites, coupled with consultant testimony and fur trade documents, we discovered that differences in the frequencies of "country food" and imported food among the various ethnic groups at different time periods were indices of these groups' economic specialization, their access to the Euro-Canadian community, and their degree of integration into the evolving fur market economy. A strong contrast emerged between "fur hunter" and "fur trade laborer" orientations for the Chipewyan and Métis Cree, respectively. Paradoxically, the Chipewyan, with the greatest subsistence self-sufficiency and geographic mobility, were no less integrated into the fur trade than Métis servants and laborers employed by firms like the Hudson's Bay Company.

Later in the 1980s and 1990s I shifted gears to issues of agrarian ecology, decision-making, and rural stratification with ethnographic field projects on farming systems in Finland and Costa Rica. At that time I focused on changes in men's and women's roles in light of agro-industrial development. Some years later Brumbach and I conducted a cross-cultural ethnoarchaeological study that examined gender dynamics and subsistence in four Circumpolar societies: Chipewyan, Iñupiaq, Khanty, and Sámi. That work grappled with reconceptualizing the sexual division of labor and with giving adequate representation and voice to women's contributions in food procurement, processing, storage, and distribution.

All of the foregoing experiences expanded my gaze from the production side toward the processing and consumption side of food systems. Working closely with both women and men in the field enhanced my appreciation of the social and ritual complexities and subtleties of meals. After attending the First International Congress of Alimentación y Cultura in Madrid in 1998, my interest in food and culture research grew. For that meeting I prepared a meal typology to help interpret how culinary styles and mediating foods are part of a symbolic means of addressing tensions and contradictions between local ecology and supra-local political economy. I have been working on variations of this theme ever since, including my first foray into the semiotics of men's mealtime conversations. Regarding the latter, I am pleased to join the evolving conversation on food and language.

Summary

From garden plots to grocery store shelves, language is important in transforming food into something both nutritionally and socially meaningful. Across the studies touched upon in this chapter, we see how researchers analyze what people actually do and say—or do not say—when they come together in food-related contexts. These contexts revolve around food and eating activities for mundane and special occasions, and in homes and marketplaces, factories and village feasts, restaurants and on the trail. The studies provide just a taste of the many possibilities for researching language around food, but they offer models for exploring not only how food and talk are interrelated, but also how such connections contribute to broader social and cultural meanings and values. Many of these studies examine the specific kinds of talk that participants produce around and about the food, but they are also concerned with broader issues of cultural and emotional significance.

As we have seen, food contexts are important for understanding discourse structure, human social organization, and the acquisition of culturally specific ways of using language and relating to the world, a topic that will be explored in more depth in Chapter 7 when we consider language *as* food. While conversation takes place in other social settings and in the absence of food, a key point of this chapter is that the pervasive co-occurrence of language and food has a significant influence on the negotiation of social relationships. Food contexts inspire the expression and construction of belief systems, language ideologies, and social identities through verbal and non-verbal communication, including specific food-situated discourse genres. They sometimes bring together individuals and groups who would not interact in non-food-related contexts, such as customers in markets and restaurants, thereby creating the potential for cross-cultural communication *and* miscommunication. They become sites for the investigation of sociocultural and linguistic change as it unfolds over time. This co-occurrence offers a prime venue for examining what it means to be human across societies, allowing us to identify universals while simultaneously exploring idiosyncratic and cultural differences.

References

Abarca, Meredith E. 2006. *Voices in the Kitchen: Views of Food and the World from Working-Class Mexican and Mexican American Women.* College Station: Texas A&M University Press.

Abarca, Meredith E. 2007. "Charlas Culinarias: Mexican Women Speak from Their Public Kitchens." *Food and Foodways* 15(3–4): 183–212.

Appadurai, Arjun. 1981. "Gastro-Politics in Hindu South Asia." *American Ethnologist* 8(3): 494–511.

Arnold, Jeanne E., Anthony P. Graesch, Enzo Ragazzini, and Elinor Ochs. 2012. *Life at Home in the Twenty-First Century: 32 Families Open Their Doors.* Los Angeles, CA: The Cotsen Institute of Archaeology Press.

Bailey, Benjamin. 1997. "Communication of Respect in Interethnic Service Encounters." *Language in Society* 26(3): 327–356.

Bakhtin, Mikhail M. 1986. *Speech Genres and Other Late Essays.* Translated by Vern W. McGee. Austin, TX: University of Texas Press.

Barrett, Rusty. 2006. "Language Ideology and Racial Inequality: Competing Functions of Spanish in an Anglo-Owned Mexican Restaurant." *Language in Society* 35: 163–204.

Blum-Kulka, Shoshana. 1997. *Dinner Talk: Cultural Patterns of Sociability and Socialization in Family Discourse.* Mahwah, NJ: Lawrence Erlbaum.

Bourdieu, Pierre. 1984. *Distinction: A Social Critique of the Judgement of Taste.* Translated by Richard Nice. Cambridge, MA: Harvard University Press.

Cavanaugh, Jillian R. 2016. "Talk as Work: Economic Sociability in Northern Italian Heritage Food Production." *Language & Communication* 48: 41–52.

Croegaert, Ana. 2011. "Who Has Time for Ćejf? Postsocialist Migration and Slow Coffee in Neoliberal Chicago." *American Anthropologist* 113(3): 463–477.

Di Giovine, Michael. 2010. "La Vigilia Italo-Americana: Revitalizing the Italian-American Family through the Christmas Eve 'Feast of the Seven Fishes'." *Food and Foodways* 18: 181–208.

Fischler, Claude. 2011. "Commensality, Society and Culture." *Social Science Information* 50(3–4): 528–548.

Gaudio, Rudolf P. 2003. "Coffeetalk: Starbucks and the Commercialization of Casual Conversation." *Language in Society* 32(5): 659–691.

Goffman, Erving. 1981. *Forms of Talk.* Philadelphia: University of Pennsylvania Press.

Goodwin, Marjorie Harness. 2000. "Participation." *Journal of Linguistic Anthropology* 9(1–2): 177–180.

Graesch, Anthony P. 2013. "At Home." In *Fast-Forward Family: Home, Work, and Relationships in Middle-Class America*, edited by Elinor Ochs and Tamar Kremer-Sadlik, 27–47. Berkeley and Los Angeles: University of California Press.

Hellman, Jörgen. 2008. "The Significance of Eating during Ramadan: Consumption and Exchange of Food in a Village in West Java." *Food and Foodways* 16: 201–226.

Jarvenpa, Robert. 2008. "Diets of Experience: Food Culture and Political Ecology in Northern Canada and Northern Finland." *Food and Foodways* 16: 1–32.

Jarvenpa, Robert. 2017. "'Women Are in the Village and Men Are Always in the Bush': Food, Conversation and the Missing Gender in Northern Dene Society." *Semiotic Review* 5: The Semiotics of Food and Language.

Jourdan, Christine. Forthcoming. "Solidarity, Agonism and Entre-Soi in the Village Meals of the Causse du Quercy." *Semiotic Review* 5: The Semiotics of Food and Language.

Karrebæk, Martha Sif. 2017. "Thai Veggies and Hair Removal Products: Space, Objects and Language in an Urban Greengrocery." *Social Semiotics* 27(4): 451–473.

Kendall, Shari. 2008. "The Balancing Act: Framing Gendered Parental Identities at Dinnertime." *Language in Society* 37: 539–568.

Kerner, Susanne, Cynthia Chou, and Morten Warmind, eds. 2015. *Commensality: From Everyday Food to Feast.* New York: Bloomsbury Academic.

Kotthoff, Helga. 2013. "Comparing Drinking Toasts: Comparing Contexts." In *Culinary Linguistics: The Chef's Special*, edited by Cornelia Gerhardt, Maximiliane Frobenius, and Susanne Ley, 211–240. Philadelphia: John Benjamins.

Kuroshima, Satomi. 2014. "The Structural Organization of Ordering and Serving Sushi." In *Language and Food: Verbal and Nonverbal Experiences*, edited by Polly E. Szatrowski, 53–75. Philadelphia: John Benjamins.

Lee, Richard Borshay. 1969. "Eating Christmas in the Kalahari." *Natural History*, December: 60–64.

Manning, Paul. 2008. "Barista Rants about Stupid Customers at Starbucks: What Imaginary Conversations Can Teach Us about Real Ones." *Language & Communication* 28(2): 101–126.

Meneley, Anne. 2011. "Food and Morality in Yemen." In *Food: Ethnographic Encounters*, edited by Leo Coleman, 17–30. Oxford: Berg.

Ochs, Elinor, and Merav Shohet. 2006. "The Cultural Structuring of Mealtime Socialization." *New Directions for Child and Adolescent Development* 111: 35–49.

Ochs, Elinor, Ruth Smith, and Carolyn Taylor. 1989. "Detective Stories at Dinnertime: Problem-Solving through Co-Narration." *Cultural Dynamics* 2(2): 238–257.

Ochs, Elinor, and Carolyn Taylor. 1995. "'The Father Knows Best' Dynamic in Dinnertime Narratives." In *Gender Articulated*, edited by Kira Hall and Mary Bucholtz, 97–120. New York: Routledge.

Philips, Susan U. 1983. *The Invisible Culture: Communication in Classroom and Community on the Warm Spring Indian Reservation*. Long Grove, IL: Waveland Press.

Riley, Kathleen C. 2016. "Learning to Exchange Food and Talk in the Marquesas." In *Making Sense of Language*, 3rd edition, edited by Susan Blum, 143–153. Oxford: Oxford University Press.

Strangleman, Tim. 2010. "Food, Drink and the Cultures of Work: Consumption in the Life and Death of an English Factory." *Food, Culture and Society* 13(2): 257–278.

Toback, Ezra. 2017. "Cross-Modal Iconism at Tully's Coffee Japan: Authenticity and Egalitarian Sociability as Projections of Distinction." *Semiotic Review* 5: *The Semiotics of Food and Language*.

Tuite, Kevin. 2010. "The Autocrat of the Banquet Table: The Political and Social Significance of the Georgian Supra." In *Language, History and Cultural Identities in the Caucasus: Papers from the Conference, June 17–19, 2005, Malmö University*, edited by Karina Vamling, 9–35. Malmö, Sweden: Malmö University.

UNESCO https://ich.unesco.org/en/RL/gastronomic-meal-of-the-french-00437, accessed December 17, 2017.

Chapter 7

Language As Food

Food is frequently talked about as a form of language, as we explored in Chapter 4. The reverse is also true—language is often metaphorically described and conceptualized as food. We begin this chapter by comparing excerpts from two written texts that illustrate this process. In the first quote from a poem by Peggy Sapphire, the Yiddish language is nostalgically likened to kasha, a nourishing porridge, and also represents her kin relationship with and socialization into Yiddish through her Aunt Ida:

> *Aunt Ida not only thrived*
> *on old country recipes*
> *she nourished us*
> *all those Sunday afternoons ago*
> *with Yiddish and kasha*
> (Sapphire 2009)

In the second quote from the American magazine *The Atlantic*, words are equated with food so that children can be starved by a supposed dearth of vocabulary in their home environments just as they can be by lack of adequate food nutrition:

> When a child is deprived of food, there is public outrage. And this is because child hunger is correctly identified as a moral and economic issue that moves people to action. We believe that the poverty of vocabulary should be discussed with the same passion as child hunger.
> (Lahey 2014)

In these examples, ideologies about food and language reflect and affect how people understand both. In some cases, such discourses can be empowering, perhaps strengthening positive attitudes toward learning a vernacular language as in Sapphire's poem. In other cases, the resulting policies and practices may, though well-intended, turn out to be detrimental to the lives of those in need. For instance, discourses of the kind found in the quote from *The Atlantic* article seek to address lower-income children's school failure by problematizing and proposing to fix their parents' language use rather than grappling with larger societal inequities. In both cases, scholars of language and food need to question the underlying assumptions created by these metaphoric connections, which highlight some visions of the world while minimizing or obscuring others.

Language *as* food, then, refers to the many ways in which people imagine language as a form of sustenance (or toxin), but also how language effectively serves as a vehicle for cultural learning and socialization. In this chapter, we first explore how the language we speak may indeed operate as a kind of sustenance, feeding us notions (nutritious or not) about the world, encoded for instance in our idioms. We consider how psycholinguistic studies of language acquisition in Western societies rest on some of these same cultural assumptions in that they conceptualize language as food for children's linguistic development. Similarly, food-and-language socialization research treats linguistic interaction as, to some degree, a process of "feeding" children and other novices much of what they know about how to speak and eat—both communicative and alimentary competence. However, this field of research has interrogated the one-way, top-down "feeding" metaphor by ethnographically investigating the complexity of diverse socializing contexts, thus recognizing that children and other novices do not simply consume all that they are exposed to. Frequently, they resist even tasting the foods they are offered; similarly, they do not simply ingest the symbolic goods indexed by the foods. In other words, we are interested in showing in this chapter how discourses about and around food are produced and reproduced in everyday food-focused contexts from home to school to imaginary play, and how their digestion or rejection contributes to cultural and linguistic transformation over time.

Do Discourses Feed Our Worldview?

Healthy debate, juicy gossip, feedback, chewing the fat, buttering someone up, spicing things up, spilling the beans, take it with a grain of salt . . . can you think of others? For American English-speakers, abundant expressions exist that equate food to language and social interaction in some fashion. And just as food communicates like language, so does language bear some semblance to food for many of us. Ideas and their communication to others are conceptualized similarly: *food for thought, raw facts, half-baked ideas, stew over that, spoon-feed our students* (Lakoff and Johnson 1980:46–47). In a nutshell, these idioms liken language and communication to food in terms of how they may nourish—or poison—our minds and communities.

Let's begin by contemplating the connections between language, culture, and thought, an enduring topic in the anthropological study of language. Central to this topic is the notion of **linguistic relativity,** also known as the   7.1

Sapir-Whorf hypothesis because it refers to the collective ideas of Edward Sapir (1884–1939) and his student Benjamin Lee Whorf (1897–1941), both of whom were influenced by the pioneering ideas of American anthropologist Franz Boas (1858–1942). In simplified terms, the Sapir-Whorf hypothesis suggests that the habitual or regular use of language influences the way its speakers view the world, thereby influencing and reinforcing the worldview of their culture. Language, which is highly patterned and conventionalized, mediates between nature and human thought and thus between the physical world and how human beings understand that physical world (see the discussion of semiotic mediation in Chapter 1). As Whorf stated,

> We dissect nature along lines laid down by our native languages. The categories and types that we isolate from the world of phenomena we do not find there because they stare every observer in the face; on the contrary, the world is presented in a kaleidoscopic flux of impressions which has to be organized by our minds—and this means largely by the linguistic systems of our minds.
>
> (Carroll 1956:213)

Language, thought, and culture are so deeply interlocked that each language is associated with a somewhat distinctive worldview that is relatively different from that of the speakers of other languages (see also our discussion of cultural relativism in Chapter 3).

Since the work of Sapir and Whorf, many researchers have accepted that there is some degree of influence of language on thought, and some have even accepted a fairly strong version of the hypothesis saying that language actually *determines* the way we think (**linguistic determinism**). According to this deterministic view, linguistic forms precede and govern thought. However, this point is controversial and can be challenged in various ways. For instance, much of the world speaks more than one language, so do speakers switch worldviews every time they switch languages? Additionally, translations from one language to another are possible even if it takes more words to express what is captured in a single word in the other language (**circumlocution**). Finally, there appear to be various non-verbal forms of thought (artistic, directional) so that if a word does not exist in a language to match those non-verbal thoughts, its speakers can create a word or borrow from another language to express the new concept or talk about the new object.

Nonetheless, there is some indication that the differences encoded in dissimilar languages through such things as **lexicon** (vocabulary), **grammatical categories** (such as tense, plurality, gender, etc.), and **idioms** (figurative expressions that frequently rest on metaphoric thinking through which one thing is understood in terms of another) may prompt their speakers to pay attention to different aspects of reality even though this operation is largely unconscious. How we use words may impact what we pay attention to, highlighting some aspects of reality—objects, experiences, relationships— over others. In terms of foodways, our language and culture help to define what counts as food through the terms we use, how we can count and measure it (pinches, handfuls, pints, quarts, gallons, ounces, milliliters, liters, bunches, some, a few . . .), how we can describe its taste and functions, and what we compare and equate it to using metaphors.

When we transfer meaning from one domain of experience to another through metaphoric thinking, meaning may be transferred as well through 7.2 the process of linguistic analogy. In Cameroon, for example, conservation efforts and the deterring of illegal game hunting at Korup National Park are complicated by the long-time use of the Cameroonian Pidgin English term *bif* ("beef") to refer to wild animals, such as *chukuchuku bif* for the brush-tailed porcupine and *watah bif* for the water chevrotain (Dr. Joshua Linder, James Madison University, personal communication). By linguistically classifying them as food, it may be easier to treat them as such.

Bruner and Meek (2011) make a similar point about seafood, critically assessing public discourses and the rhetorical strategies of organizations such as Seafood Watch that are concerned about overfishing, fishing-related environmental damage, and the health of the world's waterways. The authors find that the terms used in such discourses encode assump- 7.3 tions that need questioning: "seafood" assumes that ocean life is there for us to eat, "sustainable harvesting" assumes that humans have the right and benevolence to be good stewards, and awe-inspiring imagery of "limitless" oceans makes it hard to see and act on the actual limits. Other impersonal terms such as "bycatch," used to refer to animals unintentionally caught up and discarded by commercial fishing because they lack market value, allow for the displacement of responsibility for the killing off of as much as one-quarter of all the sea life caught in this way.

Food-related conceptual metaphors can even help sustain cultural inequalities. Hines (1999), for instance, analyzes "woman as dessert" metaphors used in everyday life, such as "tart," "cookie," and "cupcake." These pervasive linguistic expressions, Hines argues, both reflect and sustain sexism, and the idea of women as sexualized objects. These examples, like the idioms at the start of this section, need analysis for how people 7.4 may act in relation to the associations made between one area of life and another.

Language Learning: Nature, Nurture, and Language as Food

If we consider food as something that can sustain us and help us to grow and thrive, and we speak of language using similar terms, do we then evaluate language for its nourishing properties and look down upon ways of

"Stop loafing around! Your brain will turn to toast!"

Figure 7.1 Feeding our brains

communicating that do not match our own "healthful" ways? If language is "food for thought," will our minds starve and fail to thrive without it? Does language shape and sustain the mind, making up thought and world-view, as food does for the physical body?

"Nourishing" Models of Language Acquisition

7.5

Research has shown that all normally developing human children are capable of learning language and will learn one or more of them if exposed to them early enough. In other words, regardless of where and when a normally developing child grows up, they will begin using a linguistic code as long as they are somehow involved as observers of and/or participants in actual social interaction in their communities. Rare cases of children not being exposed to language during the **critical period** for language acquisition (approximately age 0–10), such as the severely abused Genie (Curtiss 1977), demonstrate that irrespective of any innately human biological predilection for language, some form of engagement in social interaction from early on in life is necessary for language learning. But the human brain's potential for acquiring and using language does not require that this social interaction happen primarily with adult caregivers or teachers; in many societies, children play a very active role in developing and transmitting the language(s) of their adult community to their peers and younger siblings. In fact, as anyone who has ever learned a play language such as Pig Latin or a form of youthspeak knows, children and youth are adept at creating new codes among themselves as well. For example, in Nicaragua, young deaf children began to develop their own sign language out of some rudimentary signs they had learned at home because they could not obtain sufficient linguistic nourishment in the classroom, where hearing teachers tried (largely unsuccessfully) to teach written and spoken Spanish via lip reading (Senghas and Coppola 2001).

7.6

It seems in many ways, then, as if language acts like food for our social brains. But just as diets range considerably across cultures, so are there different pathways for the acquisition of language. For example, across many social groups, adults alter their language when interacting with infants and young children in what has been called **babytalk** or child-directed speech (also known as "motherese" or "parentese"). Babytalk registers are characterized by varying degrees of grammatical simplification (*Baby want up?*), special vocabulary (*wawa* for water in English, *namnam* for food in Moroccan Arabic, *caca/kaka* for excrement in many languages from Spanish to Yiddish), and high-pitch prosodic features in many cultures (Ferguson 1964). As a result, some scholars have hypothesized that babytalk is beneficial or even a universal prerequisite for language acquisition, the assumption being that it is easier to "digest" than fully-formed language (e.g., Snow and Ferguson 1977; Gathercole and Hoff 2007). However, testing of this hypothesis tends to be based on data collected in laboratory settings with Euro-American middle-class subjects and does not account for cross-cultural documentation that caregivers in naturalistic settings interact in diverse ways with their infants and small children.

Language socialization studies have, in fact, demonstrated that babytalk is not universal and have helped undermine the assumption that language must in some sense be baby-fed, that is, that a modified form of language is necessary for language acquisition (Solomon 2012). Instead, language socialization research considers how children learn both language and culture as interrelated processes; in other words, children are socialized through language as they are socialized to use language, playing active roles in such processes. Studies of language socialization have focused on linguistic and cultural learning across various societies and contexts (see Duranti, Ochs, and Schieffelin 2012 for a taste of the breadth of this work).

For instance, Ochs and Schieffelin (1984) illustrated variations in communicative accommodation to language-learning children ranging from child-centered to situation-centered approaches in Anglo-American, Kaluli in Papua New Guinea, and Samoan caregiving interactions. In comparing these three "developmental stories" they demonstrated that the kind of babytalk register identified among white middle-class American families was not universal. Kaluli caregivers did not grammatically simplify language to children, as this simplification was considered to inhibit language acquisition (Schieffelin 1990). Caregivers studied by Ochs (1988) in stratified Samoan society did not employ a babytalk register either, but for different reasons. For Samoans, grammatical simplification and social accommodation is appropriate for high-ranking addressees and not for children. Local ideas about child rearing and expectations of children influence how children are engaged in social interactions, including to what extent adults and other experts modify their language use and believe that they need to "feed" children language (Paugh 2012a).

In a series of studies in the United States in the 1980s and 2000s, Ochs and her collaborators documented in fine-grained detail the ways in which **narrative competence**, communicative skills, and family beliefs and values are transmitted through mealtime conversation in middle-class American families (e.g., Ochs, Smith, and Taylor 1989; Ochs and Taylor 1992; Ochs and Kremer-Sadlik 2013). They suggest that everyday conversational narrative among family members while sharing food helps to constitute the family and construct family roles and relationships, giving shape to common values and understandings of the world and aiding family members in reflecting on happenings in their daily lives. This creates a context for probing problematic events, planning for the future, and cultivating theory-building skills among family members. Through such dinnertime co-narration, children are socialized to fill in missing pieces of stories through requesting details and more context, often leading to a reanalysis of the narrative. These "detective stories at dinnertime" aid children in the development of problem-solving and theory-building skills according to local cultural conventions that are valued (and in turn tested) in mainstream educational settings, thus preparing them for success in American society (Ochs, Smith, and Taylor 1989; Ochs et al. 1992). Everyday commensality in these families thus plays an important part in establishing the family, solidifying familial values, and socializing the next generation (Ochs and Shohet 2006).

Less Sustaining Models of Language Development

What becomes problematic is when certain patterns of communicating with children are held up as the "proper" model or institutional standard, thereby disparaging other ways of interacting as incorrect and lacking by comparison. Heath (1982, 1983) examined three communities in the Piedmont, North Carolina, and demonstrated how middle-class American strategies of reading and engaging with bedtime stories, including encouraging children to elaborate on and associate stories with their daily lives, facilitated the development of a school-based model that helped middle-class children succeed in school, in contrast to children from working-class and ethnic minority families that did not engage in literacy events in such ways. One of Heath's key points, however, was that the different strategies employed in all three communities cultivated valuable skills (such as analytic thinking and speaking) that were of importance in the wider society. But it was the way those skills were defined in schools in terms of specific communicative genres (labeling colors or show-and-tell presentations) and tested using specific question-and-answer routines that contributed to the reproduction of class differences in society in general (see also Bourdieu and Passeron 1990[1970]). All three communities had rich verbal environments that sustained certain interpretations of the world through language, but only some of those skills were prioritized in schools, at least in the early grades. Children from white and black working-class families were positioned as lacking, rendering their problems encountered at school as incomprehensible and them as responsible for the maintenance of their own second-class status.

Cross-cultural research demonstrates that the varied ways in which children learn language and different communicative strategies help them to become communicatively competent in their social groups. However, when a mismatch occurs between home and educational settings, "differences" are often conceptualized as "deficits." Such issues continue in the United States, as seen in contemporary debates about the impact of socioeconomic class on educational achievement. Some assert that wealthier families provide richer linguistic environments for their children whereas children living in poverty acquire quantitatively fewer words or less language which creates a lifetime deficit for these children (Hart and Risley 2003). These "language gap" or "word gap" discourses (Avineri et al. 2015) are widespread as evidenced by the quote from *The Atlantic* with which we started this chapter. Here Lahey (2014) likens vocabulary to food, as if some ideal 2,000-calorie-a-day diet could be applied to words and prescribed to parents, thus resolving a far heavier set of societal inequities. The problems with this logic are multiple (see also Paugh and Riley, forthcoming).

7.7

First of all, measuring how many words a child hears during the day is fundamentally different from counting food calories; while science tells us that we need particular proportions of different kinds of foods each day, nouns and verbs cannot be so easily correlated with food groups, nor are they served up in the same ways. To the contrary, social interaction requires a much more nuanced set of nutrients as so much depends on context and function. Think of how we learn through observation and experience to vary the ways we use language for both effect and appropriateness across modes (spoken/signed versus written), levels of formality, and relations of social intimacy and distance. As Cameron (2012) makes clear with her notion of **verbal hygiene**, it may be detrimental to one's academic success to use **textese** (the abbreviated style used for writing texts, full of emoticons and acronyms) when writing a paper, but one may be equally handicapped if unable to use informal youthspeak with one's peers.

Furthermore, because difference is being misinterpreted as deficiency, teachers, school administrators, and educational policy makers are missing the chance to honor, learn from, and build on the alternative ways of semiotically interacting with the world that are taught in the child's home and home culture. Instead, many untested programs have been implemented to teach parents how to speak "properly" (in societally approved ways) to their children in the home, asking them to perform linguistically in ways they have no experience with and to suppress the forms of language socialization they have learned from their own upbringing that may have many nutrient-rich benefits unrecognized by the Western educational system (Zentella 2005; Johnson and Zentella 2017). Discourses that assume that language can be so easily classified, quantified, and (de)valued can poison as much as, or more than, nourish the families and communities these discourses are designed to help.

In fact, some widespread ways of speaking that are viewed as helpful to language learning may even do more harm than good in certain contexts. For example, researchers investigating autism as a communicative disorder have found that although certain babytalk features are considered beneficial for some social groups, they can be problematic for autistic children's linguistic and social development (Ochs, Solomon, and Sterponi 2005; Solomon 2012). Other studies suggest that anxiety disorders such as agoraphobia, a fear and avoidance of situations that might cause panic or embarrassment, can be discursively transmitted across the generations through everyday storytelling (Capps and Ochs 1995). Even "normal" narratives at the family dinner table can pose risks as well as benefits. Although middle-class American children are socialized by mealtime storytelling into narrative competence, an analytic and communicative skill that is highly valued in schools, they may also attempt to avoid such tale-telling at the table, especially when they and their actions are regularly targeted for familial evaluation and moral assessment (Blum-Kulka 1997; Ochs and Taylor 1992; Ochs and Capps 2001). Additionally, a persistent concern and anxiety about the future may be socialized among children who overhear and participate in their parents' work narratives at the dinner table when adults engage in extensive speculations about the ramifications of work happenings and decisions from the past and those as yet unrealized (Paugh 2012b).

Thus, there is no single way of using language with children that is necessarily right or always nourishing in all societies and contexts. Nonetheless, some forms of social interaction are empowered and privileged over others, creating disparities between home and institutional expectations. Such disparities can have significant implications for educational outcomes, therapeutic interventions, and children's futures. Like children's socialization into language, their language socialization into foodways is also shaped by interaction and subject to ideological standards and evaluations.

Food-and-Language Socialization Across Cultures

Given that human children are dependent upon their caregivers for food, it is not surprising that these caregivers exhibit, model, and sometimes explicitly teach a range of linguistic strategies and behaviors that involve more than simply naming the comestibles that children ought to eat. Food-focused interactions are a key site for the cultural and linguistic transmission and transformation of food-related practices and ideologies as well as culture, language, and worldview more generally.

Mealtime, as a culturally organized and habitual act with discernible patterns, provides a relatively accessible context for researchers to examine

Figure 7.2 Child asks questions while watching mother prepare food in Dominica, Caribbean

Credit: Photo by Amy L. Paugh

and record interactions around, about, and through food that involve neophytes.[1] For some families, the meal becomes "an event occasioning sociability through conversation" (Blum-Kulka 1997:35). For others, talk around food may be mostly instrumental having to do with the dinner itself (passing the food, getting missing items for the table, etc.), such as in the rural French family in Margaret Mead's (1959) film *Four Families*, where talk at the family dinner entailed more activity than conversation. And, as discussed in Chapter 6, some groups prefer silence during a meal. Regardless of the quantity or type, talk about and around food is regularly about more than just physical sustenance. Children are also being figuratively fed ideologies and strategies for negotiating social interaction and relationships with others, and yet they may not swallow all of it wholesale. They may also transform those ideologies and practices through their own creative activities, thus contributing to larger processes of generational change.

From table manners to cultural classifications of food, food-and-language socialization interactions display and transmit culturally acceptable and unacceptable ways of communicating around and about food as a material object. Eating involves use of multimodal resources like verbal and non-verbal communication, use of body and posture (body placement

7.8

Figure 7.3 Family eating rice with hands in India (© Shutterstock)

vis-à-vis food, sitting up versus slouching, etc.), manipulation of food, and the serving of items. Differences abound in terms of cultural variations in appropriate topics for discussion, acceptable discourse genres (talking, joking, singing, etc.), level of formality (use of tablecloths, formal registers of talk, etc.), and rules for consumption and food sharing (burping, talking with food in one's mouth, speed of eating, taking from others' food, etc.) during the meal. For example, Blum-Kulka (1997) found that money, sex, and politics were not discussed around children at the table in Israeli and Jewish-American families. And these routine ways of feeling, thinking, and behaving are ingested deeply (along with the food), embodied, and reenacted, taking on an unconscious and powerful sense of *rightness* that Bourdieu refers to as habitus (as discussed in Chapters 1 and 4).

Food-and-language socialization occurs through direct instruction about such things via assessments, error corrections, directives, and so on, as well as through more indirect acts, such as the use of irony, inference, and silence during common mealtime genres ranging from prayer to conversational storytelling to other discursive activities about and around food. Participants interactionally construct and evaluate one another's food preferences and aversions, building normative expectations through both alignment and contestation. Researchers thus attend to participants' choice in language or language variety, their interactional patterns, and other habitual actions.

Learning to Exchange Food and Talk in the Pacific

Early language socialization research uncovered some key links between language and food in everyday life, even though this was not necessarily the focus. First of all, linguistic strategies are needed simply to access food, and these must be learned not only by children but also by other newcomers to a community. Riley (2016), for example, did not set out to study food-and-language socialization among Marquesan children, but was led to this once she realized that she did not know enough about how to use language to feed herself in the field. After arriving in French Polynesia for her first bout of fieldwork, she struggled with food insecurity in a culture where provisions are obtained through social relationships of various kinds. Like a child, she had to learn social rules for procuring, preparing, and consuming foods appropriately. All of these activities required engaging in talk and learning how to interact, first through local teasing routines that gave way to gifts of food and invitations to meals by adopted "kin." Once she became enmeshed in local social networks, her Marquesan hosts fed her both food and language.

Indeed, food procuring, preparing, sharing, and eating practices emerged as the primary socialization context for studying how children learned the cultural and linguistic beliefs and practices in Schieffelin's (1990) seminal research in Papua New Guinea. Her fine-grained analysis demonstrates how Kaluli (now referred to as Bosavi) children learned to negotiate the giving and sharing of food, and thus negotiate their social relationships. These Kaluli children were socialized not only to understand how to gather, garden, hunt, and prepare food at home and in the bush but also about who could eat what and how they could successfully ask for it. Much of this depended on contrasting social characteristics having to do with age, gender, and kinship status. For the egalitarian Kaluli, especially at this moment in history when missionaries and government administrators had only begun to make inroads into their traditional practices, reciprocity and exchange were key concerns and one needed to know how to appeal for food, but also how to assert oneself when necessary. Local theories of child rearing held that children are born helpless and already know how to appeal for food, as was evidenced by their early use of whining and begging (making others "feel sorry for" them). Children also showed their desire for food non-verbally by staring at it, or "asking with their eyes" (1990:152). This non-verbal begging was considered culturally inappropriate, and children were encouraged to verbally and directly ask for food.

It was up to caregivers, particularly mothers, to socialize assertiveness and independence in their children. A common instructional routine involved prompting children to repeat caregivers' assertions using the directive ɛlɛma "say like this"; for example, a child would repeat the phrase modeled by the caregiver to demand food from another person and to respond to the appeals of others, thus learning both to give but also to protect what was theirs when necessary. In other words, while food sharing held very high importance, so did knowing when and how to refuse to share. When Kaluli children began to use language in an assertive way, they became potential givers and could be asked to share food that they had been given by others. Caregivers used these ɛlɛma or say-it routines to encourage children's proper participation in ways that both helped them get food but also, importantly, taught them to build social relationships through (reciprocated) sharing. Older children socialized younger ones as well using strategies of appeal and assertion, often putting verbal pressure on younger children to share. This concern with sharing and reciprocity was reinforced through the action of sharing food but also articulated in verbal genres ranging from formal songs and myths to mundane negotiations over giving.

Schieffelin also demonstrated the socialization of age- and gender-appropriate behaviors through food interactions among the otherwise egalitarian Kaluli. For example, various food taboos dealt directly with language in that consuming certain foods could delay or prevent children's social and linguistic development. Children could not eat fruit pigeons, owls, and bats due to their negative impact on language learning—infant babbling is too close to the noises that flying creatures perform. Similarly, they were not allowed to eat various soft foods because developing into a full-fledged Kaluli person required a careful hardening process. Such food taboos marked age differences and hierarchy in a society that otherwise did not strongly delineate age categories.

With respect to gender, Schieffelin's food-and-language socialization research was even more revealing. To begin with, girls were taught early on to grow yams and collect lizards, while boys were directed toward hunting, fishing, and processing sago. Even the earliest feeding interactions like breastfeeding were gendered. For instance, when male infants bit the breast while nursing, mothers playfully removed them from the breast before putting them back on, beginning a teasing frame that continued and was expanded upon as the boys grew. Female infants, by contrast, were removed from the breast and reoriented toward some other activity, suggesting that feeding and playing did not mix, and that aggressive acts would not be tolerated for girls. Further, mothers gave more attention and food, especially meat, to their sons than to their daughters. Girls were socialized to offer food and objects to others, especially younger siblings, while boys were taught to make more requests in a particularly plaintive voice. Caregivers cultivated a special relationship between older sisters and younger brothers (they were taught to refer to each other as *adɛ*), and girls were socialized to take pity on and share food with their younger brothers. Kaluli myths highlight this relationship and the importance of food sharing to help constitute it, such as a story about a boy who turned into a bird when his sister refused to share food with him (1990:113). Appeals were rarely refused in the context of this relationship throughout life.

Dinnertime Socialization in the United States and Europe

As discussed in the last chapter, mealtime discourse was the primary focus in a number of other language socialization studies of largely urban, middle-class families in the United States and Europe. This research considers both how families communicate about and around food, but also what such interactions transmit about personhood, family, and "healthy" versus "unhealthy" eating practices. For example, in a foundational comparative study, Ochs, Pontecorvo, and Fasulo (1996) explored the socialization of "taste" among 20 middle-class families in Italy and the United States. They contrasted what Bourdieu (1984) called the **taste of necessity** and **taste of luxury/freedom** as manifested in the ways these families talked about food with their children. All the families discursively oriented toward food as a material good and as providing nutrition (taste of necessity) while also giving pleasure and serving as a reward (taste of freedom). Both sets of families were concerned with not wasting food—as a material good with a moral obligation, like a contractual relationship, to consume what one takes—and its role in nourishing the children. And parents in both studies offered nutrition lessons, often using an authoritative scientific register, such as the bodily need for "protein" and "leafy greens."

There were, however, cross-cultural differences, with Italian families prioritizing food as pure pleasure over other qualities, while American families gave higher priority to food as nutrition and reward, with less attention to pleasure. Italian families spent much more time discussing what both adults and children *want* to eat, with discussion of the pleasures of the process, such as planning, obtaining, and preparing food. In contrast, American families focused on what children *must* eat in order to get what they *want* to eat—a sweet dessert as a reward for finishing the required elements of the rest of the meal and a conditional pleasure that could be withdrawn if parental requirements were not satisfied. In American meals, it was also the dessert that was most positively marked, with little acknowledgement or acceptance of individual tastes and preferences regarding what was served for dinner. Italian meals, in comparison, were linguistically peppered throughout with positive affect markers (diminutives, intensifiers, refined adjectives, etc.) and discussion of how good foods tasted, with individual taste preferences considered an important component of one's personality and acceptable to be expressed. Ochs and colleagues suggest that these different ways of socializing taste contributed to more of a generational divide between American parents and their children, and much less of one for their counterparts in Italy. Interestingly, Blum-Kulka (1997) also found that Jewish Americans spoke about health-related concerns, including health foods, whereas such concerns were absent in dinner talk among Israeli families in Israel.

Further exploring such themes, Paugh and Izquierdo (2009) analyzed dinnertime interactions as well as health-focused interviews among five families involved in the UCLA CELF study (see Chapters 2 and 6) for how middle-class American families conceived of health and well-being, and managed food related conflicts and socialized strategies of negotiation over eating practices and individual autonomy. Interactional bargaining played a key role in parent-child struggles over health-related practices, values, and morality, and contributed to many parents feeling like they were not quite getting it right in transmitting "healthy" eating habits to their children. In fact, families explicitly blamed themselves for what they regarded as their children's unhealthy food consumption practices. Battles emerged over what a child "should" eat versus what they "want" to eat, how much a child needed to eat from their plate or when they needed to stop eating, and how they could work sweet treats into the meal (such as mixing a special French berry lemonade with parentally required milk to get both reward and nutrition at the same time!). These negotiations were both about food and about parental authority, individual responsibility, and control. Parents themselves struggled to "model" ideal health

Figure 7.4 Mealtime negotiations (© Shutterstock)

practices, thereby demonstrating for children the practical and moral challenges they also grappled with over what, how, and when to eat in contemporary American society.

Kremer-Sadlik et al. (2015) also studied mealtime talk in eight of the
CELF families in Los Angeles, but compared these to a complementary   7.9
study of dinners among eight French families in Paris, France. They examined how meals were organized: when and what foods were served, how
many courses, the prioritization of particular foods over others, and how
parents socialized children through mealtime talk around and about food
into fruit and vegetable consumption. They found that French meals,
served in several courses, emphasized fruits and vegetables such that children were noticed and held accountable for avoiding them. By contrast,
American families not only served fewer fruits but also served all foods
at once, so that children were able to pick and choose what they wanted,
avoiding the vegetables as well as the oversight of their parents, and thus
passed as compliant. Further, parents in the French households focused on
the taste, pleasure, and preparation of foods, whereas American parents
highlighted nutrition over taste (mirroring Ochs, Pontecorvo, and Fasulo's
findings about Italian and American families, discussed above). Kremer-
Sadlik and colleagues suggest that public health initiatives to increase the
consumption of fruits and vegetables need to take into account these different organizational and interactional frames.

Food can nourish but also be brought to bear as a discursive "weapon" or "threat" for manipulating others' actions (e.g., you'll get this food if you eat that one, you won't get dessert if you don't behave), leading to family disputes and intergenerational tensions. Dinnertime talk can socialize children into argumentative discourses and contradictory health ideologies, as well as into practices indexing inequalities and hierarchies according to age, gender, and rank. When dominated by negotiations over food, there may be no room during dinner conversation for other forms of social interaction such as stories about past and future events or for modeling ways to talk about emotions and concerns. Mealtime interactional dynamics, particularly the negotiation of control, may even play a role in the socialization of eating disorders such as anorexia and compulsive overeating (Ochs and Shohet 2006).

Vignette 7.1   Parin Dossa: Two Transnational Food Narratives

Parin Dossa teaches anthropology at Simon Fraser University and is the author of Afghanistan Remembers: Gendered Narrations of Violence and Culinary Practices *(2014).*

Rotli *(Unleavened Bread)*

An image that stands out from my early childhood experience is that of *rotli* (unleavened bread) that my mother served us on our return from school. My two siblings and I savored the taste of hot *rotlis* sprinkled with ghee. My reminiscence of *rotli* occurs in the diaspora that for me is a ruptured experience expressed poignantly through the medium of food. It is through this medium that I sought to make sense of my experience being rendered a refugee as part of the 1971 Ugandan South Asian exodus. In Canada, the host country, *rotli* is not consumed every day as was the common practice in my homeland. As I tried to understand the implication of this shift from a popular item to that of a rare one, several issues came to mind. First, the Gujarati (my mother tongue) term for *rotli* connotes abundance as *rotli* is made in batches and rarely as one piece. Its plurality connotes its consumption in a world of social relationships of kin and kith. *Rotlis* are consumed and prepared for more than one person. A different situation prevails in the Canadian diaspora with its orientation towards nuclear family units. If *rotlis* were to "speak," below is the story they would relay in the singular mode:

7.10

> *There was a time when I had a place on a table full of people and a presence as part of other food dishes, especially my companion,*

the curry. It gave me a good feeling that I satisfied so many people. I remember being kneaded into a dough and divided into small portions by a nurturing hand. I was then rolled into round shapes and roasted on a special pan called tawdhi *(clay pan). The pan was reserved for myself only. Now that I have crossed the border into another country, my pan sits alone in the corner of a kitchen shelf, its use limited to once or twice a week. I feel good when once in a while my nurturer makes 20* rotlis *that are distributed to her children. They take me to their homes but they do not consume me right away when I am fresh and desirable. They put me in the freezer, an unpleasant experience that I never had before. When they are ready to include me in their meal, they put me in a microwave. Freezing cold to very hot in a matter of minutes. Sometimes I find myself in the microwave twice when the children are late for a meal owing to the busyness of their lives. When the parents eat alone, I feel their loneliness. They do not enjoy me as much when the children are not present. I am no longer whole as I once was. I am able to express myself in language only because of my experience of rupture. I no longer exist in a house full of people who would relish me. My experience of being frozen, alone, and isolated enables me to put into words my feelings of being cut off from the world I once knew intimately.*

Eating With My Hands

I eat with my hands partly to maintain a homeland tradition and for health reasons; this is an Ayurvedic practice that enhances the process of digestion through slow eating. On one occasion, when my 10-year-old grandson was visiting on a Sunday, he asked why I eat with my hands. His tone of voice and body language indicated that he did not approve of this "archaic" practice. Ordinarily, I would have been able to explain to him how important it is not to let go cherished homeland practices and values just because these may not be publicly validated in Canada. I wished to explain to him that food constitutes an important part of our identity; it embodies symbolic, social, and cultural dimensions. I reminded him of his father's struggles when he was looked down upon for taking "South Asian" food for lunch.

It bothers me that I could not provide any kind of explanation as to the reason why I ate with my hands. Words failed me because I did not think that my grandson would understand what I had to say. Our worldviews are markedly different. My grandson has not been exposed to my mother tongue, which was undermined during the process of colonization of Uganda. English was the official language. Even the indigenous language of Kiswahili was not given official status. Further, the practice of eating with hands requires experiential understanding of its benefits and this would take time. I could not put into words what was essentially a sensual experience of using five fingers to put food into my mouth as opposed to using fork and knife. I am not suggesting that there are no points of convergence. However, in the fast-paced life of "McDonaldization," I did not think that we had a common language and grammar of food that I could use. Hence, I settled for silence.

Consuming Food, Talk, and Morality

Social interactions around and about food can construct not only eating practices and food attitudes, but also our relationships with others and our overarching moral codes. These processes are highlighted in the research of Sally Wiggins and colleagues, who suggest that eating should be viewed as "an interactional practice rather than an individual behavior" (Wiggins, Potter, and Wildsmith 2001:13; also see Laurier and Wiggins 2011). This discursive psychology approach challenges studies that rely primarily on elicitation of attitudes toward food and eating outside of situated interactions. Wiggins (2004), for example, analyzed audio-recorded mealtime interactions in 10 families in the north and midland areas of England, focusing on advice and other talk about the nutritional content of food. She identified two types of "healthy eating talk" during dinnertime: "general advice giving" that generically discussed why food is or is not healthy, and talk "focusing on the individual" that held a particular person accountable for their food choices and mealtime practices. An important point that emerged is that talk focusing on the specific eating practices of an individual may implicitly evaluate the individual's tastes and character. As in other examples described here, negative evaluations of food and food choices can spill over into judgments of the moral quality of the person, thereby impacting the experience of eating, creating interactional (mis)alignments with family members, and shaping participants' self-perceptions.

Experiences of food are to some extent interactionally co-constructed by those who eat together. In another study, Wiggins (2014) asks how children acquire the concepts, emotions, and verbal and facial expressions associated with **disgust**—a visceral and moral response to food contamination (fecal, animal, sexual, socially immoral)—by contrast with **distaste**—a sensory rejection of food. Using data collected by parents at home with preschoolers in England and Scotland, she has analyzed the everyday enactments of disgust by preschoolers and their caregivers' responses. She found, first of all, that caregivers modeled with *eugh* what they believed to be really disgusting, such as sucking on a rubber glove, and did not object to children's expressions of disgust to such objects. However, they were more likely to ignore, chuckle, or scold children for attention-getting or impolite performances of *yuck*. Children, as a result, tended to eat the foods deemed non-disgusting by their caregivers. Parents thus played an important role in socializing disgust and the ways of expressing it.

Discussions about food can become a prime site for the socialization not only of culturally specific eating habits and tastes but also notions of morality, individualism, relationships, pleasure, and consumption. Aronsson and Gottzén (2011) considered the socialization of food morality in a case study of eight Swedish middle-class families. They identified four features of food morality monitored by parents, and sometimes siblings, in the families: 1) appropriate bodily comportment and table manners; 2) following sequential rules, such as finishing something before getting more; 3) discouragement of the expression of disgust or revulsion toward foods on the table; and 4) regulation of the intake of sweets and of overeating. These food moralities were constructed and transmitted via generational positions and alignments taken up in the ongoing social interaction. In other words, they could be upheld or challenged through the ways in which a person positioned themselves or was positioned by others as a child or as an adult (such as through "childish" versus "mature" food practices) and through the ways they aligned with others in their own generation (sibling alignments, parental alignments) or across generations. Ideas about family and childhood, then, are constructed through these positionings and alignments, combined with the management of affective stances toward foods during dinner talk. Providing a detailed analysis of a single dinner in one family, they demonstrated how children could variably support and oppose their parents' food ideologies and expectations for dinnertime comportment. For example, an elder 10-year-old brother in this family alternately positioned himself as an "adult" by assuming the role of caretaker and educator of food morality for his five-year-old sibling, and as a "child" by being a playmate to that younger sibling. Thus, once again, we see how much more than etiquette and understandings about food are socialized through language use with others while in the presence of food.

In another example of how food and morality are jointly socialized, Krögel (2009) analyzed how Quechua oral narratives in Southern Peru utilized food symbolism to reinforce cultural expectations of kinship and community bonds and impart such moral knowledge to children. In four oral narratives that Krögel examined, narrators described characters who violated food-related taboos and were punished by cooks using culinary witchcraft. These domestic narratives were usually told by women in household or community settings while engaged in food-related tasks, frequently with children present, and thus served as both moral lessons and entertainment related to food. A woman, for example, left her natal home and then rejected the food offered by her family as they tried to bring her back home. By disrespecting her family and culture, she faced certain doom. Other stories described scorned wives serving their husbands adulterated meals, strangers violating local food decorum, and mothers taking revenge on wayward sons through food. In this case, language as food and as a tool of socialization took the form of cautionary tales to younger generations about what happens when people break food taboos and kinship obligations.

Language through, about, and around food, then, can be used to shore up moral codes that have been challenged. It is also a key means for identity construction according to ideas about similarity and difference: "we" eat this way while "they" eat that way. Social interactions about food and language socialize and give authenticity to cultural, familial, ethnic, and national identities. They also can undermine other identities in the process, and be impacted by larger sociocultural, political, generational, and migratory changes. This occurs especially in institutional settings.

Socializing Foodways, Discourses, and Identities at School

The ramifications of the powerful discursive connections between food and identity become visible in institutional settings such as schools. This is of particular consequence in that disparities in authority and power between adults and children are amplified, as in the teacher-student relationship, while different cultural, linguistic, and culinary practices may clash in the classroom as well as in the lunchroom, breakroom, and contexts involving snacks and celebratory foods. Teachers and administrators make decisions and comment on children's food practices, while children themselves discuss and share (or do not share) foods with peers, demonstrating preferences and dislikes for both food and the people indexed by their foodways. Food practices and knowledge, including cultural ideologies and discourses about the relation of food/food types to health, are socialized in the school setting as well as in the home.

7.11   In an ethnically diverse primary school in Denmark, for example, Karrebæk (2012, 2013a, 2013b) demonstrated the stigmatization of immigrant identities in teacher-student and peer interactions about food choices—especially what non-Danish children carried to school in their lunch boxes. Teachers adopted authoritative health Discourses as they evaluated the lunch box contents and made comments to students. In order to be good students and demonstrate respectability, minority children were expected to assimilate to the dominant food culture and health registers of the school by bringing in acceptable foods like rye bread that indexed perceived

Figure 7.5 School children at lunch in a cafeteria (© Shutterstock)

healthiness but also an authentic Danish national heritage. They were also expected to hide their disgust with pork, an iconically Dutch food, which challenged the halal norms that the Muslim children were learning in the home. Children in school thereby acquired food-related ideas and practices, but also understandings about citizenship, inclusion and exclusion, and minority-majority relations through lunchtime discourse. Given the potency of both food and language to index identity, Karrebæk (2012:2) even suggests that "it is minority-majority relations rather than just food, nutrition, and health that are negotiated at the lunch table."

Karrebæk (2014) explores such issues further by analyzing how teachers pour on messages about healthy drinks (milk versus water versus juice) via analytic activities, such as having students create healthy/unhealthy placemats, and practice-based activities, such as serving milk at snack and lunch. However, these health-related messages were not always clear, such as when a teacher confused a child who was trying to figure out whether fruit-flavored yogurt and cream belonged on the healthy side of the placemat or not. Sometimes they could be culturally pejorative, for example, telling a non-Danish child to instruct his parents that juice is not healthy because it has too much sugar, implying their parenting is inadequate because they sent him to school with it. When among their peers, the children demonstrated their preferences for "unhealthy foods," but when engaged in school activities, they would orient toward (and pressure each other toward accepting) the hegemonic "healthy food" Discourses, such as milk over water. They thereby performed "good student" behavior and excluded minority students for not following these rules, such as sanctioning a non-Danish child for drinking full-fat milk rather than reduced-fat milk.

7.12

Vignette 7.2   Martha Karrebæk: Making Meaning With Rye Bread in Denmark

Martha Karrebæk is an Associate Professor in the Department of Nordic Studies and Linguistics at the University of Copenhagen, Denmark.

I stumbled into the field of food and language by accident. As a linguist recently turned sociolinguist I was trained to focus on language and had never thought about the richness of the discourse-and-food intersection until my fieldwork in a kindergarten classroom in Copenhagen, Denmark. I had set out to analyze how language use is organized and regimented in a linguistically and culturally heterogeneous classroom in an educational system that is generally, and officially, regarded as monolingual and monocultural. Yet, I was confronted daily with the teachers' public celebrations of food characterized as "healthy" and an overwhelming preoccupation with food evaluated as "unhealthy," and thus inappropriate. Clearly, the educational agenda included food, and as food socialization happened through discourse, it was also a process of language socialization.

To give some context, in Denmark children generally bring lunch prepared by their parents to school. Traditionally, it consists of rye bread with various toppings (today also often accompanied by raw vegetables), but the rye bread has particular significance. Rye grain has been grown in the region since the Iron Age, and became, as rye bread, a dominant part of the daily diet. Even today, open rye bread sandwiches (*smørrebrød* 'butter(ed) bread') made it into the top 10 in a recent election of the national dish. In public health discourses, rye bread is promoted (very little fat, no added sugar, lots of fiber), and parents are advised to make their children eat it, regardless of its strong taste, which children may not like at first. In the classroom, the teachers adopted this discourse as part of their socialization to food understandings, especially in cases of deviation from classroom norms. When rye bread was "missing," teachers would ask the children to account for the lunch box contents: "Why didn't you bring rye bread?" or instruct them: "Remember to tell your mommy to give you rye bread." The ethnic bias in the practice was hard to miss as almost all children who brought "inappropriate" lunches had ethnic minority background. Not that the children necessarily brought food recognized as "ethnic," but they did not observe the rye bread norm and were made to feel responsible for the fact that their parents had a different understanding of an appropriate lunch box. In other words, rye bread is treated as a neutral, "healthy" food that is nonetheless being used as an ideological proxy in order to socialize children of immigrant background into "Danish" eating patterns and, implicitly, Danish identities. There were other issues, too. Pork and milk were similarly promoted by the teachers as indisputably "good" foods, something which is certainly arguable. Not the least, pork was a source of differentiation as the many Muslim children upheld a taboo against this type of meat. Such matters were never discussed by the teachers.

In Denmark, my research was met with raised eyebrows. "What's wrong with rye bread?" journalists asked me. I responded that there is nothing wrong with rye bread *per se*, but that there are wrong ways to use rye bread socially. Non-Danes with whom I have talked about this "rye bread obsession" tend to find it slightly laughable, but we know that assimilative pressures characterize many culturally heterogeneous classrooms. So, all communities have their rye bread, as food talk is used to feed children loaded ideas about morally correct, or nationally appropriate, practices, ways of life, and identities. Teaching children healthy eating patterns is a noble aim in a time and context where obesity and health-related diseases are becoming an increasing problem. However, health is not a culturally neutral phenomenon, and health education needs to be taken care of in culturally sensitive ways, which teachers need training to do.

Overall, this study taught me that we make statements about social alignment, identity, and cultural understandings through food choices and discourses about them. As a continuation of this, my recent work has expanded to include other settings in which people struggle to define what food is and who they are—in restaurants, food courts, and green grocers. I have continued to ask questions such as: What is Danish food to people in their everyday life? How do people engage with food through discourse? What work is food used to do? Health was in focus in the school setting, and in other places authenticity, high-quality, conviviality, fun, or creativity may be more important. Food and discourse lead one in many directions, but always into the core of how people create social meaning.

Riley's (forthcoming) research on food-and-language socialization in an independent school in New York City shows how both children and adults struggled over how to define "healthy" foods and how to educate children about them. Throughout the two years of the study, parents and teachers were locked in a pitched battle over what the school ought to be feeding the children and whether schools are the appropriate contexts for socializing ideologies about why healthy, sustainable, just, and culturally appropriate foods are valuable. On one side was the sustainable food camp, those who felt that these good foods and positive food values ought to be expected at an elite institution. On the other side was the freedom food camp, those who stridently voiced the opinion that this was just more evidence of the nanny state's attempt to undermine their children's freedom to choose foods that taste good by feeding them facts about environmental and personal health. Frequently, the teachers felt caught between their own preferences (at the level of both taste and politics) and the policies of the administrators that were trying to negotiate with the parents (on whose happiness and tuition dollars the school depended). As a result, they found themselves feeding the children mixed messages about who could choose what to eat when and why. Meanwhile, the children contributed their own ingredients to the food fight menu, digesting these messages in ways that were not always intended by staff or parents. For instance, while some squealed in a dining context: "Ugh, that looks healthy," others would insist, as they had been instructed: "Don't yuck my yum." And, in the classroom, while discussing world poverty, one student tattled that some kids won't eat anything that's served in the dining hall, and the teacher backtracked on her usual message about picky eaters and the need to eat variety by explaining that some children have legitimate health concerns that limit their food choices. In fact, when white bread was struck from the menu, some parents had doctors write notes insisting that their children had medical reasons for needing to eat white bread. Thus, the ideal model for food-and-language socialization unraveled.

In other cases, food messages to children in both the school and the home may be much more unified. Burdelski (2014), for example, takes a language socialization approach to studying how Japanese children are taught to feel and talk about food and others while eating with their peers at preschool and at home with family members. First, they are led by adults to voice positive assessments of the food they are eating, through terms such as 'delicious' and 'cute,' and to express empathic assessments of the food eaten by other animals, such as when feeding breadcrumbs to pigeons. Second, they are taught to finish all their food and not be wasteful so as to avoid the wrath of the Shinto gods and grandpa, to be sure that Santa will reward them at Christmas, and even to empathize with wasted rice juice ("sorry not to drink you"). Finally, they are socialized by parents, teachers, and peers to behave at the table, for example, not to scrape their plates with a fork, in empathy with the plate. Japanese caregivers use food talk to consciously fill children with cultural lessons about how to be part of a harmonious universe in which gods, elders, pigeons, plates, and rice juice are all respectfully aligned with each other, each expressing thanks for what they consume. Not that the children never resist these feedings . . . they do. But, as in other societies around the world, the language as food keeps coming.

Peer Negotiation of Food-and-Language Socialization

As touched on through these examples of sibling and peer interaction at home and at school, children also serve as socializing agents for one another. Older siblings take on adult-like roles or flout the rules pushed by caregivers in Sweden, classmates in Denmark observe and police one another's food choices in the school lunchroom, and American children do not easily ingest all the food discourses imposed upon them. In child-controlled contexts, children can explore cultural and linguistic practices and ideologies, both trying out new roles and reproducing or even transforming them in the process. From the negotiation of food sharing to imaginary play involving food, food-focused interactions give insights into the broader cultural knowledge that children are acquiring, whether about social hierarchy, rights and obligations, gender and age ideologies,

Figure 7.6 Youth night at a church in Cape Town, South Africa

Credit: Photo by Jaco Pretorius on Unsplash

or multilingualism. Peer interaction feeds children through language just as adult-child interaction does.

Sometimes children explore the social hierarchies relevant in their communities through verbal and material negotiations about and around food with peers. As illustrated by Yount-André's (2016) study in Dakar, Senegal, children often redistributed *unequally* proportioned gifts of snacks—such as two juice boxes and three bags of chips—to one another without dispute. The child who was given the snacks by the adult, or one that was designated by the other children, would divide up and hand out the portions, generally without problem. However, when the researcher gave two siblings in her study, nine-year-old Fatou and four-year-old Karim, *equivalent* snacks of juice and chips, she was surprised to find that the children pooled them together before elder sister Fatou redistributed them to Karim and herself. In fact, the incident prompted a complex verbal exchange whereby the children utilized two asymmetrical linguistic registers, "noble speech" (indexing high rank) and "griot speech" (indexing low rank), to position themselves in hierarchical roles and achieve *inequality* in their relationship. This was in contrast to the sibling *equality* that Yount-André presumed due to her own cultural background by giving the children identical snacks regardless of their rank vis-à-vis one another. Children's snack sharing practices, then, both socialized and reinforced larger caste-based differences, which adults, when asked, would instead naturalize as being simply age- and gender-based, the ideology being that older girls were more mature and thus able to divide up food.

Anthropologist Elise Berman (2014) suggests that even the category of age is produced through social interaction and the material exchange of goods such as food. Children in the Marshall Islands (Oceania), where generosity is a core value for adults, use material goods to negotiate their standing in relation to each another. They do this using practices that adults would be embarrassed to use, such as walking openly with food and not sharing it. Through such routines children socialize other children into appropriate sharing practices—including learning how *not* to share— despite the fact that they will need to begin sharing as they transition to adulthood. This, Berman argues, produces them as immature in relation to adults, thereby constructing what childhood and adulthood mean in this culture.

Children's pretend play is another prime context for exploring the relations between language, food, and society. Many of us may have heard the admonishment, common in many American households, that you shouldn't play with your food. Somewhat paradoxically, however, although real food toyed with at the dinner table generates negative commentary by adults, play food—whether transformed out of mud, sticks, or other found objects by the children's imagination or manufactured, commodified, and purposely supplied as plastic or wood food replicas by the adults in the playroom—is generally accepted or even actively promoted. Either way, when children structure their imaginary play around food, they create an opportunity to explore adult roles and broader cultural expectations and ideologies that they experience in their lives.

For instance, Sheldon (2014) took a gender and power approach to examining how boys and girls engaged in imaginary play with plastic food and kitchen equipment at a well-to-do day care center in Minneapolis in the 1980s. Here, the presence of pretend food generated an interactional context for play and socialization of gendered norms around food and eating. She found that girls commonly enacted food-related play—shopping and cooking, dining and conversing—in an orchestrated fashion. By contrast, boys tended to turn food toys into non-domestic objects, such as guns and cameras, and engaged in non-orchestrated parallel play and self-report monologue. The analysis is that girls are socialized early to produce these domestic food narratives as "'docile bodies' whose imaginations are already complicit with, and are reinscribing, gender expectations" (Sheldon 2014:276). In other words, the gendered meanings of domestic food activities are key to this exploration of how children play about and around imagined food and socialize one another into such expectations.

Paugh's (2012c) ethnography of language socialization and language shift in Dominica in the Caribbean details how material objects related to food production and processing can prompt children's multilingual role play about food in ways that do not occur in other settings or types of pretense, such as playing house or school. For example, when a group of boys discovered a pair of men's boots, usually worn to the field for agricultural work, they began a lengthy bout of imaginary role play centered on weeding potatoes. The boots and their embodied actions, bending down as if pulling weeds from the field behind their home, helped to develop the play, but it was their language choice that brought it to life. The boys code-switched from English, their regular language, into Patwa, the Afro-French creole language typically used by men when they work in the fields. This similarly occurred in other play, such as when a sheet of cardboard became the material used to cover a (pretend) slaughtered wild pig in the bush to keep flies off the meat in this same play group. The hunting and killing of the pig was narrated through Patwa, the male-associated language typically used outside the home, while other negotiations—such as about who would "cook" the food in the English-dominant home setting—were in English.

Such role-play activities provided hours of enjoyment for Dominican children while also cultivating a safe context within which they could speak the adult-associated Patwa language that was otherwise forbidden from them. Adults claimed that speaking Patwa would harm children's English acquisition, a language-as-food Discourse found in Dominican schools and elsewhere in the world where Western models of education have been incorporated. In children's play, however, material props associated with food procurement along with the outside setting and appropriate language choice created the imaginary food context that generated extensive multilingual talk and children's exploration of identities not normally available to them. It also became a key site of language socialization for children to transmit and practice Patwa amongst themselves—contributing to the potential maintenance of a local language in the face of a widespread language shift to English. Children's language about, around, and as food in imaginary play and peer interactions thus has significant real-world consequences for the reproduction and transformation of language, culture, and even foodways. In other words, children's food play may help to revalorize the "traditional" language and foodways of their communities (Patwa and local root crops and meats) despite the widespread shift to what many perceive as more "modern" varieties brought in from elsewhere (English and processed, imported foods).

Summary

As we have explored in this chapter, language may act as symbolic food, that is, as a metaphor for what does or does not nurture us. The growing body of food-and-language socialization research explores how the semiotic mediation of foodways and discourses allows for the production and reproduction of cultural practices and ideologies to do with food and language. In fact, understanding food-and-language socialization requires that we call on our full food-language framework. Language operates as food because food operates as language, with foods acting as signifiers of social significance. Further, the socialization of moral values and social stances are frequently implemented by way of language about food as food words and food narratives abound and are loaded with cultural meanings, norms, and identities. Finally, language around food is a prime context for socialization as food and talk events immerse children and other novices in social interactions that teach them how to speak, think, feel, and behave.

While these studies are rich, there are some assumptions underlying discourses about the nutrient value of food talk that bear examination—such as the idea that we (some of us) think we know best how to feed the appropriate food and food talk, food registers, and food-situated genres to others. "Language gap" discourses rest on the iconic presumption that some ways of interacting with children are healthier than others. Similarly, many members of Western society share an implicit belief that commensality—especially the family meal—is always a good thing, even though it can reinforce class distinctions, politics of inclusion and exclusion, and internal family power dynamics, frequently based on age and gender, that might not always be nourishing. Language socialization routines, negotiations over food and language, morality lessons about food and around food all reflect and produce power relations, including asymmetrical family, peer, and institutional dynamics. Through using language around, about, through, and as food, people do something in the world, in the case of socialization, shaping the next generation as well as themselves in the process.

As we have seen in our consideration of children's peer interactions, language socialization is not simply a one-way, top-down process from one generation to the next. It involves negotiations between adults and children, and among children themselves, impacting processes of reproduction and change over time and across the life span. In other words, the next generation does not always swallow whole everything they are fed by the previous generation. We continue this consideration of the performative function of food and language and the potentialities for resistance and change in the next chapter on food (inter)activism.

Note

1. Wingard (2015) offers a useful review of studies of family mealtime interaction.

References

Aronsson, Karin, and Lucas Gottzén. 2011. "Generational Positions at a Family Dinner: Food Morality and Social Order." *Language in Society* 40(4): 405–426.

Avineri, Netta, Eric Johnson, Shirley Brice-Heath, Teresa McCarty, Elinor Ochs, Tamar Kremer-Sadlik, Susan Blum, Ana Celia Zentella, Jonathan Rosa, Nelson Flores, H. Samy Alim, and Django Paris. 2015. "Invited Forum: Bridging the 'Language Gap'." *Journal of Linguistic Anthropology* 25(1): 66–86.

Berman, Elise. 2014. "Negotiating Age: Direct Speech and the Sociolinguistic Production of Childhood in the Marshall Islands." *Journal of Linguistic Anthropology* 24(2): 109–132.

Blum-Kulka, Shoshana. 1997. *Dinner Talk: Cultural Patterns of Sociability and Socialization in Family Discourse.* Mahwah, NJ: Lawrence Erlbaum.

Bourdieu, Pierre. 1984. *Distinction: A Social Critique of the Judgment of Taste.* Translated by Richard Nice. Cambridge: Harvard University Press.

Bourdieu, Pierre, and Jean-Claude Passeron. 1990(1970). *Reproduction in Education, Society, and Culture.* London: Sage.

Bruner, Michael S., and Jason D. Meek. 2011. "A Critical Crisis Rhetoric of Seafood." In *Food as Communication, Communication as Food,* edited by Janet M. Cramer, Carlnita P. Greene, and Lynn M. Walters, 271–295. New York: Peter Lang.

Burdelski, Matthew. 2014. "Early Experiences with Food: Socializing Affect and Relationships in Japanese." In *Language and Food: Verbal and Nonverbal Experiences,* edited by Polly E. Szatrowski, 233–255. Philadelphia, PA: John Benjamins.

Cameron, Deborah. 2012. *Verbal Hygiene.* Abingdon, Oxon: Routledge.

Capps, Lisa, and Elinor Ochs. 1995. *Constructing Panic: The Discourse of Agoraphobia.* Cambridge, MA: Harvard University Press.

Carroll, John B., ed. 1956. *Language, Thought, and Reality: Selected Writings of Benjamin Lee Whorf.* Cambridge, MA: MIT Press.

Curtiss, Susan. 1977. *Genie: A Psycholinguistic Study of a Modern-Day 'Wild Child'.* Boston, MA: Academic Press.

Dossa, Parin. 2014. *Afghanistan Remembers: Gendered Narrations of Violence and Culinary Practices.* Toronto: University of Toronto Press.

Duranti, Alessandro, Elinor Ochs, and Bambi Schieffelin, eds. 2012. *The Handbook of Language Socialization.* Malden, MA: Wiley-Blackwell.

Ferguson, Charles A. 1964. "Baby Talk in Six Languages." *American Anthropologist* 66: 103–114.

Gathercole, Virginia C. Mueller, and Erika Hoff. 2007. "Input and the Acquisition of Language: Three Questions." In *Blackwell Handbook of Language Development,* edited by Erika Hoff and Marilyn Shatz, 107–127. Malden, MA: Wiley-Blackwell.

Hart, Betty, and Todd R. Risley. 2003. "The Early Catastrophe: The 30 Million Word Gap by Age 3." *American Educator* 27(1): 4–9.

Heath, Shirley Brice. 1982. "What No Bedtime Story Means." *Language in Society* 11: 49–76.

Heath, Shirley Brice. 1983. *Ways with Words: Language, Life, and Work in Communities and Classrooms.* New York: Cambridge University Press.

Hines, Caitlin. 1999. "Rebaking the Pie: The WOMAN AS DESSERT Metaphor." In *Reinventing Identities: The Gendered Self in Discourse,* edited by Mary Bucholtz, A. C. Liang, and Laurel A. Sutton, 145–162. New York: Oxford University Press.

Johnson, Eric J., and Ana Celia Zentella. 2017. "Introducing the Language Gap." *International Multilingual Research Journal* 11(1): 1–4.

Karrebæk, Martha Sif. 2012. "What's in Your Lunch Box Today?: Health, Respectability, and Ethnicity in the Primary Classroom." *Journal of Linguistic Anthropology* 22(1): 1–22.

Karrebæk, Martha Sif. 2013a. "Lasagna for Breakfast: The Respectable Child and Cultural Norms of Eating Practices in a Danish Kindergarten Classroom." *Food, Culture & Society* 16(1): 85–106.

Karrebæk, Martha Sif. 2013b. "Rye Bread and Halal: Enregisterment of Food Practices in the Primary Classroom." *Language & Communication* 34: 17–34.

Karrebæk, Martha Sif. 2014. "Healthy Beverages?: The Interactional Use of Milk, Juice and Water in an Ethnically Diverse Kindergarten Class in Denmark." In *Language and Food: Verbal and Nonverbal Experiences,* edited by Polly E. Szatrowski, 279–299. Philadelphia, PA: John Benjamins.

Kremer-Sadlik, Tamar, Aliyah Morgenstern, Chloe Peters, Pauline Beaupoil, Stéphanie Caët, Camille Debras, and Marine le Mené. 2015. "Eating Fruits and Vegetables: An Ethnographic Study of American and French Family Dinners." *Appetite* 89: 84–92.

Krögel, Alison. 2009. "Dangerous Repasts: Food and the Supernatural in the Quechua Oral Tradition." *Food and Foodways* 17: 104–132.

Lahey, Jessica. 2014. "Poor Kids and the 'Word Gap'." *The Atlantic,* October 16. www.theatlantic.com/education/archive/2014/10/american-kids-are-starving-for-words/381552/, accessed August 23, 2017.

Lakoff, George, and Mark Johnson. 1980. *Metaphors We Live By*. Chicago: University of Chicago Press.

Laurier, Eric, and Sally Wiggins. 2011. "Finishing the Family Meal: The Interactional Organisation of Satiety." *Appetite* 56: 53–64.

Mead, Margaret. 1959. *Four Families*. National Film Board of Canada.

Ochs, Elinor. 1988. *Culture and Language Development: Language Acquisition and Language Socialization in a Samoan Village*. Cambridge: Cambridge University Press.

Ochs, Elinor, and Lisa Capps. 2001. *Living Narrative: Creating Lives in Everyday Storytelling*. Cambridge, MA: Harvard University Press.

Ochs, Elinor, and Tamar Kremer-Sadlik, eds. 2013. *Fast-Forward Family: Home, Work, and Relationships in Middle-Class America*. Berkeley and Los Angeles: University of California Press.

Ochs, Elinor, Clotilde Pontecorvo, and Alessandra Fasulo. 1996. "Socializing Taste." *Ethnos* 61(1–2): 7–46.

Ochs, Elinor, and Bambi B. Schieffelin. 1984. "Language Acquisition and Socialization: Three Developmental Stories and Their Implications." In *Culture Theory: Essays on Mind, Self, and Emotion*, edited by Richard Shweder and Robert LeVine, 276–320. New York: Cambridge University Press.

Ochs, Elinor, and Merav Shohet. 2006. "The Cultural Structuring of Mealtime Socialization." *New Directions for Child and Adolescent Development* 111: 35–49.

Ochs, Elinor, Ruth Smith, and Carolyn Taylor. 1989. "Detective Stories at Dinnertime: Problem-Solving through Co-Narration." *Cultural Dynamics* 2(2): 238–257.

Ochs, Elinor, Olga Solomon, and Laura Sterponi. 2005. "Limitations and Transformations of Habitus in Child-Directed Communication." *Discourse Studies* 7(4–5): 547–583.

Ochs, Elinor, and Carolyn Taylor. 1992. "Family Narrative as Political Activity." *Discourse & Society* 3(3): 301–340.

Ochs, Elinor, Carolyn Taylor, Dina Rudolph, and Ruth Smith. 1992. "Storytelling as a Theory-Building Activity." *Discourse Processes* 15(1): 37–72.

Paugh, Amy L. 2012a. "Local Theories of Child Rearing." In *The Handbook of Language Socialization*, edited by Alessandro Duranti, Elinor Ochs, and Bambi B. Schieffelin, 150–168. Malden, MA: Wiley-Blackwell.

Paugh, Amy L. 2012b. "Speculating about Work at Dinnertime: Dinnertime Narratives among Dual-Earner American Families." *Text & Talk* 32(5): 615–636.

Paugh, Amy L. 2012c. *Playing with Languages: Children and Change in a Caribbean Village*. New York: Berghahn Books.

Paugh, Amy L., and Carolina Izquierdo. 2009. "Why is This a Battle Every Night?: Negotiating Food and Eating in American Dinnertime Interaction." *Journal of Linguistic Anthropology* 19(2): 185–204.

Paugh, Amy L., and Kathleen C. Riley. Forthcoming. "'Deficit' or 'Difference'? Poverty and Children's Language." *Annual Review of Anthropology*.

Riley, Kathleen C. 2016. "Learning to Exchange Food and Talk in the Marquesas." In *Making Sense of Language*, 3rd edition, edited by Susan Blum, 143–153. Oxford: Oxford University Press.

Riley, Kathleen C. Forthcoming. "'Don't Yuck My Yum': Semiotics and the Socialization of Food Ideologies at an Elite Elementary School." *Semiotic Review* 5:
The Semiotics of Food and Language.

Sapphire, Peggy. 2009. "Steamy Sundays." In *In the End a Circle*, 70. Simsbury,
CT: Antrim House.

Schieffelin, Bambi. 1990. *The Give and Take of Everyday Life: Language Socialization of Kaluli Children.* Cambridge: Cambridge University Press.

Senghas, Ann, and Marie Coppola. 2001. "Children Creating Language: How
Nicaraguan Sign Language Acquired a Spatial Grammar." *Psychological Science*
12(4): 323–328.

Sheldon, Amy. 2014. "'I Needa Cut Up My Soup': Food Talk, Pretend Play, and
Gender in an American Preschool." In *Language and Food: Verbal and Nonver-
bal Experiences*, edited by Polly E. Szatrowski, 257–277. Philadelphia, PA: John
Benjamins.

Snow, Catherine E., and Charles A. Ferguson, eds. 1977. *Talking to Children: Language Input and Acquisition.* New York: Cambridge University Press.

Solomon, Olga. 2012. "Rethinking Baby Talk." In *The Handbook of Language
Socialization*, edited by Alessandro Duranti, Elinor Ochs, and Bambi B. Schieffelin, 121–149. Malden, MA: Wiley-Blackwell.

Wiggins, Sally. 2004. "Good for 'You': Generic and Individual Healthy Eating
Advice in Family Mealtimes." *Journal of Health Psychology* 9(4): 535–548.

Wiggins, Sally. 2014. "Family Mealtimes, Yuckiness, and the Socialization of Disgust Responses by Preschool Children." In *Language and Food: Verbal and Non-
verbal Experiences*, edited by Polly E. Szatrowski, 211–231. Philadelphia, PA:
John Benjamins.

Wiggins, Sally, Jonathan Potter, and Aimee Wildsmith. 2001. "Eating Your Words:
Discursive Psychology and the Reconstruction of Eating Practices." *Journal of
Health Psychology* 6(5): 5–15.

Wingard, Leah. 2015. "Family Dinner Interaction." In *The International Encyclopedia of Language and Social Interaction*, edited by Karen Tracy, Cornelia Ilie,
and Todd Sandel, 603–612. Malden, MA: Wiley-Blackwell.

Yount-André, Chelsie. 2016. "Snack Sharing and the Moral Metalanguage of
Exchange: Children's Reproduction of Rank-Based Redistribution in Senegal."
Journal of Linguistic Anthropology 26(1): 41–61.

Zentella, Ana Celia, ed. 2005. *Building on Strength: Language and Literacy in
Latino Families and Communities.* New York: Teachers College Press.

Chapter 8

Applying the Food-and-Language Model

"There's war, disease, poverty, and violent crime all
over the world...and your greatest concern is
me not eating peas!"

Figure 8.1 Finish your peas!

As we have documented over the course of this book, food and words are produced, consumed, processed, and exchanged in many different ways in various social settings across cultures. Foodways are evocative, suggestive, and multisensuous. We dig our hands in the soil and glance at food displays, crunch on a chip, and smell the stew as it simmers. Similarly, our ways of communicating through, about, around, and as food are multimodal and multifunctional. We may pray to our gods to express thanks for the meal or post our dinner with friends on Instagram to confirm our friendships. The ways in which we talk about food reinforce what the food signifies; our social interactions in its presence nourish us in meaningful ways.

Sometimes the interaction between foodways and discourses is a source of pleasure and play, emotion and aesthetics. Other times the entanglement is fraught with troubling social and political import.[1] Focusing on how this happens, bringing it to consciousness in our own lives, and then applying that knowledge to understanding how others in the world are doing something both similar yet different can provide the basis for improved communications across linguistic or cultural barriers and political or social divides.

In this final chapter, we look at how studying food through-about-around-as language may be a way not only to enrich our experience of cultural diversity, but also to improve the participation of everyone in the food-and-language riches of the world. We sketch out the ways in which food activists use social interaction and semiotic mediation to frame and help resolve problems in the food system. In doing this, we ask if and how social research about the use of language through, about, around, and as food can contribute to what we call **food (inter)activism**.

The Semiotic Mediation of Food Activism: Food (Inter)Activism

Food activism is a form of political activism that has emerged over the last half-century to focus on the role of food in recalibrating human relationships on this planet (Counihan and Siniscalchi 2014; Holt-Giménez 2017; Nestle 2002; Poppendieck 2010; Watson and Caldwell 2005; Wilk 2006; Williams-Forson and Counihan 2012). Food activists may be jour-

8.1

nalists, educators, farmers, community organizers, chefs, refugees, and/or parents, and can be found in a range of more or less institutional settings from household gardens and street demonstrations to governmental offices and transnational non-profit organizations. Some individuals work within

8.2

institutions formed for the purpose of regulating the **food system**, that is, the systemic ways in which food is produced, distributed, and consumed at local, national, and/or global levels. Others engage in this work out of a passion to improve the world, their lives, and the lives of others (Gottlieb and Joshi 2010; Holt-Giménez 2011). This is not to say that the former are never impassioned or that the latter have no right to work on these issues. Either way, these actors focus on a range of overlapping concerns involving individual health, environmental balance, and social and economic justice.

The term **sustainability** is frequently used to encompass all of these, the overarching goal being to identify and address flaws in some aspect of the

8.3   food system.

We have coined the hybrid term **food (inter)activism**—*food* plus *inter* from *interaction* plus *activism*—to draw attention to forms of food activism that depend on the role of interpersonal and intercultural communication to successfully implement constructive food change.[2] That is, we consider food activism to be food (inter)activism when the activists show some awareness of the role discourses play in shaping understandings of food systems and their problems. Food (inter)activism seeks to cure what is viewed as a flawed food system by analyzing what is wrong and how it may be fixed and then communicating the possible cures in palatable ways to those empowered to make the changes and to those who will benefit from them. The idea is that food messages go down more easily when they are served up in sensuous packages—such as in tasty and healthy dishes prepared by celebrity chefs or movies steeped in food, emotion, and memory.

8.4

Food (inter)activism has been sprouting up in many ways around the world. By way of illustration, we offer several examples from New York City, where Riley has conducted research and lived for much of her life. First of all, due to intervention by lots of school food activists, vegetable gardens now flourish in schools from Brooklyn to the Bronx with the goal of teaching children where food comes from and how to prepare and enjoy it. Festive farmers markets offering local and organic fare (and seasonal food samples) are open on a regular schedule throughout the year with the objective of bringing consumers closer to their producers and engaging them in learning how to cook with fresh produce. Community-supported agriculture opportunities have emerged even in neighborhoods once considered food deserts (such as Harlem), which allow residents to access fresh food as well as visit with farmers on the farms where the produce is grown. A chef at a soup kitchen in the Upper West Side offers delicious lunches accompanied by presentations about the cultural roots of the cuisine du jour. Each of these initiatives attempts to deliver tasty, healthy, sustainable, and meaningful food and food knowledge to consumers while also engaging them in a participatory role in the initiatives. That is, participants are not only invited to consume the foods and foodways discourses offered but also to engage as empowered interlocutors and producers in their own right, to help make the programs what they want them to be.

8.5

In this section, we examine in more detail how food activists whom we would identify as practicing food (inter)activism use language through, about, around, and as food to discursively frame and voice their concerns. More specifically, we assess here how they draw on meaningful food imagery to construct messages about food problems, frequently in contexts where food is actually or virtually present, to feed to actors who they hope will be able to do something about the problems.

8.6

Vignette 8.1   Cynthia L. West: Food (Inter)Activism in the College Classroom

Cynthia L. West taught in the Humanities Department at Johnson State College for 35 years and has been involved in the food movement in northern Vermont as a gardener and gleaner for most of her adult life.

When I first saw Julia Child on TV pronounce the French noun *pommes de terre* (potatoes) and then learned that it translated literally into 'apples of the Earth,' I knew I would study French. First in high school, then college, finally graduate school. Living in France as a young adult just added to the personal passion for food I had developed as a child. So, after finishing my Master's research on a French poet (Saint-John Perse), I conducted an oral history project on the changing foodways of Franco-Americans in the Northeast Kingdom of Vermont. Some dishes were based on old Norman recipes, using the farm ingredients they could raise themselves in those northern climates on either side of the Atlantic. The food, like the language, had transformed slowly over 400 years in Quebec, and then much more rapidly over the past century in the US.

Many years later, this interest in how language, culture, and food come together inspired me to collaborate with my colleague Kathleen Riley on developing and teaching an interdisciplinary and interactive class called "Cultures through Cuisine." I had always imagined that the topic would captivate college students, especially the students in a small state college in Vermont, many of whom had never tried a bite of anything other than the meat-and-potatoes (or hamburger-and-pizza) diet they had grown up on. It did indeed. Our guest cooks (some professional chefs and some domestic but committed cooks) from France, Japan, Mexico, Thailand, Germany, and Italy were enthusiastic to share their food culture. When they left their kitchens to come into ours, they created a true classroom *atelier*, bringing their groceries, languages, stories, and recipes. Prior to the day of cooking and eating, students researched the food items required for the meal—from potatoes to lemongrass; their presentations contributed fodder for our unique culinary and cultural exchange. Then, with the guest cook's guidance, we prepared and cooked the dishes chosen for the day.

For some students, it was the first time that they had ever paid attention to taste, aroma, quality, or texture. We savored what we prepared, conversing about table manners, food service, presentation, and consumption. All of us soon realized how each ingredient, each culinary technique, each way of dining held a world of information, just awaiting discovery. We learned about political systems and economic exchange from studying the history of tea, tomatoes, and cabbage. We learned about the roots of globalization in the spice trade and the semiotic differences of "fine dining" in French and Japanese foodways. We learned that in most cultures, food vocabulary adds a flavor of its own. For example, the French word *compagnon* (comrade) translates literally into 'the one you eat your bread with,' and *restaurant* is from a 16th-century word for 'a food which restores health.' In fact, it was originally a locale where one could order this concoction.

Food was the vehicle that brought us together and language the air we breathed. Teachers, students, and cooks became a community of interactive learners. For many of us, this was a life-changing experience, encouraging a consciousness that would go on to inspire our choices as consumers, our aesthetic appreciation of how humans interact differently around the world, and our understanding of how food ties humanity together on this planet.

(Inter)Activism About and As Food

One way in which food (inter)activism takes place is through carefully crafted discourses intended to feed others information about perceived problems in the food system, which can come in the form of books, films, and websites, as well as through institutions such as schools. Let's take for example the topic of **agribusiness,** a portmanteau[3] term that was originally used to discuss any agriculture-related business but has been adopted by food activists to critique a corporate approach to farming wherein the primary goal is to maximize output and profit. The scale of most agribusiness is huge in terms of the amount of resources used (land, technology, energy, and capital) and the massive amount of food produced. Food activists criticize this form of conventional agriculture for using a variety of techniques that are understood to be unhealthy and unsustainable for humans, other species, and the environment (Shiva 2016; Garnett 2016).[4] We look here at a couple of the techniques that are most virulently critiqued and how the critiques are semiotically framed by food activists in ways meant to persuade others of the problem.

First of all, agribusiness usually involves planting and harvesting a single commodity crop, such as corn or soy, over vast areas without variation, a practice known as **monocropping**. Effects of monocropping include cutting down on the benefits of biodiversity while using GMO seeds,[5] chemical fertilizers, and pesticides[6] to make up for the exhaustion of the soil. Manual

8.7

laborers in agribusiness are exposed to these toxins in the fields, and/or large (energy-guzzling) machines are used to cut labor costs. One publication designed to convince readers of the dangers of agribusiness by contrast with small-scale, biodiverse production is called *Fatal Harvest: The Tragedy of Industrial Agriculture* (Kimbrell 2002). By placing vivid photos of the two types side by side, it evokes what is wrong with the one and right with the other through appeals to our aesthetic sensibilities: monoculture appears visually monochrome and dull while biodiversity appears colorful and appetizing. The book also attempts to debunk what Kimbrell calls seven "myths of industrial agriculture" (for instance, that it will provide sufficient cheap, healthy food to feed the world) by providing scientifically researched facts about the two forms of agriculture as well. This myth-debunking approach has a long history in food activism circles concerned with food insecurity around the world (Lappé, Collins, and Rosset 1998).

8.8

Startling photographs interspersed with food facts are also marshalled to bring the topic of global food inequities to public consciousness in the book entitled *Hungry Planet* (Menzel and D'Aluisio 2007). And Delpeuch et al.'s (2009) *Globesity: A Planet out of Control* uses charts, graphs, and talking points to draw connections between climate change and what is framed as a global obesity pandemic (using another catchy portmanteau, as discussed above regarding agribusiness).

8.9

In another agribusiness practice known as **factory farming,** animals (especially pigs, cows, and chickens) are raised in cramped quarters and fed foods, antibiotics, and hormones that are meant to produce more meat faster but are critiqued by activists as unhealthy for them and their human consumers. They are also butchered in ways that activists target for being inhumane to the animals and unsafe for the workers and for contributing to the spread of pathogens that infect our foods (Kirby 2010).[7] An affecting investigation of factory farming at the beginning of the 20th century can be found in Upton Sinclair's indictment of the stockyards of Chicago in *The Jungle* (2004[1906]). More recently, *Fast Food Nation* (Schlosser 2012), also written as hard-hitting journalism, has incited many Americans to rebel against the unhealthy and unjust food system underlying their favorite meal of burgers and fries. Finally, the symbolism implicit in the title of the book, *The Face on Your Plate* (Masson 2009), and made explicitly graphic on the front cover through the image of a sweet-looking calf standing on a white dinner plate, is clearly intended to bring pathos to the topic of animal abuses in the factory farming system while the subtitle, *The Truth About Food*, again indexes the idea that corporate agriculture is creating myths and obfuscating reality.

8.10

Additionally, a number of filmmakers have taken on the task of identifying and representing the governmental and corporate, national and international players thought to be responsible for making the food system unhealthy and unsustainable. For instance, the film *Food, Inc.* (Kenner

2010) attempts to show how individuals are employed first by the United States government and multinational food corporations and back again in a sort of revolving door situation that leads to bias and self-interest in governmental policy making. That is, government employees end up making decisions based on the needs of their previous corporate employers rather than for the good of the citizenry. Another film, *Cowspiracy* (Andersen and Kuhn 2014), focuses in particular on how animal agriculture threatens the environment through carbon emissions and is supported by powerful corporate lobbies in the United States. Both of these films use both pathos (personal narratives, sensuous photography) and logos (facts, diagrams, talking heads) to push their points about the food system.

(Inter)Activism Through and Around Food

Food (inter)activism also uses the powerful significance of food while interacting around the food to encourage humans to enact change. This approach is particularly relevant in **food sovereignty** movements, that is, those directed at restoring the ability of individuals and communities to participate more directly and sustainably in the production and consumption of healthy and culturally meaningful foods. Such movements frequently try to change the food system by organizing community gardens, food cooperatives, and communal kitchens. The idea here is that by people getting their hands dirty together and interacting around and about the food, the food system will change literally from the grassroots up (Holt-Giménez 2011; Gottlieb and Joshi 2010; Sacharoff 2016; Winne 2008).

In one analysis of a specific community garden, Seegert (2012) explored the importance of treating a community garden space, and the vegetables grown there, in a "blighted" neighborhood in Salt Lake City, Utah, as a text with many meanings to be read. She interpreted the acts involved—re-conceptualizing the "empty lot," applying for a city grant, designing the space, building and decorating the raised beds, planting and weeding, eating and communicating with other bodies (human and not) in and around the garden—as signs of **resignification**, the process by which signs are given new meaning. Here, a previously abject community reconfigured how it fed and felt about itself, thus creating new urban-agricultural forms of visibility (aesthetic and political) that put down roots in the soil. In other words, the community was able to take charge not only of the means of production but also their ways of presenting themselves to the world through food.

Many individuals act on and communicate their beliefs by choosing to eat foods that symbolize particular moral stances (language *through* food). For instance, by choosing to eat organic, vegetarian, local, or fair-trade foods, they are indexing their concern for the health of themselves and the environment, their economic community, and/or the workers who helped produce their food. They hope through these choices not only to

Figure 8.2 A community garden (© Shutterstock)

help undermine but also to communicate their resistance to what they view as a corporate food system more concerned with profit than the health of human communities or the planet. While individual choices may have only a minimal material impact on the food system (Lavin 2012; Morris and Kirwan 2012), the symbolic effect is not negligible as food movements such as these have the power to create democratic civil spaces within which values can be transformed (Hassanein 2012). Meaningful food choices may, in the course of becoming a topic of conversation around food, also become an instigator of change. Some everyday foodways discourses even turn up as internet trends that go viral or in books that become bestsellers (as in Barbara Kingsolver's 2007 *Animal, Vegetable, Miracle* on the topic of eating local for a year).

8.11

Other food (inter)activists explore community-based strategies that build on individual food choices while working to take charge of and transform the means and relations of production and consumption. Examples range from community organizers who promote urban gardening (for example, Ron Finley, the "Gangsta Gardener" of Los Angeles) to gleaning initiatives in which committed volunteers collect crops leftover after commercial harvesting and redistribute these to food shelves (for example, the non-profit Salvation Farms in Vermont). In a study of communal dinners, LeGrand

8.12

(2015) discusses her fieldwork with an environmental NGO in Lisbon that organized a weekly vegan dinner. These dinners were open to anyone but were attended mostly by international students. Through commensality, they engendered political commitment to the environmental causes represented by the (significance-laden) vegan food being served up on those evenings. First of all, the meal was intended to model for eaters the potentialities of how eating dishes without animal based foods could taste good and lack for nothing; secondly, the meal provided a setting for discussing how veganism could contribute to changing the food system.

One grassroots online campaign used environmental aesthetics to nourish food sovereignty activism (Todd 2011). Roger Doiron, head of Kitchen Garden International (KGI), wanted to promote household food production for environmental reasons. He hoped to take back local space and aesthetically revalue the land as edible garden versus suburban sod, and to contribute to real change through food production not just passive consumer consumption. The KGI campaign to "plant high-impact food gardens in high-profile places" was rhetorically successful because Doiron used catchy phrases such as "Eat the View!," "edible landscapes for all," and "this lawn is your lawn," combined with iconic images of him digging up his own suburban lawn next to the first family digging up the White House lawn to put in vegetable gardens. Such tactics were aimed at inspiring nationalist feelings of self-reliance and embodied action—in other words, every American family can dig in and feed themselves in healthy, sustainable ways.

8.13

Finally, Frye (2012) examined how and why the ultimate self-sacrifice—suicide—of social activists can rhetorically feed social movements. In this case, South Korean farmer-activist Lee Kyung Hae committed suicide as part of an international revolt against the imposition of the World Trade Organization's policies supporting corporate agriculture and undermining smaller farmers' ability to sustainably produce food for themselves and their communities. Such self-sacrifices function rhetorically as heroic acts, rather than as anti-social forms of insanity, to fuel the movement. Ideologically, Lee paved the political way with prior hunger strikes and verbal signage: "WTO Kills Farmers." He then used the physical setting of the WTO meeting in Cancun, Mexico, by climbing to the top of a barrier separating protesters from WTO insiders. Finally, Lee plunged a Swiss army knife in his heart, manifesting with this synecdoche the reality of international agents (the Swiss) killing farmers. Lee's public suicide was the rallying cry that disrupted the WTO trade agreement proceedings in 2003 and his online memorial continues to fuel the movement. One is left asking: is this what it takes?

If we recall the performative function of language, we can begin to understand how the forms of semiotic mediation discussed in this section can be powerful in the best and worst senses of the word. That is, foodways

8.14

discourses may be used to support and facilitate the understandings and actions of individuals and communities regarding food; they may also be used to erase or undermine participation in a food system that seems to be out of anyone's control. We have seen how in settings both mundane and ritual, discourses and foodways support specific power-laced social structures. For instance, at the most intimate level, dinnertime conversations are orchestrated by age and gender differences whereas at global levels, access to meaningful and sustaining food is shaped by inequitable systems of class and nationality. However, discourses and foodways are also frequently enlisted as semiotic resources to address social injustice, especially as it manifests in an unsustainable food system. In the next section, we explore how applying our model for studying language through-about-around-as food can also be used to inform researchers' attempts to address problems in the food system.

What Food (Inter)Activist Research Adds to the Soup

A growing number of researchers from various disciplines, including anthropology, nutrition and food studies, and communications and rhetoric have been studying how the food system may be changed (Counihan and Siniscalchi 2014; Cramer, Greene, and Walters 2011; Frye and Bruner 2012; Watson and Caldwell 2005; Williams-Forson and Counihan 2012). Some of these researchers study the phenomenon by critically analyzing public discourses available in various textual formats from print to online, and we will look at a few such studies first. However, from our linguistic anthropological perspective, we are particularly interested in understanding if and how studying food (inter)activism in ways that are themselves interactive and participatory can add to scientific understanding and/or to the activist missions themselves. The final section will be devoted to this topic.

Rhetorical Analyses of Food-and-Language: Counting the Calories

Many policies and programs are developed at local, national, and international levels to address perceived problems with the food system and/or to address other social problems via food. Some of these initiatives are launched by governments and some of them are specifically non-governmental and led by self-styled food activists. Either way, scholars in communications and food studies level a range of critiques at these initiatives frequently to do with the ethnocentric or classist assumptions of those who have designed them. Frequently, these programs are decried for being neoliberal, that is, of being biased by the ideology that market forces will bring about necessary social transformations through individual willpower and action (see Harvey (2005) for an overview of neoliberalism). In other words, the objection is that these policies and movements are not attempting to take on the larger structural issues that constrain individuals' food and lifestyle choices but are relying on the notion that individuals can be educated to simply make better choices in order to improve their own and their community's well being. We look here at several of these critiques.

National governments may administer policies intended to impact the family, the educational system, and wider media discourses. For instance, as discussed by Kimura (2011), the Japanese government developed a range of policies to address several food problems: 1) the lack of food self-sufficiency on the island nation due to a reduction in local agricultural output; 2) the rise in obesity and related health problems caused by imported consumption habits; and 3) food contamination and falsification of food components, including GMOs, pesticides, and unapproved additives. To address these problems, the government formed an education research committee and established laws and food education programs to promote eating a balanced diet of Japanese foods that are locally produced, especially rice, and prepared at home and eaten together by the family. These food policies, however, depend on gender inequality in the "traditional family" with women staying home as the good wife and mother to make homemade meals, socialize children, and supply cheap, part-time corporate labor when needed. Kimura is especially critical of the neoliberalism of this approach and that it asserts old nationalistic discourses, such as the need to make Japan and its workers strong in the global marketplace.

Focusing on a recent effort to regiment the American diet, Seiler (2012) unpacks the prescriptive messages about food to be found in Michelle Obama's Let's Move program. On the one hand, Seiler credits Obama with making references to the structural constraints that affect individuals' healthy food choices and contribute to the societal problem of obesity. On the other hand, the author faults Obama for not delving more openly into the gender, ethnic, and class-based barriers that contribute to, for example, the prevalence of food deserts in some neighborhoods over others or the socioeconomic barriers, such as lack of a living family wage, that create the conditions for socializing a taste for unhealthy fast foods. Instead, Obama relies on neoliberal discourses about rational individuals and relates stories from her own childhood mealtimes to illustrate how educating parents about food and nutrition can lead to change. She does not employ alternative discursive resources to probe the societal causes of obesity and thus discover community-level solutions. Seiler suggests that "the more easily *digestible* and hegemonic narrative of individual responsibility has made it difficult to promote socially rooted and environmentally sensitive public health initiatives" (2012:167, emphasis added).

8.15

An attempt to use food to promote international dialogue can be found in the Slow Food movement based in Italy. For instance, Parkins and Craig (2009) analyze, the first conference of Terra Madre, an alternative global food network intended to nourish "virtuous globalization." They look at how this is an attempt at consciously positive form of globalization that would bring small-scale "local" producers from all over the world together in a cultural space where they could, while eating together, exchange information about producing their products and create relationships to improve their distribution networks. Slow Food also promoted farmers markets to provide cultural spaces for experimenting with new forms of sociality and community, activated by engaging through co-presences in new tastes and feelings. The authors' concerns were that, although the stated goal of these projects was to resist and remake the food system, local producers were being on the one hand co-opted by global capitalism and on the other being drawn in to some degree by a reactionary elitist ideology about returning to an idealized past.

8.16

Indeed, the power of sitting down, talking, and eating together with others as a means to resolving our differences may be overestimated. For instance, Meneley (2016) critiques a film called *A Slim Peace* that followed the progress of a program designed to create dialogue among Jews and Muslims in Israel-Palestine by getting women together to talk about dieting. The working assumption was that food and dieting is such a globally relevant topic for women that a multi-faith dieting group would inevitably create a mediating space for these women from opposite sides of the highly politicized conflict in Israel-Palestine to come together across the ideological divide. However, the film concluded by showing that a year after the film was made, these women were no longer in contact, nor had they necessarily lost weight. To the contrary, according to Meneley, the sort of self-surveillance that dieting requires seemed to have added very little to the lives of the Palestinian women, who were already facing state-level surveillance at every checkpoint.

8.17

Vignette 8.2   Garrett M. Broad: Giving Voice to Food Justice

Garrett M. Broad is a food activist and communication researcher, now teaching in the Department of Communication and Media Studies at Fordham University in New York City.

I moved to Los Angeles for graduate school at the University of Southern California's Annenberg School for Communication and Journalism only a few weeks before I attended the first organizational meeting for what would later be named Fountain Community

Gardens. My motivations were two-fold: I was eager to get involved in a productive project in my new neighborhood, but also curious as to whether my participation might open up potential opportunities for ethnographic research. Urban agriculture and community gardens were starting to get a lot of attention in those days—highlighted by the likes of Michael Pollan and Michelle Obama—and I was excited by the enthusiastic stories advocates told, insisting that food could serve as a powerful tool for building community, promoting health, and advancing ecological sustainability in cities across the country.

When the meeting commenced, my enthusiasm was quickly tempered by concern. Where were the Latin@s? The Armenians? The Thais? My neighborhood was one of the most diverse in the city, a mix of working-class immigrants, long-time residents, and aspiring Hollywood newcomers. But as I surveyed the room, it was clear that most everybody looked and talked like me—white, English-speaking, highly educated professional and artistic types. Could we really call this a community garden if only the most privileged segment of the community was being represented? What cultural and agricultural insights would we miss if we were not a fully inclusive space? What practical steps could we take to promote a more egalitarian model for garden interaction, participation, and governance?

Those questions became a driving force for the scholar-activist work I would develop in the years ahead. The more I explored the intersection of community activism and food systems, the more I realized that dominant discourses about the problems and solutions of urban food had been crafted by well-intentioned but disconnected people of social and economic advantage. The stories they told about the power of food and community were overly romantic, exaggerating the positive impacts and overlooking the real challenges and tensions that urban food activists face. Discourses about school gardens, for instance, often espoused what I call the "magic carrot approach" to food activism: if young children in low-income neighborhoods of color follow the journey of a carrot from seed to plate, these narratives suggest, then almost like magic the children and their families will finally have the opportunity to live a healthy life. My experience in the field, however, suggested that no carrot was magical enough to overcome racism, poverty, and sustained inequality.

This is not to say that I lost my enthusiasm for food and its potential to encourage social and environmental justice. Instead, I become more devoted to identifying the conditions that need to be met in order for true food justice to be achieved. Central to that project, I soon learned, was ensuring that the voices and perspectives of those most marginalized by the food system were emphasized and given the opportunity to lead. So, at Fountain Community Gardens, I took on the role of treasurer, working with others to develop active initiatives that promoted long-term inclusivity. And, as one of my first projects as a graduate student researcher, I solicited narratives from gardeners to understand the array of motivations and knowledges they brought to the soil and the garden community.

Soon thereafter, I found myself collaborating with community food advocates in other parts of Los Angeles and across the country, ethnographically exploring the efforts of people-of-color-led organizations that use food as a tool for economic development and racial justice in historically oppressed African-American and Latin@ communities. I wrote my first book, *More Than Just Food: Food Justice and Community Change*, as a way to understand the communicative and cultural challenges that food justice advocates face, as well as to articulate the principles that must be in place in order for them to achieve their social transformation goals. Today, now on the east coast of the United States, I continue to parlay my scholarly insights into community practice, maintaining action research collaborations with groups in cities that stretch from Los Angeles to Philadelphia and New York.

I have learned a great deal from this journey of engaged scholarship, but one primary insight comes through clearly: the most effective projects are those that begin from a place of legitimate community-based collaboration. When projects and programs are guided by the needs and desires of local residents themselves, with community-based storytelling used to identify and amplify their visions for change, a healthy and just food system becomes a real possibility.

Researchers Digging in the Food (Inter)Activist Garden

Anthropologists and other social scientists have been working for decades to decide if and how to make our research activities and findings relevant to our research subjects. To begin with, we now tend to self-consciously call them our "participants" rather than our "subjects" or "informants" as in the past. Similarly, we have debated at length whether the effort to have a positive impact in our field sites deserves a subdisciplinary label of its own; as a result, **applied anthropology** now exists as a fifth subdiscipline in many anthropology departments. However, other labels— activist, participatory, engaged, or public—have also been proposed and are now included as categories in many university, association, and

publication settings. In this section, we briefly touch on this question with
relation to food (inter)activism by looking at several fieldwork studies that
have applied an engaged approach to studying food activism, asking our   8.18
readers and ourselves whether this succeeds in facilitating the activist mis-
sion on the one hand while on the other hand also increasing our understanding of how humans engage with each other via food and language in
various settings.

In 1943, anthropologist Margaret Mead (2008) asked how anthropologists could use their research skills to address the "problem of changing
food habits" in large, complex societies such as the United States. At that
point, the "problem" had to do with immigrant communities and war-
time rationing. She suggested that research needed to investigate a range
of things, beginning with the impact of foods and foodways, such as nutrients, production, preparation, and social desirability, on consumers' health.
She wanted to probe the food habits of regional and ethnic subcultures,
including the cultural practices, values, tastes, and socializing patterns that
form children's tastes through sanctions and media. She also recommended
using psychological studies to investigate how and why people resist or
accept foods depending on how they were offered, for example, by friends,
government, movie stars, or home economic experts. Next, she identified
some results from studies that had already been conducted in the United
States. For example, European peasants had brought with them the belief
that diets based on purified grains, sugar, and daily meat carry status. The
Puritan notion that healthy food should taste bad had been retained, neces-
sitating a system whereby unhealthy, delicious foods (aka sweets) are used
to reward the eating of healthy, disliked foods. By contrast, in the southeast, an emphasis on one's personal relationship to food and taste was
promoted. A new interest in pure, processed, no-muss, packaged foods was
on the rise; and across this cultural diversity, there was a tendency to serve
foods separately, simply cooked without spicing and with condiments on
the side. She concluded: "[T]he food habits of the future will have to be
sanctioned not by authoritarian statements which breed rigid conformity
rather than intelligent flexibility, but by a sense of responsibility on the part
of those who plan meals for others to eat" (2008:25).

In other words, Mead suggested that if and when changing our foodways becomes necessary but appears difficult, we need to first analyze how
culturally socialized patterns and political circumstances influence foodways and then apply this knowledge in non-authoritarian but persuasive
and nourishing ways. This recommendation from a key figure in our discipline must have a ring of familiarity for many who attempt to engage in
food (inter)activist research. For instance, Kaplan et al. (2011) theorized
that if children were engaged in family food decision-making, they would
learn to eat "better." To explore this possibility the researchers conducted
multi-generational focus groups to discuss who makes the food decisions

at home and how much children are involved in these discussions. This became both a means to prove their hypothesis—indeed the children who were included in discussions of what to eat and why appeared to have the healthier foodways—as well as to actively encourage this form of talk. Creating successful programs along these lines is tricky because it involves making prescriptions about two very sensitive subjects: telling people what they ought to eat and feed their children and telling them how they ought to be talking with their children. As we discussed in Chapter 7, programs such as these, whether directed at changing the way we feed children language or how we use language to feed children information about how they should eat can be easily flawed by culturally biased assumptions about what is "good" for people, whether good language or good food. However, the article explored some suggestive participatory possibilities for using focus groups as an activist tool to open real dialogue and nurture healthy eating.

In another compelling instance of what we would label food (inter)activist research, Thorpe (2006) makes a powerful call for the place of participatory ethnography in the project of food activism. She spent four years researching an elementary school garden project in Michigan, one that is now typical of the school food change movement's drive to enrich the science and social science curriculum by having the children get their hands dirty. For instance, by planting a "three sisters" garden of pumpkin, corn, and beans, they learned not only about the symbiosis of nutrient-fixing plants and nutrient-needy plants, but also about Native American cultures and their respect for the land. Or by planting a pizza garden of garlic, onions, tomatoes, and peppers, they learned not only about how these vegetables are bulbs and fruits, but also about where they originated in the world and how they can be put together into a tasty pizza. The significance of Thorpe's research has less to do with her findings and more to do with the originality of how she wrote them up in her book-length ethnography, *The Pull of the Earth*, using not only photos of the children and garden, but also the journal entries, poems, and other writings about the garden by the children, teachers, and research assistants. From the perspective of food (inter)activism, what she clarifies is how all of this communication about and around food also filled the food with meaning and nourished the children with language. As she wrote: "I came to Jonesville School to help children connect to the earth and found in the process that we became connected to one another" (2006:43).

However, in a study of a community food program that emerged over many years out of the Black Panthers movement in South Los Angeles, California, Broad (2016) cautions us that not all food justice problems can be cured through school gardens. That is, he is critical of what he considers neoliberal moves to sell the food justice brand to "philanthrocapitalists," individuals who use their money made through capitalism to try to solve the

Figure 8.3 School garden in New York City with food origins map in the background

Credit: Photo by Kathleen C. Riley

problems wrought by capitalism. These individuals donate money for small community projects because the larger system is not about to change (and in fact their assets depend on the system remaining fixed). By contrast, Broad illustrates through his food (inter)activist research how it takes complex and long-term forms of community organizing involving local food growing and exchange, dialogue, and education to reach these goals. Broad engaged in five years of participant observation, interviews, and discourse analysis to understand how this community used food to attain forms of social justice as opposed to using social organizing to change the whole food system. He took a "communication ecology" perspective, that is, the idea that communication operates like other ecological systems via feedback. Based on his participatory research with this particular group, he presents a complex picture of how to build social networks and tell narratives that go viral in ways that can over time impact the larger system. For example, the Metamorphosis Project that first took root in Los Angeles following the 1992 riots has now flowered into an activist research project housed at the University of Southern California devoted to understanding the role of storytelling and local communication in promoting sustainable change, especially in communities influenced by globalization, immigration, and now the internet.

8.19

In another affecting study of food and children in Mwanza, Tanzania, Flynn (2008) critiques Sen's (1982) **entitlement** approach to explaining food insecurity and proposes instead her own ethnographic analysis of how street children actually acquire food and other necessities. According to Sen, entitlement is socially structured by rules such that those with more resources to begin with are necessarily entitled to receive more in return. By contrast, Flynn proposes that far more complex variables to do with age, gender, and even ethnicity facilitate and undermine street children's access to food. Further, both the children themselves as well as individual almsgivers and charitable organizations are caught up in a system of instantiating and expressing "street credit," which becomes then the basis for a particular kind of entitlement in the global charity business. From our food (inter) activist perspective, what is significant to analyze in this research is how the children use language as a tool for eliciting sustenance (both food and other forms of nourishing sociality) from others, whether it be by begging or depending on snacks dispensed at charity centers, sex work or small jobs at food stands, theft, strategic bullying, and/or sharing with others. Those with more street credit—in this case, the ability to extract food in this way—garner more resources. Additionally, the charity system seems structured to provide donors with a similar form of street credit for giving charity to the most "needy" in this system. From Flynn's ethnographic report, we learn the importance of engaging slowly and carefully with a vulnerable population such as this, living in conditions hard for most to imagine much less immerse in. Additionally, we learn that food (inter)activist research must work from the premise that we cannot possibly know in advance all of the factors influencing how our subjects are engaging with their environments to access food; instead, we need to learn about the various ways in which actors in our field sites are using language to communicate through, about, around, and as food. Flynn's research provides a necessary window into both the hardships and the resourcefulness of children engaged in semiotic mediation as a means to access food.

However, the role of food (inter)activist research is not only to provide a window onto the unimaginable, but to empower others to find their food voice with which to express their lives. Dossa's engaged research (2014; see also Vignette 7.1) is an illustration of this work as she explores the role of food and narrative among Afghan women, some of whom were still living in the war-devastated remains of their homes in Kabul and others who had immigrated to Canada. Her ethnography works at several levels: first to chronicle how individual women used the significance of food to respond with strength and persistence to their struggles; second to listen and act as witness to their lives and narratives of personal agency; and finally to disseminate their powerful stories of distress, displacement, and resilience to a world that would not otherwise pay attention. The food itself (particularly fruits and meat) carries significance for these women as signs of a past life when food was more plentiful and their families undisrupted. Also highly significant are the ways in which they continue to prepare food for friends and family who remain (many others have died or emigrated elsewhere) using the foods they can procure (scarce in Kabul and culturally inappropriate in Canada) to express hospitality and conviviality despite their reduced circumstances. Finally, and perhaps most deeply significant are the ways in which they tell tales while eating in ways that nourish them still.

Applying the Food-and-Language Model in Situations of Foodways Endangerment

Food (inter)activist research may also be attempted in parts of the world where indigenous foodways are endangered, putting food sovereignty at risk. Food in these contexts is neither reliably plentiful nor nutritious and safe, not only because the indigenous knowledge of how to produce food out of the land and water are at risk, but also because traditional ways of storing and preserving, processing and preparing foods are being lost (Nabhan 2008a; Peña et al. 2017). This loss of cultural knowledge and practices related to food is frequently compared to, and goes hand in hand with, the loss of biodiversity and linguistic diversity in the world. Thus, the term for it, **endangered foodways,** is modeled on the notion of endangered species and **endangered languages.** Here again we have a parallel in the development of terms from food studies and linguistics. The linguistic marketplace (discussed in Chapter 1) influences the vitality of minority languages in much the same way that indigenous foodways are at risk due to the global production and distribution of homogenous foods and foodways. At present, half of the world's 7,000 or so languages are in danger of disappearing by the end of this century, and language shift and endangerment has developed into a veritable field of study in its own right over the last quarter-century, beginning with Fishman's seminal work on

8.20

language shift and maintenance (e.g., Fishman 1991) and now included in most introductory linguistics textbooks.

Investigative research can be put to use in very specific ways in settings such as these. For instance, Nabhan (2008b) used his research into the causes of diabetes among Indians in Arizona (Pima and Papago) and northern Mexico (Seri) to organize a 12-day hike through the Sonoran Desert that was healing in several ways. His research had revealed that the high rate of diabetes in this population was likely caused by the recent replacement of their former diet of high-fiber, slow-release desert plants such as cacti and acorns with the typical North American diet high in saturated fats, sugars, and low-fiber and fast-burning carbohydrates. The hike was intended to reproduce their former subsistence strategy of foraging for desert foods, a lifestyle that had over several millennia apparently influenced the genes of this population in ways that have made them particularly vulnerable to the fast-food lifestyle of present-day Americans. The hike was a success because, first of all, this form of daily and long-term exercise is recommended for diabetics. Additionally, the hikers experienced the desert foods to be "nutritious, satisfying, and filling enough to sustain our arduous pilgrimage" (Nabhan 2008b:379), and indeed the foraging hike allowed the participants to reconnect with their cultural roots. While the article does not make any claims for the long-term impact on this particular population, the model for food change is inspiring.

However, just as many researchers studying language endangerment and the **language revitalization movements** intended to revive these languages proceed with caution lest they project their own romantic fantasies of saving the small languages of the world (Hill 2002), so must researchers studying endangered foodways and the accompanying **foodways revitalization movements** be somewhat wary. We may inadvertently invest these "authentic" foodways with meanings of our own, projecting our own interventionist desires into the semiotic mediations of those residing in our field sites, those who actually live with the impact of these emerging foodways and foodways discourses. Similarly, we may find ourselves working only with elites in these contexts, people who are less invested in the good of the community and all its members and more in their own status as movement leaders. Thus, just as both Riley (2007) and Paugh (2012) have worked cautiously on the language revitalization movements found in the Marquesas and Dominica, so have we been treading lightly as we investigate the food (inter)activist movements emerging on these islands. Our intention is to conduct what we consider a critically compassionate form of participatory research in which we allow our participants to set the parameters for if and how they wish for us to engage with their food sovereignty projects.

Nonetheless, from our research we can report a bit about the possibilities and difficulties of pursuing food (inter)activism in island settings such as these. Island inhabitants have understood, sometimes for many centuries, that dependence on foods from elsewhere is at times necessary and at other times risky. For instance, the first residents of Polynesia had to import and adapt foods from the mainland (originally Asia and later South America) in order to inhabit these islands where few human food crops had arrived carried by the waves or birds (Pollack 1992). Once they managed to cultivate foods in these new contexts, it was tempting but perilous to give up producing them locally in exchange for the convenient dried and canned foods (flour, rice, tinned beef, and salt cod) that were imported by the more recent explorers, traders, and colonists from the continents (Gewertz and Errington 2010). These foods could only be bought at the price of investment in an uncertain global economy, whose rhythms the islanders did not control. In this vein, Riley has been working to chronicle the role of language in Marquesans' attempts to reclaim their indigenous foodways, the ways in which they talk around and about food to organize the production, preparation, and marketing of local crops and dishes. Although richly semiotic in their own right for the older generation, some of these ways of doing food need to be packaged in ways that are also appetizing for children who are otherwise exposed only to global advertising and French educational regimes that do not always represent local foods in the best light.[8]

On those islands in the Caribbean where the cultivation of food crops such as manioc and breadfruit gave way to the production of cash crops such as sugar or bananas, the population's food supply has become precarious due to their dependence on the world market demand for the commodities they produce and the global pricing of the foods they now need to import. Their precarious dependence becomes especially evident in the face of natural disasters, such as hurricanes, earthquakes, and tsunamis. For instance, the 2017 hurricane season in the Caribbean brought Puerto Rico to its knees—an island that operated on the assumption that it could call on the full support of the United States for water, food, energy, and medical aid in times of need.

Similarly, Hurricane Maria flattened the island nation of Dominica, where Paugh's research has been situated for many years. It left a disastrous lack of *food* in its wake, and initially also a lack of nourishing *talk* as families and friends waited for news for days (Paugh 2017). At first, all telecommunication networks were taken out, and no one could tell what was happening as the hurricane prevented immediate outside contact and aid. It was left to amateur ham radio operators on the island to communicate with amateur radio operators in the United States who picked up their sporadic broadcasts; then internet radio station TDN radio, based in Houston, Texas, and owned by two Dominican ex-patriots, broadcasted the intermittent updates. Over the next hours and weeks, four radio announcers originally from Dominica and now in distant parts of the world—Houston, Texas; New York; Toronto; and South Sudan—began covering the storm and fielding phone calls from transnational family and

8.22

friends in the Caribbean, United States, Canada, United Kingdom, and elsewhere. They provided whatever information they could gather, compiling lists of people's names from concerned callers desperate for news. The unpaid volunteer announcers fed their starving audience with talk about the "resilience" of Dominicans, interspersed with upbeat Dominican music that, according to one announcer, sustained people with the sound of the "sweetness" of home, even if they didn't understand all of the Afro-French Patwa lyrics, given that most now learn English as their mother tongue. Once some cell service was restored days later, TDN radio took calls from islanders telling their relatives they were safe and relayed daily government press briefings and assessments from outside aid organizations.

However, the initial language-as-food discourses ("have you seen or heard from my mother, father, spouse, child, sister, brother . . . ") shifted soon enough to language *about* the desperate need for food and water. In short, the category 5 hurricane's catastrophic 160 mph winds and torrential rainfall had caused flooding and massive devastation to infrastructure; it had wiped out almost all crops, livestock, and fisheries, and disrupted the commercial food supply chain. The initial weeks warned of severe food shortages and malnutrition, especially in isolated areas. Public discourses

Figure 8.4 Trees, stripped of their vegetation and fruits, block streets on the Caribbean island of Dominica after Hurricane Maria on September 18, 2017 (© Shutterstock)

about food concerned aid deliveries and their fair distribution as well as the need for fast-growing crops and seedlings to restore local and regional food security given Dominica's role as the "food bowl" of the eastern Caribbean. Dominica's post-colonial legacy of poverty, debt, reliance on external support, and vulnerability to global markets and natural disasters all helped set the stage for the current situation.

Fortunately, during the months of recovery after the hurricane, Dominicans were able to rely on many "traditional" foods that survived the wind and rain—hardy root crops such as tuberous yams and dasheen, commonly called "ground provisions." But they also depended on the tinned meats and dried foodstuffs from foreign aid donors, these being foods that the Health Ministry simultaneously cautions are unhealthy for many who are struggling with diabetes and hypertension. These foods themselves speak to the ravages of the hurricane—a language of disaster *through* food—as people collected what they could from the ground, and boxes of aid and food labels indicated the names of their foreign countries of origins. Six months later, as this book went into production, many of Paugh's friends were still lacking access to food, clean water, and electricity even as the foreign aid slowed and much of the hardy root crops were consumed. In this case, she has identified her food (inter)activist role as that of communicating to nourish: bearing witness, spreading the word to the world, and fundraising for needed aid.

Summary: Putting the Food-and-Language Model to Work

We hope this chapter has made clear that the language through-about-around-as food model is not meant to be only a way to analyze the world but also a way to act in it. Food, language, and research about them may all be to some degree destructively dumped as toxic waste or ethically recycled as fruitful compost. In this final chapter, we have focused on how food (inter)activism attempts to avoid the former and engage in the latter, and how researchers study and may contribute to this. Our food-and language model may be of use both in reflecting about and acting upon the food-and-language issues we take note of in our world.

As we have explored throughout this book, the values of food and talk are produced and processed, cooked and consumed, both economically and symbolically. Foodways are semiotically read as a form of structured communication. Discourses (both the discursive activities and the ideological Discourses they carry) about foodways include not only referential representations but also performative acts about both the food and everything it signifies. Discourses around food not only reference but also index the co-present food, reproducing and transforming old understandings of food values. Finally, discourses operate as metaphorical and instrumental forms of sustenance, nutritious or not. And in this chapter, we have focused on how the values at stake include health and taste, climate change and interspecies relations, social justice and identity politics. In other words, ideologies about food and language are both reflected in and forged by discursive food exchanges, sometimes prompting acts of resistance to systems of miscommunication and efforts to renovate ailing food systems and revive endangered ones.

8.23

There are nonetheless areas that have still to be explored and connections yet to be made. For instance, while several studies have focused on how age and gender norms and hierarchies are socialized in the home and how neoliberal ideologies about ethnicity and class are frequently acquired at school, much important research could be conducted on how everyday racism is socialized via food and language in many domestic settings. Researchers have examined how foods are labeled and advertised, how branded foods are strategically used to dismiss or elevate others, and how food fads and panics are set off and mediatized, but studies have yet to be done on the real-time discussions (many of which probably happen "over" coffee and bagels or wine and cheese) by NGO program directors addressing the latest food crisis or World Bank officers making plans for structural adjustment due to or in spite of chronic food insecurity, or state representatives debating the legalization of marijuana in the form of edibles. Researchers have observed how meals prepared from endangered species may serve political ends and how deeply unsettling forms of interspecies semiosis occur in slaughter houses, and yet no one has yet found a way to examine the overall impact of these semiotic food chains on our human consciousness.

In other words, the possibilities for food-and-language research are endless. This research is needed for the sake of our species and our planet, and it is needed for the sake of understanding how humans communicate through, around, about, and as food, an essential element of our existence. Much of this food-related communication brings us great meaning, comfort, and pleasure, and it may also be key to sustaining ourselves and our world.

Notes

1. And we would be remiss if we did not mention that for some human beings, food seems to be merely an inconvenience. Some would take a pill for all their nutrients if they could. See for example this instance of techies in Silicon Valley who reportedly subsist on the product known as Soylent: www.washingtonpost.com/news/wonk/wp/2017/06/13/how-one-company-plans-to-change-your-mind-about-genetically-edited-food/?utm_term=.e1cca522c6dd.

2. Riley developed this term in her classes and organized a panel discussion at Rutgers in 2017 entitled: "Food (Inter)activism: Changing the Food System through Interaction." See also Riley (2017).

3. A portmanteau is a word created by merging two or more other words. It comes from the French for "carry" and "coat" and meant the kind of luggage that opened up like a portable closet. In this case, the two words packed up together are *agriculture* and *business*.
4. Intelligent critiques of food activists' critiques of agribusiness are also launched. For instance, in *Just Food*, the historian McWilliams (2009) cautions that the construction of a sustainable food system cannot be attained through quick, simplistic fixes (for example, local and organic food fads) but through open-minded scientific exploration and adaptation. He along with many others does not agree that all synthetic chemicals or GMOs are necessarily evil; instead the problem is with the ways in which they are applied. He also cautions that not all local foods are better for the environment than some lower-impact product from far away. In other words, not all food activists agree on the problems, much less the solutions.
5. For a review of the possible risks involved in the use of GMOs, see Smith (2003) and Shetterly (2016).
6. The dangers of chemical fertilizers and pesticides began to be documented midway through the last century through Rachel Carson's (1962) seminal research.
7. The term used these days for factory farming by food activists is the acronym CAFO (Concentrated Animal Feeding Operation). While acronyms such as this are frequently used to be efficient, they also index complex, bureaucratic structures for which such terms are needed to be rational and efficient and which may also attempt to obscure through euphemism any related problems. In this case, the fact that food activists have adopted this term used by the food industry can be taken as a self-conscious and discursively ironic move.
8. See Donaldson and Riley (2018) on the rise and fall and resurrection of the richly semiotic breadfruit in the Marquesas by contrast with the French baguette.

References

Andersen, Kip, and Keegan Kuhn. 2014. *Cowspiracy: The Sustainability Secret.* A.U.M. Films & Media and First Spark Media.

Broad, Garrett M. 2016. *More Than Just Food: Food Justice and Community Change.* Berkeley: University of California Press.

Carson, Rachel. 1962. *Silent Springs.* Boston: Houghton Mifflin.

Counihan, Carole, and Valeria Siniscalchi. 2014. *Food Activism: Agency, Democracy and Economy.* New York: Bloomsbury Academic.

Cramer, Janet M., Carlnita P. Greene, and Lynn M. Walters, eds. 2011. *Food as Communication, Communication as Food.* New York: Peter Lang.

Delpeuch, Francis, Bernard Maire, Emmanuel Monnier, and Michelle Holdsworth. 2009. *Globesity: A Planet Out of Control?* London: Earthscan.

Donaldson, Emily, and Kathleen C. Riley. 2018. "Speaking Breadfruit: Phyto-Communicability in the Marquesas Islands." Panel presentation at the Society for Linguistic Anthropology Conference, Philadelphia, PA, March 10.

Dossa, Parin. 2014. *Afghanistan Remembers: Gendered Narrations of Violence and Culinary Practices.* Toronto: Toronto University Press.

Fishman, Joshua. 1991. *Reversing Language Shift: Theory and Practice of Assistance to Threatened Languages.* Clevedon: Multilingual Matters.

Flynn, Karen Coen. 2008. "Street Credit: The Cultural Politics of African Street Children's Hunger." In *Food and Culture: A Reader*, 2nd edition, edited by Carole Counihan and Penny Van Esterik, 554–571. New York: Routledge.

Frye, Joshua J. 2012. "Lee Kyung Hae and the Dynamics of Social Movement Self-Sacrifice." In *The Rhetoric of Food: Discourse, Materiality and Power*, edited by Joshua J. Frye and Michael S. Bruner, 139–154. New York: Routledge.

Frye, Joshua J., and Michael S. Bruner, eds. 2012. *The Rhetoric of Food: Discourse, Materiality and Power*. New York: Routledge.

Garnett, Tara. 2016. "Plating Up Solutions." *Science* 353(6305): 1202–1204.

Gewertz, Deborah, and Frederick Errington. 2010. *Cheap Meat: Flap Food Nations in the Pacific Islands*. Berkeley: University of California Press.

Gottlieb, Robert, and Anupama Joshi. 2010. *Food Justice*. Cambridge, MA: MIT Press.

Harvey, David. 2005. *A Brief History of Neoliberalism*. Oxford: Oxford University Press.

Hassanein, Neva. 2012. "Practicing Food Democracy: A Pragmatic Politics of Transformation." In *Taking Food Public: Redefining Foodways in a Changing World*, edited by Psyche Williams-Forson and Carole Counihan, 461–474. New York: Routledge.

Hill, Jane H. 2002. "'Expert Rhetorics' in Advocacy for Endangered Languages: Who is Listening, and What Do They Hear?" *Journal of Linguistic Anthropology* 12(2): 119–133.

Holt-Giménez, Eric, ed. 2011. *Food Movements Unite! Strategies to Transform our Food Systems*. Oakland, CA: Food First Books.

Holt-Giménez, Eric. 2017. *A Foodie's Guide to Capitalism: Understanding the Political Economy of What We Eat*. New York: Monthly Review Press.

Kaplan, Matthew, Lynn James, Frances Alloway, and Nancy Ellen Kiernan. 2011. "Youth Empowerment in Family Conversations and Decision-Making about Food." In *Food as Communication, Communication as Food*, edited by Janet M. Cramer, Carlnita P. Greene, and Lynn M. Walters, 337–358. New York: Peter Lang.

Kenner, Robert. 2010. *Food, Inc.* Los Angeles: Participant Media.

Kimbrell, Andrew, ed. 2002. *Fatal Harvest: The Tragedy of Industrial Agriculture*. Washington, DC: Island Press.

Kimura, Aya Hirata. 2011. "Nationalism, Patriarchy, and Moralism: The Government-Led Food Reform in Contemporary Japan." *Food and Foodways* 19(3): 201–227.

Kingsolver, Barbara. 2007. *Animal, Vegetable, Miracle: A Year of Food Life*. New York: HarperCollins.

Kirby, David. 2010. *Animal Factory: The Looming Threat of Industrial Pig, Dairy, and Poultry Farms to Humans and the Environment*. New York: St. Martin's Griffin.

Lappé, Frances Moore, Joseph Collins, and Peter Rosset. 1998. *World Hunger: 12 Myths*, 2nd edition. New York: Grove Press.

Lavin, Chad. 2012. "The Year of Eating Politically." In *Taking Food Public: Redefining Foodways in a Changing World*, edited by Psyche Williams-Forson and Carole Counihan, 576–591. New York: Routledge.

LeGrand, Yvonne. 2015. "Activism through Commensality: Food and Politics in a Temporary Vegan Zone." In *Commensality: From Everyday Food to Feast*, edited by Susanne Kerner, Cynthia Chou, and Morten Warmind, 51–63. New York: Bloomsbury Academic.

Masson, Jeffrey Moussaieff. 2009. *The Face on Your Plate: The Truth about Food*. New York: W. W. Norton & Co.

McWilliams, James E. 2009. *Just Food: Where Locavores Get It Wrong and How We Can Truly Eat Responsibly*. New York: Back Bay Books/Little Brown and Company.

Mead, Margaret. 2008(1943). "The Problem of Changing Food Habits." In *Food and Culture: A Reader*, 2nd edition, edited by Carole Counihan and Penny Van Esterik, 17–27. New York: Routledge.

Meneley, Anne. 2016. "Checking Your Waistline at Qalandiya Checkpoint: Dieting as a Peace Initiative." *Jerusalem Quarterly* 68: 90–103.

Menzel, Peter, and Faith D'Aluisio. 2007. *Hungry Planet: What the World Eats*. Napa, CA: Material World Books and Berkeley, CA: Ten Speed Press.

Morris, Carol, and James Kirwan. 2012. "Vegetarians: Uninvited, Uncomfortable or Special Guests at the Table of the Alternative Food Economy?" In *Taking Food Public: Redefining Foodways in a Changing World*, edited by Psyche Williams-Forson and Carole Counihan, 542–560. New York: Routledge.

Nabhan, Gary Paul. 2008a. *Renewing America's Food Traditions: Saving and Savoring the Continent's Most Endangered Foods*. White River Junction, VT: Chelsea Green Publishing Company.

Nabhan, Gary Paul. 2008b. "Rooting Out the Causes of Disease: Why Diabetes is so Common among Desert Dwellers." In *Food and Culture: A Reader*, 2nd edition, edited by Carole Counihan and Penny Van Esterik. 369–380. New York: Routledge.

Nestle, Marion. 2002. *Food Politics: How the Food Industry Influences Nutrition and Health*. Berkeley: University of California Press.

Parkins, Wendy, and Geoffrey Craig. 2009. "Culture and the Politics of Alternative Food Networks." *Food, Culture, and Society* 12(1): 77–103.

Paugh, Amy L. 2012. *Playing with Languages: Children and Change in a Caribbean Village*. New York: Berghahn Books.

Paugh, Amy L. 2017. "Disaster in Dominica." Roundtable presentation at the 116th American Anthropological Association Annual Meeting, Washington, DC, December 2.

Peña, Devon G., Luz Calvo, Pancho McFarland, and Gabriel R. Valle, eds. 2017. *Mexican-Origin Foods, Foodways, and Social Movements: A Decolonial Reader*. Fayetteville: University of Arkansas Press.

Pollack, Nancy. 1992. *These Roots Remain: Food Habits in Islands of the Central and Eastern Pacific since Western Contact*. Laie, HI: The Institute for Polynesian Studies.

Poppendieck, Janet. 2010. *Free for All: Fixing School Food in America*. Berkeley: University of California Press.

Riley, Kathleen C. 2007. "To Tangle or Not to Tangle: Shifting Language Ideologies and the Socialization of Charabia in the Marquesas, F.P." In *Consequences of Contact: Language Ideologies and Sociocultural Transformations in Pacific*

Societies, edited by Miki Makihara and Bambi B. Schieffelin, 70–95. New York: Oxford University Press.

Riley, Kathleen C. 2017. "Food Talk Matters: How Health, Wealth, and Security Are Semiotically Produced, Consumed and Unequally Distributed." Roundtable at the 116th American Anthropological Association Annual Meeting, Washington, DC, December 2.

Sacharoff, Shanta Nimbark. 2016. *Other Avenues Are Possible: Legacy of the People's Food System of the San Francisco Bay Area*. Oakland, CA: PM Press.

Schlosser, Eric. 2012. *Fast Food Nation: The Dark Side of the All-American Meal*. Boston: Houghton Mifflin.

Seegert, Natasha. 2012. "Resignified Urban Landscapes: From Abject to Agricultural." In *The Rhetoric of Food: Discourse, Materiality and Power*, edited by Joshua J. Frye and Michael S. Bruner, 121–138. New York: Routledge.

Seiler, Abigail. 2012. "Let's Move: The Ideological Constraints of Liberalism on Michelle Obama's Obesity Rhetoric." In *The Rhetoric of Food: Discourse, Materiality and Power*, edited by Joshua J. Frye and Michael S. Bruner, 155–170. New York: Routledge.

Sen, Amartya. 1982. *Poverty and Famines: An Essay on Entitlement and Deprivation*. New York: Oxford University Press.

Shetterly, Caitlin. 2016. *Modified: GMOs and the Threat to Our Food, Our Land, Our Future*. New York: Penguin Books.

Shiva, Vandana. 2016. *Who Really Feeds the World? The Failures of Agribusiness and the Promise of Agroecology*. Berkeley: North Atlantic Books.

Sinclair, Upton. 2004(1906). *The Jungle*. New York: Pocket Books.

Smith, Jeffrey M. 2003. *Seeds of Deception: Exposing Industry and Government Lies about the Safety of the Genetically Engineered Foods You're Eating*. Fairfield, IA: Yes! Books.

Thorpe, Laurie. 2006. *Pull of the Earth: Participatory Ethnography in the School Garden*. Lanham, MD: Altamira Press.

Todd, Anne Marie. 2011. "Eating the View: Environmental Aesthetics, National Identity, and Food Activism." In *Food as Communication, Communication as Food*, edited by Janet M. Cramer, Carlnita P. Greene, and Lynn M. Walters, 297–315. New York: Peter Lang.

Watson, James L., and Melissa L. Caldwell, eds. 2005. *The Cultural Politics of Food and Eating*. Malden, MA: Blackwell Publishing.

Wilk, Richard, ed. 2006. *Fast Food/Slow Food: The Cultural Economy of the Global Food System*. Lanham, MD: Altamira Press.

Williams-Forson, Psyche, and Carole Counihan, eds. 2012. *Taking Food Public: Redefining Foodways in a Changing World*. New York: Routledge.

Winne, Mark. 2008. *Closing the Food Gap: Resetting the Table in the Land of Plenty*. Boston: Beacon Press.

Glossary

Acts specific actions; as used in this book, communicative or discursive acts, such as jokes, compliments, or complaints

Agonism respectful rivalry and non-antagonistic conflict between groups

Agribusiness a portmanteau term that was originally used to discuss any agriculture-related business, but has been adopted by food activists to critique a corporate approach to farming wherein the primary goal is to maximize output and profit

Alimentary related to foodways

Alimentary Competence the knowledge of what specific foods and foodways mean and how to interact around and with them in particular contexts and relative to the participants' social statuses and relationships (see **linguistic competence** and **communicative competence**)

Anthropology the holistic study of human beings and their many different ways of giving meaning to experience, past and present, through the biological, archaeological, cultural, and linguistic subfields

Anthropophagy cannibalism

Applied Anthropology the application of anthropological methods and theories to solving human problems; exists as a fifth subdiscipline in many anthropology departments

Arbitrary Signs signs without a natural connection but linked by conventional usage to their meanings (see **non-arbitrary signs**)

Artifacts objects found in an archaeological site that humans transformed for use, such as utensils for cooking and eating food (see **ecofacts**)

Assemblages collections of different objects and ideas from different places that mediate human interactions in different ways

Authenticity the discursively valued characteristic of peoples, cultures, languages, foods, clothes, practices, etc., that are understood to have emerged out of unique and specific locales and traditions

Babytalk a linguistic register directed at infants and young children, also known as child-directed speech, "motherese," or "parentese"

Boundary Objects objects that work to both define a cultural community that values them while also mediating the boundary between communities

Carnism   the ideology that human animals have the right to raise, slaughter, and consume other animals

Circumlocution   the use of several words to express a single idea; for example, the need to use more words in one language to express what is captured in a single word in another language

Code-Switching   the alternation between two or more languages between or within sentences

Columbian Exchange   the circulation of foods, and also diseases, between Europe and the Americas as a result of Columbus sailing in 1492 from Spain to the Caribbean in search of India

Commensality   the act of eating together (from Latin *com* = 'with' and *mensa* = 'table')

Communicative Competence   the ability to communicate in various social situations in ways deemed appropriate by a given social group (see **linguistic competence** and **alimentary competence**)

Communitas   a shared experience of community, such as through a rite of passage or communal meal, wherein hierarchical barriers may be both respected and momentarily dissolved

Context   spatial, temporal, and/or social setting within which events take place

Conviviality   taking lively pleasure in the company of others (from Latin *com* = 'with' and *vivere* = 'to live' and *comvivere* = 'carouse together')

Creolized   blended or mixed, as in foods or languages

Critical Period   the period from birth to approximately age 10 during which language is more readily acquired

Cultural Relativism   attempt to understand unfamiliar practices or beliefs within their cultural context (see **ethnocentrism**)

Decontextualized   when objects such as foods or linguistic forms are removed from their original contexts of use (see **recontextualized**)

discourse   the activity of communicating (linguistic and paralinguistic); language use above the level of the sentence

Discourse(s)   dominant ideology or ideologies circulated via discourse (everyday and formal)

discourses   material and symbolic practices involved in the production and consumption of language and language ideologies in both everyday and formal settings

Discourse Events   occasions in which people engage in some form of contextualized social interaction

Discursive   relating to discourse(s) and Discourse(s)

Disgust   a visceral and moral response to food contamination such as fecal, animal, sexual, or socially immoral (see **distaste**)

Displacement   a feature of human language that allows for communication in the present moment about events in the past and future or elsewhere

Distaste   a sensory rejection of food (see **disgust**)

Domains   culturally relevant categories of experience, a main focus of ethnosemantics

Ecofacts   objects found in an archaeological site that humans used but did not transform for use, such as remains of what people ate (see **artifacts**)

Ecomuseums   museums focused on the cultural heritage of a place, with participation by community members who may re-enact traditional practices

Endangered Foodways   indigenous and other foodways that are at risk of disappearing due to the global production and distribution of homogenous foods and foodways (see **endangered languages**)

Endangered Languages   languages that are at risk of disappearing due to demographic changes or to the fact that their users are shifting to the socially dominant languages of their area (see **endangered foodways**)

Engaged Anthropologists   anthropologists who attempt to design their research to be relevant and useful for their participants (see **applied anthropology**)

Entitlement   concept that highlights how rights to, for instance, food, are socially structured by rules that ensure that those who begin life with more resources also end up with more

Ethnocentrism   the assumption that our own community's ways of acting, thinking, and feeling are the normal or right ways (see **cultural relativism**)

Ethnographic Fieldwork   consistent, immersive, on-the-ground research with a social group over an extended length of time

Ethnography   the activity of using immersive fieldwork to understand and document another culture; both the method of investigation and the process of creating a written account (*ethnos* = 'people' and *graphy* = 'writing')

Ethnography of Communication   a more current term for Dell Hymes's ethnography of SPEAKING in order to include other communicative modes beyond the spoken word: written, signed, and embodied

Ethnography of SPEAKING   a key research framework for documenting and analyzing naturally occurring speech events

Ethnonym   the name used to refer to a group of people (see **linguonym**)

Ethnosemantics   the field of study that collects, classifies, and taxonomizes local terms related to a number of domains, food being a particularly productive one

Factory Farming   the large-scale industrial raising of animals (especially pigs, cows, and chickens) in ways that may threaten the welfare of the animals and their human consumers

Field Notes   the qualitative notes recorded by researchers while engaged in participant observation and used for later analysis

Focus Groups   a research method in which researchers gather a group of participants to discuss various questions, whether open-ended or directed, about particular topics such as food

Food Activism   a form of political activism that has emerged over the last half-century to focus on the role of food in recalibrating human relationships on this planet

Food Bilinguals   persons who are fluently engaged in more than one foodway

Food Chain   global commodity chains of production and distribution by which animals and plants are raised, processed, and marketed as food; see also **food paths**

Food Deserts   urban neighborhoods or rural areas devoid of outlets where healthy food (or sometimes any food at all) can be accessed

Food Ideologies   ideologies about foods and foodways, including the nature and significance of food's production, exchange, and consumption

Food Insecurity   the lack of dependable sources of food in many sectors of society and many parts of the world

Food (inter)activism   a term that combines 'food' plus 'inter' from 'interaction' plus 'activism' in an effort to draw attention to forms of food activism that depend on the role of interpersonal and intercultural communication in implementing constructive changes to the food system

Food Paths   the global paths traveled, past and present, by particular foods and foodways (see also **food chains**)

Food Registers   socioculturally and contextually specific variations in people's foodways (see **linguistic registers**)

Food Social Space   a concept first developed by Jean-Pierre Poulain to refer to the ways in which food meanings emerge out of human interaction within specific foodscapes

Food Socialization   the process by which individuals learn alimentary knowledge and practices (see **language socialization** and **food-and-language socialization**)

Food Sovereignty   goal of food activist movements designed to create or restore the ability of individuals and communities to participate more directly and sustainably in the production and consumption of healthy and culturally meaningful foods

Food System   the systemic ways in which food is produced, distributed, and consumed at local, national, and/or global levels

Food Talk   discourses about foodways

Food Voices   a concept developed by Carole Counihan to facilitate the (inter)activist goal of amplifying a people's power in the world through the expression of their relationship to food

Food-and-Language Socialization   the interlinked processes by which food and foodways are learned through language and by which language is learned through food and foodways (see **food socialization** and **language socialization**)

Food-Centered Life Histories   personal and social histories revolving around significant food memories

Foodography   the melding of food and photography

Foodscapes   the inundation of social space with food, both actual at the supermarket and virtual in the media (see **linguistic landscapes**)

Foodways   material and symbolic practices related to the production and consumption of food and food ideologies in both everyday and formal settings

Foodways Journals   a research method that asks participants to keep track in written form of how they procure, prepare, consume, and talk about food on a regular basis for a period of time

Foodways Revitalization   movements directed at reviving endangered or threatened foodways (see **language revitalization**)

Fusion Foodways   foods and food practices melded as a consequence of cross-cultural contact and semiotic mediation

Gastro-Politics   concept used to explain how food carries political significance for interactants based on social and religious beliefs to do with age, gender, kinship, caste, etc.

Gastrotourism   tourism that revolves around the search for unique alimentary experiences

Genres   types or ways of communicating, such as prayers, gossip, or lectures

Globalization   the circulation of ideas, commodities, and people around the world, increasingly facilitated and controlled by new forms of transportation, communication, and political economic organization

Glocalized   global goods, practices, and ideas that are transformed by local users

Grammatical Categories   morphological and syntactic categories, such as tense, plurality, and gender

Habitus   deeply embedded ways of being in and understanding the world

Haute Cuisine   the forms of food preparation and service first associated with the upper classes of France that have since spread (the particular foods, practices, and ideologies) to other areas of the world

Heritage Food   a food handed down through the generations and celebrated as symbolic of this particular tradition (see **heritagize**)

Heritagize   the process by which practices (such as foodways) are transformed into the valued patrimony of a region or ethnic group (see **heritage food**)

Homogenized   used to refer to foods or other objects that are mass-produced to be the same no matter where they are made or eaten

Honorifics   linguistic features used to index respect and submission

Hybridized goods, practices, and ideas produced out of a synthesis of two or more previously distinct elements

Icons non-arbitrary signs whose meanings are based on some form of natural resemblance

Ideologies cultural beliefs, values, and assumptions held by individuals even if not in their best interests; ideologies are made powerful by media pronouncements and daily interactions (see **Discourses**)

Idioms figurative expressions that frequently rest on metaphoric thinking through which one thing is understood in terms of another

Indexes non-arbitrary signs that point like an index finger at the intended meaning in the current context

Informed Consent the process of informing potential research participants about the research to be conducted and the risks and benefits related to their participation before asking them if they are willing to give their consent and participate in the research project

Interlocutors conversational partners

Intertextual the links that are created when discourses are circulated across texts whether oral, signed, written, or mediated (see **decontextualized** and **recontextualized**)

Interviews a research method in which questions are asked to elicit information from participants; can be highly structured, semi-structured, or informal

Involvement Politeness politeness strategy that relies on telling friendly jokes, showing personal interest through narratives, and making offers (in contrast to **restraint politeness**)

Jargons specialized languages, such as the technical language used in legal documents

Language a system consisting of conventionally agreed upon symbols used for communication; employed in this book to refer to the many ways in which humans communicate

Language Ideologies ideologies about how languages are structured, acquired, and used

Language Revitalization efforts directed at reviving endangered or threatened languages (see **foodways revitalization**)

Language Socialization the social interactional process through which individuals learn language ideologies and practices, that is, an understanding of language and how to use it (also see **food-and-language socialization**)

Lexemes the meaningful units that make up the vocabulary of a language (see **lexicon**)

Lexicon the vocabulary of a language (see **lexemes**)

Lingua Francas simplified languages used for communication in multilingual contexts, especially trade languages

Linguacentrism the assumption that our own community's ways of communicating are the normal or right ways (see **ethnocentrism**)

Linguistic relating to language in written, signed, and spoken modes; linguistics is the discipline devoted to the study of language

Linguistic Anthropology the branch of anthropology that looks at language use as a social activity across cultures

Linguistic Competence the knowledge needed to put together a well-formed and grammatically meaningful sentence in a particular language (see **alimentary competence** and **communicative competence**)

Linguistic Determinism a strong version of linguistic relativity claiming that language determines the way we think

Linguistic Landscapes the inundation of social space with language in the form of signage, whether as official warnings, billboard advertising, or trashed newspapers (see **foodscapes**)

Linguistic Marketplace societal structures organizing the value of particular linguistic varieties according to the prestige of those who speak them and constraining who has access to them

Linguistic Registers the ways of speaking socioculturally associated with particular activities or contexts of use, such as sports or cooking (see **food registers**)

Linguistic Relativity the notion that the habitual use of language influences the way its speakers view the world, thereby influencing and reinforcing the worldview of their culture, also known as the **Sapir-Whorf hypothesis**

Linguonym the name of a group's language (see **ethnonym**)

Logos communication that appeals to logic or rationality (see **pathos**)

Longitudinal conducting research over a considerable length of time, such as when investigating language development

Mediated Texts written and audio-visual materials found on the radio, TV, internet, etc.

Metalinguistic referring to communication about language

Metapragmatic referring to communication about how language is used

Middens refuse heaps, in archaeological terms

Monocropping the planting and harvesting of a single commodity crop, such as corn or soy, over vast areas without variation

Morphemes the smallest meaningful linguistic units, including both words and elements of words; morphology is the study of morphemes

Multifunctional serving many functions, referential and performative in the case of language

Multimodal involving multiple modes such as vocal and facial expressions, hand and body gestures, spoken or manual language, paper and electronic writing, music and dance, visual images, and food

Multisensual involving multiple senses including taste, smell, touch, sound, and sight

Multivalent involving multiple meanings

Narrative Competence the ability to tell and interpret a narrative according to cultural conventions

Narratives   stories about personal and public events that are told according to cultural conventions in spoken, signed, or written form

Naturalistic   type of data collected as research participants go about their daily lives in everyday contexts, by contrast with data collected experimentally in a laboratory setting

Neocolonial   referring to the control of ex-colonies by ex-colonial states, frequently via multinational corporations and global trade policies

Neoliberal   the ideological Discourse that market forces will bring about necessary social transformations through individual willpower and action without the structural intervention of governments

Non-Arbitrary Signs   signs with a natural link to their meanings, such as smoke indicating fire (see **arbitrary signs**)

Norms   unspoken social rules or conventions

Observer's Paradox   the fact that observers inevitably alter if only in small ways the very reality they wish to observe when doing naturalistic and other research

Oinoglossia   wine talk

Ontogenic   related to individual development

Orthographies   writing systems

Orthopraxia   an ideology related to our attempts to correct a set of practices (*ortho* = 'straighten'; *praxia* = 'practice')

Orthorexia   an ideology related to our attempts to correct our yearnings, such as for food (*ortho* = 'straighten'; *orexia* = 'desire')

Paralinguistic   alongside language, including voice quality, vocalizations, facial expressions, and body language, as well as dress, hairstyle, and perfume

Participant Framework, Participant Structure   the configuration of actors in a communicative event

Participant Observation   the research method of observing while participating in everyday life

Pathos   communication that appeals to the emotions (see **logos**)

Performative, Performativity   how language enacts and does things in the world

Phonemes   the contrastive bits of sound used to form words; phonology is the study of phonemes and other sound patterns

Photo Elicitation   a research method that uses photographs as a point of departure for eliciting people's opinions and beliefs concerning food or other topics

Phylogenic   related to species evolution

Plantation System   European system of using enslaved labor from Africa and indentured labor from Asia and Oceania to produce a few valued food commodities such as sugar in the colonies

Questionnaires   list of questions used for eliciting information from participants whether anonymously or through face-to-face interactions

Rapport positive, ethical, working relationships that an anthropologist establishes with research participants

Ratified Participants listeners who are directly addressed by speakers in a given communicative event (in contrast to **unratified participants**)

Recontextualized when objects (foods or linguistic forms) are shifted into new contexts (see **decontextualized**)

Redistributive Feasts occasions at which leaders collect food produced by their followers and redistribute it in ways that manifest the leader's powerful affiliations

Referential, Referentiality how language conveys information about the world

Resignification the process by which signs are given new meaning

Restraint Politeness politeness strategy that relies on making indirect requests, being apologetic, and not demanding another's attention (in contrast to **involvement politeness**)

Ritual Insults insults that are culturally ritualized and socially acceptable discourse genres (often playful), in contrast to personal insults

Sapir-Whorf Hypothesis the phrase used to refer to the ideas of Edward Sapir and his student Benjamin Lee Whorf, based on the principle of **linguistic relativity**, which suggests that languages influence thought and worldview

Semiosis processes involving signs

Semiotic Mediation semiotic forms that mediate social interaction and organization

Semiotics the study of signs and semiosis

Shifters indexical signs that shift their meaning depending on the situation, such as using 'you' for the person being addressed

Sign something that stands for something else

Socialization the process by which individuals learn ideologies and practices from parents, teachers, peers, and media

Sociolects ways of speaking that index where we come from regionally, ethnically, and/or socioeconomically

Speciesism the ideology that the human species has the right to consume all of earth's resources, including all other species

Standard a language variety with high symbolic capital, usually close to the standardized written form used in government, commerce, mass media, and schools

Structural Anthropology a school of thought in anthropology that examines cultures in terms of their structurally related elements, such as kinship and mythology

Suprasegmental Prosody how sentences take on significance due to intonation

Surveys systematic method for gathering information from a large pool of participants using questionnaires, frequently implemented in writing or by phone in ways that conceal the identities of respondents; the resulting data are frequently analyzed using statistics

Sustainability   concerning the maintenance of individual health, environmental balance, and social and economic justice, via food and language for instance

Symbolic Capital   the amount of value and prestige associated with semiotic resources such as language variety, taste preferences, and food etiquette

Symbols   arbitrary, conventional signs; most languages are primarily constructed out of symbols

Syncretic Foods   new foods created out of a mix of two or more meaningful foodways, such as those of indigenous peoples and colonial settlers

Syntax   the rules that govern how **morphemes** are combined into sentences

Taste of Luxury/Freedom   a class-based formulation of taste, referring in this case to the freedom of choice in food preferences available to the upper class (see **taste of necessity**)

Taste of Necessity   a class-based formulation of taste, referring in this case to how the need for substantial, nourishing foods shapes food preferences among the lower classes (see **taste of luxury/freedom**)

Terroir   the notion that foods carry the taste of the specific soil and climate in which they are cultivated

Text Type   type of food text, such as a recipe or food blog

Textese   the abbreviated style used for writing texts, which tends to make use of many emoticons, abbreviations, and acronyms

Transcription   the process of writing down, using a particular set of coding conventions, what has been said during audio- and video-recorded interactions and including varying degrees of contextual details; produces a transcript

Unratified Participants   listeners who merely act as overhearers in a given communicative event (in contrast to **ratified participants**)

Verbal Hygiene   efforts aimed at "cleaning up" or correcting language usage and preventing language change

Vernaculars   the informal languages used at home and in the local community rather than at work or in the capital

Vocal Gestures   semi-words such as *yuck* and *yum* in English

Vowel Triangle   a model from linguistics in which vowels are seen to be distinguished by the way the tongue moves through the mouth when forming them

Vulnerable Population   people, such as children or prisoners, considered vulnerable because they are understood to be unable to give their autonomous, informed consent to participate in research

Appendix

Ethnography of SPEAKING-and-FEEDING

Riley has formulated this method for studying the **foodways-discourse** events, that is, events involving both food and communication such as a fishing trip, an outing to the farmers market, a baking get-together, an everyday family meal, or holiday feast. These events must be examined within the context of a relevant food-focused **community of practice**, that is, a community organized around a set of interactive practices. Food-related communities of practice include, for instance, members of a food co-op, baristas and regular customers at Starbucks, and Marquesan participants in after-church bingo-and-snack events.

To begin, choose a foodways-discourse event and ask the participants for their consent to be observed and studied. Second, conduct participant observation during the event and take notes using the two mnemonic charts (ethnography of SPEAKING and ethnography of FEEDING) to help you organize your observations. The first mnemonic, the ethnography of SPEAKING, was formulated in the 1960s by the linguistic anthropologist Dell Hymes in an attempt to systematize a method for the cross-cultural and ethnographic study of everyday communications, what he labeled "speech events," in the ethnolinguistic context of what has come to be called our "speech communities." Borrowing from his approach, Riley created an additional methodological mnemonic: the "ethnography of FEEDING" (see Chapter 3 for more on these methods).

Next, take field notes on the kinds of foodways-and-discourse data listed in both of these mnemonics. There is no correct way to write field notes—no necessary format or amount! Simply write down everything you notice at the time—using the questions in the charts to inform your observations in whatever shorthand or technologically mediated way you want (pen and paper, iPad, etc.). Then, type these up as soon after your fieldwork experience as possible because you'll find yourself remembering details to add as you write, which may be forgotten later. Finally, extract data from these notes and put both general observations and illustrations into two charts.

To see examples of how these data may be charted, see the eResources page under "Student Research Examples."

1. *Ethnography of SPEAKING*	2. *Ethnography of FEEDING*
Setting = when and where is the discourse event taking place (macro and micro)? • macro: neighborhood/city/country, month/year • micro: time of day, specific location and use of space (e.g., tables and chairs) **Participants** = who is present and participating in the discourse event (consider age, gender, social class, ethnicity/nationality, social roles, etc.) **Ends** = what are the goals, intentions, and effects of participants' specific discursive acts and of the discourse event as a whole? **Acts** = what types of small discursive actions are engaged in during the event (e.g., commands, pleas, greetings, insults)? **Key** = what emotional moods or emotions are expected or created during specific interactions or the event as a whole? **Instrumentalities** = what channels and codes are used for communicating? • channels: speaking, writing, texting, manual signing, body language, etc. • codes: languages, dialects, registers, etc. **Norms** = what discursive rules and expectations govern the event? • what topics are normal and what topics are taboo? • what discourse features are normal: how do people address one another? how much silence and/or overlap is appropriate? how much switching between codes (code-switching) occurs? what acts, instrumentalities, and genres are appropriate according to participants' social characteristics, roles, etc. **Genres:** what discourse genres are used (e.g., prayer, song, joking, teasing, storytelling)?	**Food** = what food items are present during this event? **Employment** = what specific practices or activities are involved in procuring, preparing, serving, and eating the food (e.g., hunting, boiling, passing food family-style, keeping one hand in the lap)? **Etiquette** = what cultural rules seem to shape this event (e.g., social politeness, religious ritual, political principle, health or safety guidelines)? **Display** = how are the foods arranged and presented during this foodways-discourse event (practically, aesthetically . . .)? **Implements** = what equipment is used to produce, prepare, package, serve, consume the food at this event (e.g., gardening tools, bread knife and ladle, the family china, chopsticks, TV tables)? **Notions** = what ideas and beliefs about food are expressed or manifested during this event (e.g., what makes food good, tasty, healthy, meaningful, sustainable)? **Gender** = who has the right and/or obligation to do what with the food according to their socially constructed identities (e.g., based on age, gender, sexuality, ethnicity, class) and/or sociocultural roles (e.g., boss, mother, family clown)?

Index

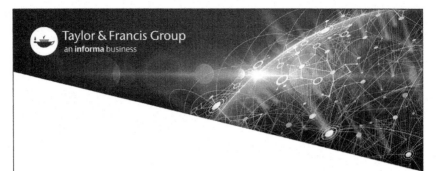